"While the world rallies and holds yet another seminar on equity, diversity and inclusion – Crosby offers a real path forward, rooted in truth and the individual and collective work that needs to be undertaken to create a more just society. His words carry the intended and unintended pain of racism, the deadly disease that continues to be spoon fed to generation after generation. The cure, as Gilmore shares, begins with a simple, time-tested framework of communication, planning, implementation and assessment. Let's do what needs to be done for our children's sake. Thanks for this stimulating and heartfelt reminder."

Nnamdi O. Chukwuocha, LMSW
State Representative- Delaware
State of Delaware Poets Laureate

"*Diversity Without Dogma*, a new book by Gilmore Crosby, has the potential for redirecting much of our racial angst and anxiety to substantive racial change and equity. It breaks new ground by challenging people/organizations to not only think about race and racial inequality but doing something to change the racial outcomes. It is more than talk, but action. It is more than idle proscriptions but actual group/organization therapy. He recognizes that much of the conversation about racism deals with intangibles such as unconscious biases, behaviors, etc., but that the focus needs to be on practical ways in which we can challenge the racial structures and systems. He asserts that the name, blame, and shame industry that so many in DEI operate in is not only counterproductive but wrong. Such an approach does not lead to any significant change, it only adds weight to the system as those targeted become more entrenched in their beliefs. The frequent failure of such practices only serves to buttress the racist structures and practices. In the process we begin to doubt our ability to change, the rationality of such change, and in frustration give up on any real attempt to change. Crosby asserts that the path is difficult, and we are concerned with a process not an event. Dealing with systemic racism can only be brought about by reducing the confusion and tensions that are part and parcel to unequal structures. Good intentioned people, unaware of these dynamics, wind up blaming the people rather than the system. The resulting homeostasis is strengthened. The alternative is engaging groups in identifying those systemic elements that preserve inequality, routing them out, and helping people to understand how they can foster real organizational change. As he demonstrates 'In other words, trying to change individuals without changing the social environment within which they live is like building one's house on sand.' I encourage any who are interested in true meaningful organizational and social change...look at Crosby's *Diversity Without Dogma*."

Dr. Rodney Coates
Professor of Global and Intercultural Studies at Miami University (Ohio)
Co-author of *The Matrix of Race*, 2nd Edition

"Issues of inclusion, diversity, social justice, and equity (DEI) have a long and important history in social psychology going back to the crucial work by Kurt Lewin showing how change in this area has to involve group based norms. Fortunately, the great wisdom that came out of Lewin and his students is brought back in this important book because what was learned in the last seventy years is highly relevant to how to approach these issues in today's complex world. This book provides not only the important linkages to how the DEI issues need to be conceptualized but reviews usefully how existing theory can help to deal with those issues in today's more volatile and complex world."

Edgar H. Schein
Professor Emeritus, MIT Sloan School of Management
Author with Peter Schein of *Humble Leadership (2018)* and
Humble Inquiry, 2d Ed. (2021)

"The first step to improve organizational issues of diversity, equity and inclusion is to appoint a Senior Vice President of DEI or, perhaps more broadly, a SVP of Social Justice. WRONG! This kind of action relieves everyone else in the organization of the responsibility for addressing and taking steps to improve issues of social justice, especially those represented by diversity, equity, and inclusion. In other words, 'I do not need to worry about these sticky problems. We have a SVP in charge.' Gilmore Crosby has it RIGHT! First, social justice is everyone's concern, especially those of us who are leaders and managers. And, second, social justice is systemic and touches all of us. It is buried in the organization's culture, a matter of context, and an organization's history. Gil Crosby is a master interpreter of Kurt Lewin's theories. Follow his lead regarding these critical issues that underlie an organization's ability to change."

W. Warner Burke, PhD
Professor Emeritus of Psychology & Education
Teachers College, Columbia University

"It is the practicality that makes Gil's latest book so moving. In an age dulled by so many slogans and shiny platitudes, Gil's well thought out message is even more salient. And when you read his book, use a marker...there are passages you will no doubt want to revisit."

Allon Shevat
OD Professional, Tel Aviv

"Few people can say that they grew up in the world of OD. Gil Crosby can. He is the son of Robert P. Crosby, who brushed shoulders with early Organization Development luminaries from Kurt Lewin's inner circle. This, Gil Crosby's latest writing, highlights Lewin's post-WWI Polish-German experiences as a bedrock for Lewin's theories on 'minority relations' and his action research methods for what to do to truly create 'a status of equity.'

Diversity Without Dogma belongs on every Diversity, Equity, and Inclusion practitioner's bookshelf alongside Andrea Pitzer's *One Long Night: A Global History of Concentration Camps*, Mehnaz M. Afridi's *Shoah Through Muslim Eyes*, Harriet A. Washington's *Medical Apartheid*, David Roediger's *Working Toward Whiteness*, Matthew Frye Jacobson's *Whiteness of a Different Color: European Immigrants and the Alchemy of Race*, Derald Wing Sue's *Race Talk and the Conspiracy of Silence*, and Heather McGhees' *The Sum of Us: What Racism Costs Everyone*, and that is where you will find it in my office.

As part of an academic canon, *Diversity Without Dogma* sits beside Washington's book, giving examples of historic traumas resulting from systemic biases, including lobotomies on the LGBTQ community and Caesar Lombroso's books *Criminal Man* and *The Female Offender*. It pairs well with Pitzer and Afridi's books in that it adds to the existing literature on antisemitism and the Jewish diaspora from the rise of Hitler. And it can be partnered with Roediger's and Frye Jacobson's work for teaching the emergence of eugenics, racial constructs, and the creation of 'Whiteness.' Whether you read *Diversity Without Dogma* as a stand-alone text or paired with canonical Diversity, Equity, & Inclusion (DEI) or Justice, Equity, Diversity, & Inclusion (JEDI) books, you will find it a valuable addition to your OD and DEI library."

Renée A. Freeman
CDO and Principal, Freeman Consulting & Associates, LLC
T-Group Facilitator at the Museum of Tolerance in Los Angeles, CA
Academic researcher of Faith, Culture, Texture, and
Color: Inclusivity Above the Neckline

"Gil Crosby's *Diversity Without Dogma* is a beautiful and powerful introduction to one of the taproots of the DEI 'family tree.' I am referring to the work of Kurt Lewin, The Grandfather of Applied Behavioral Science. Not everyone knows that his 1946 action research project in Connecticut was 'aimed' at racial issues in school systems and communities. But Gil Crosby knows! Thank you for this contribution to the fast-expanding DEI world, Gil. You make it very clear that these issues will not be resolved with training programs but only as mind-and heart-altering experiences embedded in culture-change (OD) initiatives."

Dr. John J. Scherer
Founding Partner, Scherer Leadership Center
Author of *Facing the Tiger: Five Questions that Change Everything*

"Gilmore Crosby's new book, *Diversity Without Dogma*, is a much-needed guide to both implementing organizational change to increase equity; and also to understand what actually leads to increasing equity. Spoiler alert: simply having a training where people may learn some of the history of codified inequality or engage in personal introspection is insufficient. I recall a time when a congenial and generally justice-minded colleague declared a voluntary DEI training to be a success. The smiling pause in the conversation implied it was my turn to heartily agree and move on to other topics. Dismay registered on their face when I disagreed and dissolved into further discomfort when they could not just brush me off as 'not being the target audience.' Without an attempt to recognize the systemic nature of racism, ableism, and sexism coupled by concrete action to rectify the same, DEI trainings often end up assuaging the inquietude of those who are worried about being blamed for -isms, wounding those who are negatively impacted by these -isms and doing nothing to improve an organization. *Diversity Without Dogma* provides the needed context for equitable organizational transformation and the blueprint to initiate and evaluate the action plans and trainings that are the key components to organizational change. *Diversity Without Dogma* is not just a book you read; it is a book you do."

Julie Pierce Onos, MBA
Professor of Business Administration at Fitchburg State University
Author of the forthcoming *Business Eco-Systems and Identity*, 1st Edition

"The interpersonal space is a myriad theater. It takes arduous, methodical, and caring focus to decipher from observation, then internalize integrative experiences, and finally socialize for impact. It takes a communicative intent as Gilmore here has epitomized to tie origins of applied behavioral science fundamentals to contemporary dynamics. This work again reminds us that in the social media barrage of cascade and dissentions, it is easy to forget basics while the epidemic of bias, prejudice, and even baseless hate rage on. Another inimitable essential reading for facilitators of human agency and goodwill. A masterful embodiment of Lewinian thought for times to come."

Joseph George Anjilvelil
Founder, Workplace Catalysts LLP, Bangalore, India
Author of *BEING PEOPLE: Life- histories of Six HRD Professionals of India*

"*Diversity Without Dogma* is a fascinating read! Crosby offers a thorough perspective of the road we have traveled to the current commitments to diversity equity and inclusion in organizations and in contemporary culture. He does so from a theoretical, historical, and practical/praxis perspective. I read Crosby's book with several lenses: As a consultant working with clients committed to creating more inclusive work cultures and enhancing diversity, equity and belonging in their organizations and their communities, as a board member of The Lewin Center, and as a fellow author who has explored how we make sense of and create our social worlds in our relationships with each other. In this book, Crosby has covered a lot of ground. Building on his prior scholarly work, he has done an excellent job weaving the gifts of Lewin's many theories and frameworks throughout in addressing the complexity of DEI initiatives. Specifically, force field analysis, action learning, how we create our social worlds, and engaging in healthy conflict. Lewin's work is timeless and Crosby's integration and synthesis of Lewin's work with considerations of how we recognize the gift of our differences is timeless and ever more critical to reference as we navigate today's discursive forces."

Ilene C. Wasserman, Ph.D.
President, The Lewin Center
Senior Leadership Fellow, Lead Executive Coach and Learning Director –
McNulty Leadership Program and Executive
Education at the Wharton School

"Gil Crosby has written a unique and valuable perspective on how we need to work with DEI in today's society. As a Lewin scholar, he weaves Lewin's social science throughout what is needed in approaching diversity, differences, conflicts, and dialogues. This book provides many reasons why so many approaches have produced limited results and new thinking on how to apply proven methods to improve communications among people with differences and systems with 'isms!'"

David W. Jamieson, Ph.D
President, NTL Institute for Applied Behavioral Science

"Gilmore Crosby is a wonderful writer, just as he is a wonderful human being. We write what we are. He and I can talk about anything and everything. It is funny, I was afraid to read his writing, but not to talk to him. I'm self-conscious about my lack of a formal education. However, the way Gilmore writes covers that completely. He writes for all people. One paragraph caused me to flash back to the supper table when I was 7 in North Carolina. My Dad and his brothers were talking and every other word was the 'N' word. Finally, I said Why do you guys TALK LIKE THAT. Mr Chesson (helper on the farm) is a very nice man and he would never talk like the way you guys are. My dad, feeling uncomfortable with his BROS, as they had gotten very quiet and were just staring at LITTLE ME, said, 'ROY, I DON'T KNOW WHY WE TALK LIKE THAT, IT IS THE WAY WE WERE RAISED, IT IS WHAT WE DO!' I looked at these guys and said 'WELL YOU ARE NOT GOING TO RAISE ME THAT WAY, I WILL NEVER TALK LIKE YOU DO, and I LOVE MR. CHESSON!' I jumped up and ran to the woods, but not before I heard one uncle say to my dad, 'BRO, YOU GOT YOUR HANDS FULL WITH THIS ONE!' And so he did. Also, in reading Gilmore's thoughts about LBGTQ, we are far more critical and rude to each other in our community than society could ever be. My Partner and I were so free that Gay people were afraid of us and ridiculed us constantly in the 70's. Mr. Crosby's intelligent yet understandable approach and his fearless belief that 'any prejudice begets more prejudice' is a breath of fresh air this country and world sorely needs."

Roi Barnard
Author of *Mister, Are You a Lady?*

"I was impressed with the analysis, at the outset, with reference to the reality and impact of race and class in Jamaica. Mr. Crosby's full and dynamic treatment of the subject of race and class are consistent with the extensive discussion by the late Professor Rex Nettleford (1970), especially in his book *Mirror Mirror*. In his book, *Identity, Race and Protest in Jamaica*, Nettleford (1970) highlights the intractable challenge of race and identity in Jamaica, and the reality of classism in this post slavery society. It is this challenge that Crosby takes on directly with his approach to diversity, equity, and inclusion, an approach which is referred to in other spheres as communication for development. A development agenda which takes the interest, welfare, and wellbeing of people seriously means putting people at the center of progress and taking into account what Nettleford (1970) refers to as the dynamic and diverse aspects of the Jamaican people. It is this dynamism which Robert Nester 'Bob' Marley sings about as 'One love, one heart, let's get together and be alright.' This bringing or coming together of diverse aspects of Jamaican or American society include lessons for the global families of peoples. Though the book is largely related to the American context, it is vital that we learn from, support, and implement this vision of diversity over dogma in the global community."

Rt Reverend Garth Minott
Bishop of Kingston
Episcopal/Anglican Church of Jamaica

"Gilmore Crosby has provided more than the technical and practical understanding one needs to appreciate and apply my grandfather's ideas in this book. Crosby has also captured the heart, the values, and the high respect for the individual that drove all of Kurt Lewin's work. I am glad he is continuing to share and pass along this valuable insight about Lewin's legacy, which is needed as much now as anytime since his death."

Michael Papanek
Leadership and OD Consultant, Grandson of Kurt Lewin

"Many people skip reading the introduction of a book. Please don't skip this one! Gil has started this book with a bang. Great insights and truths that in themselves change the conversation and actions related to race and diversity."

Frederick A. Miller
CEO, The Kaleel Jamison Consulting Group, Inc.
Co-author, with Judith Katz, of *The Inclusion Breakthrough*
(2002) and the forthcoming *Creating Inclusive Cultures with
Change Champions: A Dialogic Approach* with
Judith Katz and Monica Biggs

Diversity Without Dogma

Social Scientist Kurt Lewin said, "No research without action, and no action without research." Too much of the current DEI (diversity, equity, and inclusion) approach is insight-based instead of action-based. Even though institutional racism is identified as the root problem, the change effort is focused on looking inward for bias instead of taking action to eliminate institutional racism and other isms. A Lewinian approach, in contrast, is balanced. What people think *is* important, but no more important than what people *do*. If you bring people together to change things, this will change what people think! We don't need therapy nearly as much as we need action based on dialogue! Instead of spending your energy soul-searching for evidence in your thoughts and behaviors that you have unconscious biases, this book helps put your energy into doing something practical about racism.

To get there, this book uses Lewin's social science to build a framework for sorting through the many approaches to and positions held on race, racism, diversity, and related topics. While the framework is and must be applicable to any prejudice, systemic or individual, the bulk of this exploration is focused on racism, which to a large degree has become the primary social justice focus of our times. Painfully aware that conversations about race can easily deteriorate into polarization, the author lays a path toward finding common ground.

Diversity Without Dogma
A Collaborative Approach to Leading DEI Education and Action

Gilmore Crosby

Routledge
Taylor & Francis Group
A PRODUCTIVITY PRESS BOOK

Cover Image Credit: Norman Hathaway

First Published 2023
by Routledge
605 Third Avenue, New York, NY 10158

and by Routledge
4 Park Square, Milton Park, Abingdon, Oxon, OX14 4RN

Routledge is an imprint of the Taylor & Francis Group, an informa business

ISBN: 978-1-032-37175-7 (hbk)
ISBN: 978-1-032-37174-0 (pbk)
ISBN: 978-1-003-33568-9 (ebk)

DOI: 10.4324/9781003335689

Typeset in Minion Pro
by KnowledgeWorks Global Ltd.

"The burden of being black and the burden of being white is so heavy that it is rare in our society to experience oneself as a human being. It may be, I don't know, that to experience oneself as a human being is one with experiencing one's fellows as human beings. It means that the individual must have a sense of kinship to life that transcends and goes beyond the immediate kinship of family or the organic kinship that binds him (or her) ethnically or 'racially' or nationally. He has a sense of being an essential part of the structural relationship that exists between him and all other men (and women), and between him, all other men (and women), and the total external environment. As a human being, then, he belongs to life and the whole kingdom of life that includes all that lives and perhaps, also, all that has ever lived. In other words, he sees himself as part of a continuing, breathing, living existence. To be a human being, then, is to be essentially alive in a living world."

Howard Thurman (1965, p. 94)

"When you plant lettuce, if it does not grow well, you don't blame the lettuce. You look into the reasons it is not doing well. It may need fertilizer, or more water, or less sun. You never blame the lettuce. Yet if we have problems with our friends or our family, we blame the other person. But if we know how to take care of them, they will grow well, like lettuce. Blaming has no positive effect at all, nor does trying to persuade using reason and arguments. That is my experience. No blame, no reasoning, no argument, just understanding. If you understand, and you show that you understand, you can love, and the situation will change."

Thich Nhat Hanh (Hahn, 1991, p. 78)

"Anytime you have an opportunity to make a difference in this world and you don't, then you are wasting your time on earth."

Roberto Clemente

"Where do we go from here? Chaos or community?"

Martin Luther King, Jr.

"United we stand, divided we fall."

Aesop

I dedicate this to Thich Nhat Hanh, a relentless crusader for world peace who passed away as I was in the process of completing it. Also, to Roberto Clemente, Howard Thurman, and Kurt Lewin. Especially to my father, Robert P. Crosby, my wife, Alecia, and my grandchildren, Loki, Chloe, and Makia.

Contents

SECTION III   IT'S NOT ALWAYS ABOUT RACISM

SECTION IV   LEADING DEI EDUCATION AND ACTION

Introduction – Why We Need a Better Approach

The society is the enemy when it imposes its structures on the individual. On the dragon there are many scales. Every one of them says "Thou shalt." Kill the dragon "Thou shalt."

Joseph Campbell (Osbon, 1991, p. 21)

This book has been written to slay the dragon "Thou shalt." The dragon in this case is racism and any other form of prejudice. The dragon is also dogma in the fight against racism. The dragon of dogma, "we hold the truth about you," burns collaboration to ashes with its fiery breath.

A collaborative approach is needed because societal dynamics like racism, sexism, and any and all forms of individual prejudice and systemic oppression, breed confusion. This confusion gets in the way of the "sense of kinship...to all that lives and...all that has ever lived" spoken of in the opening quote by Howard Thurman[1] (1900–1981) (Thurman, 1965, p. 94). It leads to proclamations of "thou shalt." It allows those of us who are committed to equality to be divided. We will be prone to confusion and division as long as there is inequality, and confusion and division help perpetuate the problem we are trying to solve.

That was the conclusion of a man ahead of his time, social scientist Kurt Lewin (1890–1947). Lewin's social science, if we choose to use it, provides a foundation for understanding and addressing the contemporary dynamics of prejudice. This book lays out a "Lewinian" framework to decrease polarization and guide dialogue and action on social justice issues. Lewin's methods are inclusive. Whatever our position in the system, whether we have privilege or lack it, we must each step up and help each other if we are to get unstuck from past and present imbalances. As Lewin put it, "... so-called minority problems are in fact majority problems" (Lewin, 1946, 1997, p. 151).

Lewin said, "No research without action, and no action without research." Too much of the current DEI (diversity, equity and inclusion) approach is insight-based, instead of action based. Even though institutional racism is identified as the root problem, the change effort is focused on looking inward for bias instead of taking action to eliminate institutional racism and other isms. Lewin's approach is balanced. What people think *is important*, but no more important than what people *do*. If you bring people together to change things, *this will change what people think!* We don't need therapy; we need action based on dialogue. That will be the best therapy! It's time for a bias for action! Instead of spending your energy soul-searching for evidence in your thoughts and behaviors that you have unconscious biases, put your energy into doing something practical about racism (the reader will find plenty of examples of what that might be in this book, especially in Chapter 14)! Even if you have prejudice, do things to rid the world of racism! That is better than having no prejudice and doing nothing! We don't have to wallow in guilt and/or be saints! "Search yourself," as Bob Marley said, but when push comes to shove, favor action over insight!

This text then will use Lewin's social science to sort through the many approaches to and positions held on race, racism, diversity, and related topics. While the framework is and must be applicable to any prejudice, systemic or individual, the bulk of this exploration will focus on racism, which, for many reasons, has become the primary social justice focus of our times.

Like anything that matters, the topic of racism sells, and people become emotionally attached to what they have created or bought into. Because the topic is so highly emotional, it can be difficult to talk about it and difficult to differentiate what is a quality approach from what is not. Despite the difficulties, it is important to do exactly that so as to minimize backlashes and erosion of confidence in what can and should be done and to guide constructive action.

Part of what divides those of us who are struggling against racism is semantics. Most people think of racism as prejudice held toward another group. Historian Ibram Kendi defines racism this way: "… to say something is wrong with a group is to say something is inferior about that group … My definition of a racist idea is a simple one: It is any concept that regards one racial group as inferior or superior to another racial group in any way" (Kendi, 2016, p. 5). In other words, any negative stereotype held about other people that you think of as a "race" is racism.

The categorization of groups by race is not scientific; it is social (in the eyes of the beholder). Such categorization may include a mix of geographical, religious, and ethnic commonalities and usually includes generalizations regarding superficial physical differences (such as skin color). If you go to virtually any region in the world, you will find local prejudices based on concepts of race. Jamaica, a culture full of love (which I love deeply, consider my second home, and mean no disrespect towards!), can nonetheless help us understand Kendi's concept of racism. Jamaica is a useful contrast to the US because it is primarily what most people would consider a "black" population. Applying Kendi's definition, this does not mean there is no racism. Having spent decades working there (and with the added insight from my marriage to a Jamaican), I know there are negative racial stereotypes held in Jamaica (as there are pretty much everywhere) toward "whites" (including prejudice *favoring* pale-skinned Jamaicans, known as "brownings"), toward Chinese, toward immigrant Indian businessmen, toward Muslims, and no doubt toward others.

Let us turn here to Sociologist Robin DiAngelo, a leading voice on DEI and author of the best-selling book *White Fragility*. As if the subject of race is not touchy enough, talking about DiAngelo is just as touchy, and there is a risk of losing some readers by either agreeing or disagreeing with her. Hopefully, the reader will take a slow, deep breath and read the full introduction more than once if they have a strong reaction; otherwise, misunderstanding and reactivity may close the mind to what follows. That is good advice in all attempts at DEI related dialogue and indeed in all attempts to talk about difficult subjects.

The approach to DEI presented here aligns with DiAngelo in some ways but differs with her in others. Her work has played a significant role in raising the DEI conversation to a much broader audience. A downside is that there are many who are passionately attached to her and/or her message and are quick to jump to her defense. This is partially because DiAngelo offers no clear framework for how to have dialogue (mutual exploration) or how to give and receive feedback. When she leads a much-needed conversation on racism, the conversation predictably digresses into polarizing debate. She herself predicts it, writing that reactive debate happens over and over again during her workshops. She ascribes the cause to the "defensiveness" of the white participants, not to how she is relating to them.

In contrast, this book provides an approach that encourages dialogue instead of debate. The million-dollar question is whether the writer and the reader will find common ground long enough to get past initial reactions, if strong, so the reader can give this approach a chance.

Let's return to the example of prejudice in Jamaica. DiAngelo's approach wouldn't consider any of the aforementioned Jamaican behavior "racism." Neither do many Jamaicans. In my wife's eyes, the national motto, "Out of many, one people," is how Jamaicans truly see each other. They are one people regardless of their ethnic roots or the color of their skin. Given that perspective, Jamaicans tend to think that racism is something that occurs elsewhere and that it is perpetrated by "white people." DiAngelo's thinking essentially agrees. She asserts that "racism – like sexism and other forms of oppression – occurs when a racial group's prejudice is backed by legal authority and institutional control" (DiAngelo, 2018, p. 20). The people who have held that "authority and institutional control" in recent history across most of the globe are "whites." This power-based definition, while being accepted more and more in academic and sociological circles, is not how most people think, at least not in the US. Consequently, DiAngelo is constantly dealing with "defensive" responses when she asserts that "only whites can be racist" (DiAngelo, 2018, p. 22). Scattered in her writing are explanations that what she means is that whites are part of and beneficiaries of a system that is racist, but that is not how many people hear it. She further blurs her own meaning with statements such as, "All white people are invested in and collude with racism" (DiAngelo, 2018, p. 116) and that white people have "unaware yet inevitable racism" (DiAngelo, 2018, p. 113). The people she is lecturing, if they think of themselves as "white," can understandably hear these messages as a blanket accusation of prejudice.

Further complicating a topic that is complicated enough already, some African-Americans who hear the "only whites can be racist" message understandably think it means they cannot be racist. Technically, by Ms. DiAngelo's definition, they are right. African-Americans do not have the power structure of racism behind them, so they do not fit into this definition of racism.

Unfortunately, looking at it that way takes a very nuanced perspective, and it is easy to miss DiAngelo's purported meaning. Instead, minorities may understandably take this definition of racism as permission to say whatever they want to "white" people and to dismiss any of the predictably defensive responses as more proof of "racism" in a similar fashion as DiAngelo. They are grasping one end of two poles: individualism and systemic thinking. Because they are in a systemically racist system, they may think DiAngelo (and others) mean they have no personal responsibility for their own reactions. In the intensity of such conversations, if one does talk of responsibility at the interpersonal level, the message is predictably dismissed as "blaming the victim." That imbalance in conversations is not the intent of DiAngelo's message, but it is part of the impact (an impact she doesn't acknowledge … at least not in her book and other writings to the best of my knowledge).

Rather than trying to fight the needless and uphill battle of confronting the majority and attempting to teach them what DiAngelo means when she says, "only whites can be racist," we need to find a way to come together against racism. This means adopting Kendi's definition of racism instead of DiAngelo's. Prejudice is a tense enough topic and problem without us adding to the tension! As Rodney Coates, the co-author of *The Matrix of Race,* put it to me, "… micro-aggression and blind spots are the wrong way to start conversations about diversity" (Crosby, 2021a, p. 119). Starting with fighting words and expecting people to come together is a mistake! To some extent, I have already done that by laying out my differences with DiAngelo, but I think that contrast is important as we explore what to do and what not to do. Hopefully, the reader will bear with me.

We must slay the dragon of needless polarization to find common ground. Addressing race relations by telling people "thou shalt" is counterproductive. Policing words and behaviors is polarizing. Teaching that racism is unconsciously within all whites, that only the "other" people are to blame for interpersonal tension, or that judgments about others (such as they are "being defensive") are incontrovertibly true is the dogma referred to in the title. The Merriam-Webster definition of *dogma* is "a belief or set of beliefs that is accepted by the members of a group without being questioned or doubted." *Dogma* is undemocratic and adds to the confusion and inflames the fight-flight responses, including defensiveness, of those trying to engage in dialogue about racism and other DEI issues. It's time for an approach that is less focused on judging what we think and say and more focused on building alliances and getting things done.

Besides a passion for change, one such common ground shared by DiAngelo, Lewin, Kendi, and others is the assertion that race is a false hypothesis. There are real cultural and ethnic differences, but the concept of race does not stand up to scientific scrutiny on a biological level in any way, shape, or form beyond skin pigmentation and other superficial characteristics. Even those don't fall neatly into categories. Race is a twisted example of the "social construction of reality." We believe it because we have been taught it.

Many trace the assertion of racism as we know it to the papal decree in 1493, giving the Catholics of Spain and Portugal dominion over the new world (along with the cause of converting everyone in it). It was codified into Virginia law in 1691 to divide the servant classes and prevent uprisings (see Chapter 5) and further legitimized by "scientists" such as the German anthropologist Johaan Blumenbock who asserted in 1795 that blond, blue-eyed people were the most beautiful and had originated in the Caucus mountains (Raj Bophal, 2007, pp. 14). Such widely un-factual "scientific" conclusions have been adopted by those who were looking to justify power, in this case, the power of pale-skinned people over all others. The myth of the Caucuses has stuck to this very day as the term "Caucasian."

Power imbalance and the coveting of the same is the root of this evil, and Lewin demonstrated that as long as there is significant power imbalance, both the people who "hold power" and the people who are relatively powerless will be confused and twisted by the inequality. That does not mean one cannot wield power in a positive way. We need the "power" of leadership to create change. How to effectively lead and be led will be part of this framework and is explored carefully in Chapter 12.

What seems forgotten in current discussions of racism is that power imbalances and abuse have been true throughout history. That is not an excuse. It is a cold hard fact that can shed light on our current dilemmas. Women have been relatively powerless throughout recorded history, and many have blamed themselves for failings that were rooted in patriarchy and sexism. As Howard Thurman illuminates in his *Jesus and the Disinherited*, Jews during the time of Jesus were powerless under Roman rule, and many must have asked themselves whether they had somehow brought their lot upon themselves. The Old Testament is full of beliefs that it is the chosen people's own fault that they are suffering. In Lewin's mind, the powerless are forever on the margin, never sure if what is holding them back is their own behavior or the racism/sexism of the people they are dealing with. Am I being held back or reacted to in this moment because I am black? Because I am a woman? Are people against me because I am a white male? Am I struggling because of personal shortcomings and behaviors I need to address? How can I tell the difference? That is the foggy territory we tread.

Most people on Lewin's "margin" will long to be part of the good life being lived by the group in power, even to the point of identifying with, imitating, and trying to fit into that group while simultaneously feeling something akin to repulsion to some degree toward those very same people. For example, many (far too many!) dark-skinned people in Jamaica, India, and no doubt elsewhere, attempt to lighten their skin with bleach and other "treatments" to look more like those who have held power, wealth, and socially constructed standards of beauty. Beauty is in the eye of the beholder and, as such, is universal to all shades, but racism has blinded countless numbers of the oppressors and the oppressed to that fact. The damage to self-esteem to anyone who does not think their skin pigmentation meets the standard of how a person should look is reason enough to fight racism.

Lewin's person "on the margin" will also long to feel pride in their own group even while feeling resentment and embarrassment over the disadvantages, self-doubt, and often-desperate behavior that powerlessness brings with it. They may vacillate from pride to anger to despair. They belong firmly to neither world and can easily be plagued by confusion and doubt as long as the inequality they are living in continues to exist. To some extent, we are all on that margin, and consequently *we are all fragile.* The individual experience is important in this puzzle, but the puzzle itself is systemic.

The person in the group "in power," despite the real advantages, is also in a confusing position. Far too many whites in the US today defensively cling to the illusion of individualism and racial superiority and/or deny that institutional racism still exists. Even if they see and acknowledge racism, others wallow in confusion, guilt, and fear of black violence. On a recent call to a colleague in Ukraine, I asked if she was fearful of a Russian invasion. She told me that life in her city was completely unaffected by the Russian troops amassed on the border and that the whole thing was being blown out of proportion by the media[2]. Then, she asked me if I was ok. She had just talked with colleagues in Los Angeles and San Francisco, two white women, and both feared that blacks would commit violence in their neighborhoods. I was stunned and assured her that I had no such fears, nor any reason to and that I doubt the women were in any danger either. That sample of how some white Americans perceive the world is nonetheless part of the puzzle we must solve.

We have our work cut out for us, and we need to invite all the help we can get, including those two women. As Lewin put it, inequality is a problem for the majority and the minority. Equality, as much as can be achieved by human society, is the only solution. Lewin was effective in using his "action research" methods to address prejudice and move toward equality.

His methods, mostly forgotten, are still available. My sincere hope is that this framework, based on Lewin's social science, will help create dialogue and action in the direction of real and lasting change.

Objectivity! Humility! Forgiveness! Dialogue! Collaboration! Action! That is what needs to be instilled into the struggle for equity! Most of all, even if we are not perfect, we must act out of love! If you have gotten this far, thanks for joining this journey!

Disclosure: I am writing this from and mostly about the United States. While some global history and perspective are included, I focus primarily here on the nation I call home. If well received, perhaps a second volume will attempt a more global reach. This is more a matter of scope than value. I also believe wholeheartedly that the DEI framework presented herein can be adapted and applied anywhere.

A note on the acronym "DEI." The language for describing the issue is always evolving, and I recognize that DEI is only one of many evolving ways to talk about racial and other personal and institutional prejudices. By the time I am done writing this, another letter may have been added to the common jargon. I ask the reader to bear with me as I stick with what is the most common usage at this time.

I also ask the reader to join me in the spirit of exploration. This is a serious subject, and I am dead serious about relentlessly pursuing the goal. At the same time, we must figure out how to lighten up, or instead of having a dialogue, we are certain to get bogged down into polarized debate. That will lead to further division and failure. The intent of this framework is to help people figure out how to talk about these issues without constant tension. Tension puts the reptilian brain in charge, with fear-based reactions of fight (constant oppositional "logic") and flight (avoidance). It is time to be playful yet serious and to treat one another with kindness. It is also time to experiment together and not get hung up on expressing our thoughts just right or using the right jargon. Such rigidity kills creativity and keeps things stuck. We'll explore those dynamics further, especially in Chapter 11, Conflict Beliefs and Behaviors.

Disclaimer: I struggle with using words like "white" because they were popularized as part of the system of racism introduced in the US, as we shall see in Chapter 5. It is possible that using terms created to segment the population as a means to assert inequality, such as White, Black and Asian, will perpetuate more of the same. More accurate language would describe pigmentation, starting with the palest pale and ranging to the darkest dark. As my father has often pointed out, his skin isn't white; the background of this page is white. His skin and mine are difficult to accurately describe using available colors, but we are some sort of blend of very light brown, with perhaps pink and yellow. The Native American term "Pale Skin" is certainly more accurate than "White." Nonetheless, perhaps because I have been accultured to these terms, I chose to mostly use the word white when referring to light-colored people and black when referring to dark-colored people. I put them into quotation marks at times in an attempt to remind the reader that such categorizations of people are opinions that keep shifting with the sands of time, as we shall see.

In a similar vein, I use a plethora of historical sources and have not tried to update the language from quotes into the common usage of today; hence, the language in quotes is often patriarchal, and the reader is asked to be patient with outdated terms such as the word negro.

I also ask the reader to bear with me as I switch at times from third person to first person. I primarily do so when I am using my own experiences to illustrate this emotionally charged topic and when I want to be clear that I am speaking for myself (which is a much-needed behavioral skill). While my goal is to lend as much objectivity to this topic as possible, I do not want to hide behind a veil of objectivity. The truth requires a blend of subjectivity and objectivity.

A final note to the reader. As in my previous book, *Planned Change*, I have relied heavily here on Kurt Lewin's writing. There are many quotes and citations. Many of his papers are collected in two wonderful anthologies published by the American Psychological Association (APA). The first, *Resolving Social Conflicts & Field Theory in Social Science*, was published in 1997, and the second, *The Complete Social Scientist*, in 1999. To acknowledge these anthologies, I have chosen to cite the original source by year and add the APA dates and pages (since the two APA books are where most readers are likely to access the material). Hence, you will see citations like this throughout this manuscript: (Lewin, 1943, 1997, p. 73).

NOTES

1. Regarded by many as the father of the civil rights movement. Thurman was pastor to both Martin Luther King, Jr. and to my father at Boston University.
2. That was before the invasion. She holds no such illusions now.

Section I

Building a Foundation

1

A Framework for DEI Education and Action

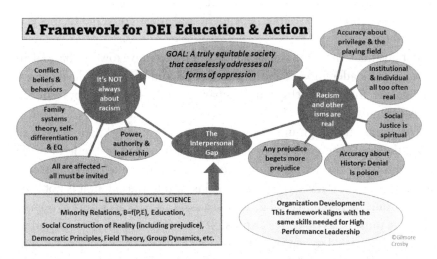

FIGURE 1.1
A framework for DEI education and action.

Here is an explanation of the framework in a nutshell:

People are teaching about diversity, equity, and inclusion without any clarity about how to approach the topic. This can easily make things worse instead of better. White people, in particular, often exit such trainings feeling blamed and less open-minded afterward instead of more. We need as inclusive an approach as possible, beginning with having a shared understanding of how to approach the topic (Figure 1.1).

I don't care if everyone uses this model, but they should try to organize their thinking in some way and make it transparent to the people they are teaching!

DOI: 10.4324/9781003335689-2

Having said that, let me be clear that you do have my permission to use the model or to adapt it to your needs with proper credit please. For more on adapting versus adopting, read Appendix D.

The framework begins with Kurt Lewin's social science as the foundation. Lewin applied it successfully to addressing racism and other forms of prejudice, so we don't need to reinvent the wheel! We can use his methods.

Next comes John Wallen's *Interpersonal Gap* as a way of understanding communication, how easy it is to screw it up, and what to do to fix it. We are responsible for ourselves, whether sending or receiving!

Then, we diverge toward understanding racism in one direction and toward understanding conflict and issues that are not racism (but may occur simultaneously with racism) in the other direction.

The two branches are interdependent and must converge to move us toward the goal.

For business, the same skills that are needed to move toward the goal are essential to leadership and performance. DEI and leadership development can be one, instead of being taught separately and competing for resources as is common practice today.

For a more thorough understanding of this framework, one must start with the goal. The goal, in turn, must be understood in the light of the elements of the framework. Equity, for example, must include an objective assessment of how level the playing field is, and to the extent it is not level, action must be taken to level it. To ceaselessly address all forms of oppression, we must be as objective as possible about what oppression is, and we must not be afraid to confront it.

The goal is pursued through application. Any event now or historically could be influenced by the poison of racism, sexism, or any other form of prejudice and/or systemic/institutional oppression. Any event may simply be the result of interpersonal and other tensions that have nothing to do with prejudice or "the system." If we don't have an objective framework for considering both, we will create needless conflict by blaming people who are innocent, and we will obscure conditions that need to be addressed.

When leading DEI learning in organizations, one need not separate it from other organizational needs. If DEI is thought of as something you are supposed to do ("thou shalt") but not as something related to performance, the likelihood of sustained effort and real change diminishes. Trying to convince decision makers that having more diversity will automatically improve performance is a thin argument, not backed by most studies on the topic, and so easily refuted. Using this DEI framework bridges that gap. The framework is grounded in the same leadership, conflict, and dialogue skills needed for high individual, group, and organizational performance. There is plenty of data to back that up, starting with Kurt Lewin's research (some of which is covered in Chapter 2) and continuing into the present day. The goals of true equity and organizational performance can be pursued simultaneously.

Next in the framework comes the foundation, the social science of Kurt Lewin. We will explore that in detail in the next chapter. By way of introduction, Lewin believed that sociological and psychological phenomena, including prejudice based on any criteria (such as race or gender), must be understood and addressed in a scientific manner. He devised and tested a scientific approach that worked both in his experiments and in the efforts of others. By experiments, I mean he used his methods in real-world situations, in industry, and in society. He also applied them at the level of the individual, the group, and as we shall see, the same methods almost certainly influenced the reconstruction of Germany and Japan.

IMAGE 1.1
Kurt Lewin and Elanor Roosevelt, Copyright © Michael Papanek. (Used with permission.)

Lewin believed an effective social science should be applicable to all situations, be they small or large. If a person is interacting with someone who is different from themselves in some generally obvious way, such as gender, and there arises tension in the interaction, a solid DEI framework should help the people involved understand what is happening. It is possible the tension has nothing to do with gender, and so, the intrapersonal (within the individual) and interpersonal (between the individuals) must be considered. It's possible the tension is about gender at an interpersonal and intrapersonal level but is not related to anything else. An example would be that one or both parties hold stereotypes of how gender should behave that the other party does not hold or unresolved anger toward a parent. It could also be that larger institutional dynamics are at play, such as a belief, supported by others, that certain jobs and skills are only suited to one gender. That would almost certainly be an example of institutional sexism. There could also be larger dynamics at play that result in tension between individuals and groups that have nothing to do with institutional isms, such as goal misalignment between groups (maintenance and production, for example, or a location and a corporate headquarters) or different roles in the organization (such as management and labor). To further complicate the possible root cause of the tension, other types of prejudice could be at play (racism, etc.). Figure 1.2 illustrates these different levels and dynamics.

It would be nice if it was simpler, but as Lewin's social science demonstrates, as long as there is inequality, there will be increased ambiguity. That's why it is easy to blame the innocent and to hide the guilty, and that is why we will all be a little crazy until true equality is achieved. Assuming it is one thing or another is tricky business, and error-likely. Seeing through this fog as accurately as possible requires social science clarity and is explored from various angles in this framework but especially by applying a model known as *The Interpersonal Gap* in Chapter 3. If we take the shortcut of dogma (all white people are racist, for example), we head down the slippery slope of fighting prejudice with prejudice, leading to predictable and understandable polarization.

This framework instead asserts that any prejudice begets more of the same and is more harmful than helpful to the overall goal. Furthermore, any such divisive approach works against the framework standard of *All are affected – All must be invited*. In other words, everything in this framework is linked together and is important to pursuing the goal.

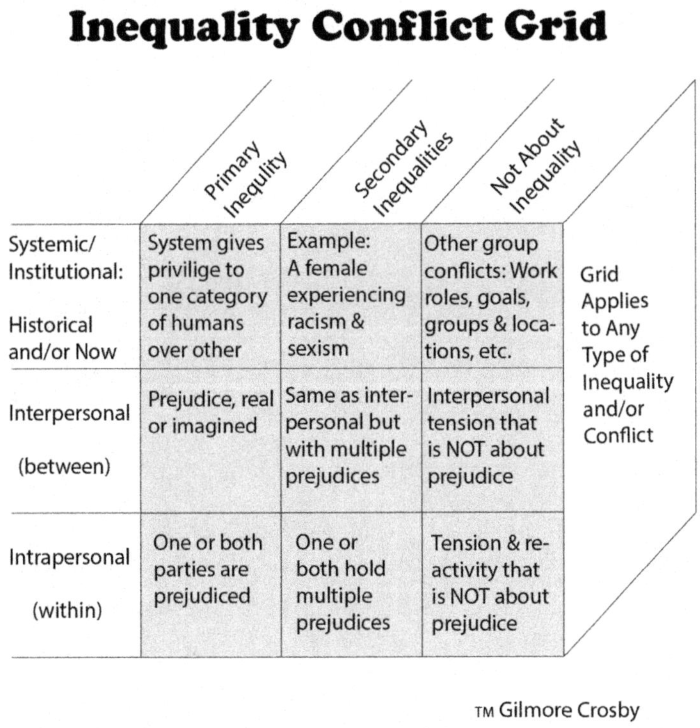

Inequality Conflict Grid

	Primary Inequility	Secondary Inequalities	Not About Inequality	
Systemic/ Institutional: Historical and/or Now	System gives privilige to one category of humans over other	Example: A female experiencing racism & sexism	Other group conflicts: Work roles, goals, groups & locations, etc.	Grid Applies to Any Type of Inequality and/or Conflict
Interpersonal (between)	Prejudice, real or imagined	Same as interpersonal but with multiple prejudices	Interpersonal tension that is NOT about prejudice	
Intrapersonal (within)	One or both parties are prejudiced	One or both hold multiple prejudices	Tension & reactivity that is NOT about prejudice	

™ Gilmore Crosby

FIGURE 1.2
Inequality conflict grid.

Sections II and III explore each element of the framework in detail, while Section IV moves on to application and action. That's what we need, so let us begin!

2

Lewinian Social Science[1]

Social Science Concepts Relevant to Prejudice and Inequality

Minority Relations - *Inequality places us all in ambiguity about identity and what is causing behavior*

B=f(P,E) - *Behavior is a function of the Personality and the Environment*

The Social Construction of Reality - *Race is a social construction, not a biological fact*

Democratic Principles - *Inequality is antithetical to real democracy*

Field Theory - *Systems tend towards homeostasis*

Group Dynamics - *Positive peer pressure is the most reliable path towards individual change*

Prejudice as a False Hypothesis - *Prejudicial thinking can be shown to be based on false premises*

Re-education - *People must be able to think for themselves or change won't stick*

Action Research – *Anyone can be trained to conduct effective social change methods*

FIGURE 2.1
Social science concepts relevant to prejudice and inequality.

KURT LEWIN INVENTS HIS SOCIAL SCIENCE

Kurt Lewin was born in 1890 in Mogilno, in the Prussian province of Posen (now part of Poland, then part of pre-WWI Germany). Lewin was a Jewish male in Germany during the rise of Hitler. He experienced racism firsthand and also the triumph of authoritarianism over democracy.

As if that wasn't enough to deal with, Lewin mounted his trusty steed and charged the windmills of the separation of scientific methodology from the field of psychology and related studies of human behavior (Figure 2.1).

DOI: 10.4324/9781003335689-3

Giants of the field, such as Freud, elaborated theories that had never been tested. Lewin went about the business of borrowing research methods from the physical sciences and applying them to the study of being human.

Above all else, Lewin had faith that if humanity is to build a path for creating a better world, that path must be based on *reason*. In Lewin's words, "To believe in reason is to believe in democracy, because it grants to the reasoning partners a status of equality. It is therefore not an accident that not until the rise of democracy at the time of the American and French Revolutions was the goddess of reason enthroned in modern society. And again, it is not an accident that the very first act of modern Fascism in every country has been officially and vigorously to dethrone this goddess and instead to make emotions and obedience the all-ruling principles in education and life from kindergarten to death" (Lewin, 1939, 1997, p. 67).

We will address those founders, warts, and all, later on. Meanwhile what's important, and worth celebrating, is that Lewin went about the business of creating what he called "social science," with the ambition of developing theories that could address real social problems, such as racism, whether the focus was at the level of the individual, group, or society as a whole.

The hypothesis of this framework is that he succeeded and that the same Lewinian methods used to address organizational challenges by my father before me (starting in 1953), and in my own career (beginning in 1984), are exactly what is needed to create dialogue based on reason and real change in pursuit of social equity.

MINORITY RELATIONS

Minority relations, as Lewin put inequality, are a practical example of his social science framework in action. Lewin was clear that inequality influences how we think and interact with each other, and that a golden age where everyone is granted equal rights and perceived with equal respect won't come by minority individuals pulling themselves up by their bootstraps one person at a time into the majority culture, even though "fitting in" has long been an understandable and crazymaking aspiration of the oppressed. Inequality and prejudice are systemic issues and require systemic answers. Let us allow an excerpt from Lewin's prolific writing, in this case published in 1939, to speak for itself:

It is well to realize that every underprivileged minority group is kept together not only by cohesive forces among its members but also by the boundary which the majority erects against the crossing of an individual from the minority to the majority group. It is in the interest of the majority to keep the minority in its underprivileged status. There are minorities which are kept together almost entirely by such a wall around them. The members of these minorities show certain typical characteristics resulting from this situation. Every individual likes to gain in social status. Therefore the member of an underprivileged group will try to leave it for the more privileged majority. In other words, he will try to do what in the case of Negroes is called "passing," in the case of Jews, "assimilation." It would be an easy solution of the minority problem if it could be done away with through individual assimilation. Actually, however, such a solution is impossible for any underprivileged group. Equal rights for women could not be attained by one after the other being granted the right to vote; the Negro problem cannot be solved by individual "passing." A few Jews might be fully accepted by non-Jews. This chance, however, is today more meager than ever and certainly it is absurd to believe that fifteen million Jews can sneak over the boundary one by one.

What then is the situation of a member of a minority group kept together merely by the repulsion of the majority? The basic factor in his life is his wish to cross this insuperable boundary. Therefore, he lives almost perpetually in a state of conflict and tension. He dislikes or even hates his own group because it is nothing but a burden to him. Like an adolescent who does not wish to be a child any longer but who knows that he is not accepted as an adult, such a person stands at the borderline of his group, being neither here nor there. He is unhappy and shows the typical characteristics of a marginal man who does not know where he belongs. A Jew of this type will dislike everything specifically Jewish, for he will see in it that which keeps him away from the majority for which he is longing. He will show dislike for those Jews who are outspokenly so and will frequently indulge in self-hatred.

There is one more characteristic peculiar to minority groups kept together merely by outside pressure as contrasted with the members of a minority who have a positive attitude towards their own group. The latter group will have an organic life of its own. It will show organization and inner strength. A minority kept together only from outside is in itself chaotic. It is composed of a mass of individuals without inner relations with each other, a group unorganized and weak.

Lewin (1939, 1997, p. 119)

Lewin's following topographical drawing[2] (Figure 2.2) depicts the minority person on the margin between the majority group and their own group.

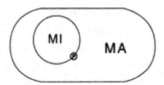

The marginal man. The person (*P*) standing on the boundary between the minority group *MI* and the *majority* group *MA*.

FIGURE 2.2
The marginal person.

Being on the margin has many subtle and insidious effects. The margin is where institutional inequality and individual prejudice intersect. Faced with resistance, the individual cannot know whether what they are experiencing is systemic, interpersonal, or just their spider senses alarming them because everything has begun to look like evidence of oppression. Have they come up against the glass ceiling or is it that they are really not the best candidate? Is their personal resistance to inequality a strength or do they have a bad attitude that is causing needless tension? Is the person or group that is not promoting them prejudiced or are they simply making the best decision based on fair criteria?

Lewin, facing the same ambiguity in his Jewish experience, explains this way: "*Unclearness* as to whether, in a given case, a set-back is due to the individual's lack of ability or due to anti-Semitism. If the young Jew is refused a job, is not invited to a birthday party, is not asked to join a club, he is usually not fully clear as to whether he himself is to blame or whether he is being discriminated against. A person who knows that his own shortcomings have caused his failure may do something to overcome them, or, if that is not possible, he can decide to apply his efforts in other directions.

If he knows that his being refused has nothing to do with his own abilities he will not blame himself, and instead may try to change the social reality. However, if he is in doubt as to whether his own shortcomings are the cause of his experience, he will be disorientated. He will intermittently blame himself and refuse responsibility, blame the others and be apologetic. In other words, this unclearness necessarily leads to a disorganized emotional behavior on the area of self-esteem..." (Lewin, 1999, p. 329).

Thus, ambiguity, which is already a fact of life, combines with mistrust in every interaction in an unequal system. What's real gets missed or easily denied, and what's innocent gets viewed with suspicion. False certainty and creeping doubts poison interactions, as we shall see in Chapter 3. Only by relentlessly working toward systemic equality can we truly decrease the confusion and tension which inequality add to the social fabric.

B = f(P,E)

Lewin boiled things down into formulas that could visually summarize and represent social science concepts. B = f(P,E) was important at the time and is still important today. B stands for behavior, P stands for personality, E stands for the environment, and f means that behavior is a function of personality and the environment. In other words, individual behavior at any given moment is both about nature (what is inside you) and nurture (the environment you are in and have grown up in).

This is another way of saying what we have already been covering. The individual is an important variable, as is the context. Social change must recognize and address both.

THE SOCIAL CONSTRUCTION OF REALITY

No one is born hating another person because of the color of his skin, or his background, or his religion.

Nelson Mandela

The social construction of reality is a concept that takes B = f(P,E) to the next level. It basically boils down to this – everything we think and believe *is a social concept*. If you accept this hypothesis, then you are free to influence and alter your social construction of reality. I am attempting to do so with this book. The possibility of altering the social construction of reality is why DEI learning can make a difference.

The social construction of reality implies that we are all a product of our environment, including the sum of what has come before us. Language is an example. You and I didn't just make it up. It is socially constructed by the generations before us. It comes in a variety of forms based on history and culture. Depending on when and where one is born, one learns to speak and think in terms of a primary language, and possibly secondary languages, emerging blends, and so on.

Having been born into a part of the world that was once ruled or at least influenced by the British Empire, I speak English (and apparently, you read it). Individuals born in other places and times speak the mother tongue of their culture and learn the beliefs of the people who raised them. If you were born in Greece, 500 BC, for example, you would speak the local version of Greek. To a very large degree, you would think what everyone else thinks, such as that the Gods are petty and can be cruel, that slavery is acceptable (and that slaves are part of the family), that patriarchy and private property are the way things are, that war is a necessary and manly part of life, that the world is flat, that a man should weep when faced with sorrow, and depending on where and when in Greece you were born, that democracy is more civilized than autocracy (more on this in Chapter 13).

The social construction of reality is a widely accepted sociological concept and applies to each and every one of us. Where and when we were born, our gender, our social status at birth, etc., have a huge impact on how we view ourselves and the world. Only in adulthood are we likely to get that our way of being and thinking isn't the only way. Even in the face of powerful evidence to the contrary, we may cling to our old beliefs as being "right." Clearly, many people have and still do believe they are in some way superior to others, with gender and skin pigmentation being two of the favorite excuses for holding such a belief. Some accept it and act on it even if they don't believe it, just like some preachers don't believe what they are preaching, and flimflam artists don't believe what they are selling.

Lewin explains the social construction of reality this way: "Cultural anthropology has emphasized recently that any constancy of culture is based on the fact that children are growing into that culture. They are indoctrinated and habituated in childhood in a way that keeps their habits strong enough for the rest of their lives" (Lewin, 1943, 1997, p. 290). As he put it later in a paper titled *Conduct, Knowledge, and Acceptance of New Values* (an important topic as we shall see),

> ...what exists as reality for the individual is, to a high degree, determined by what is socially accepted as reality. This holds even in the field of physical fact: to the South Sea Islander the world may be flat; to the European it is round. Reality therefore is not an absolute. It differs with the group to which the individual belongs...the general acceptance of a fact or a belief might be the very cause preventing this belief or fact from ever being questioned.
>
> **Lewin (1945, 1997, p. 49)**

The social construction of reality is one of the keys to unlocking the grip of inequality on humanity. We can assess our own beliefs and consider new ones. There is a fundamental truth that the concept of the social construction of reality holds for racism. It is this: race is a social construct, not a biological fact. On this, the varying and often conflicting voices on DEI agree. Let us turn to my colleague Professor Rodney Coates to explain. On page 5 of the preface of their book, *The Matrix of Race*, Coates et al explain their hypothesis this way: "The 'matrix' in the title refers to a way of thinking about race that can help readers get beyond the familiar 'us versus them' arguments that can lead to resistance and hostility. This framework incorporates a number of important theories and perspectives from contemporary sociologists who study this subject: (a) Race is socially constructed; it changes from one place to another and across time. (b) When talking about racial inequality, it is more useful to focus on the structures of society (institutions) than to blame individuals. (c) Race is intersectional; it is embedded in other socially constructed categories of difference (like gender, social class, ethnicity, and sexuality). And (d) there are two sides to race: oppression and privilege. Both are harmful, and both can be experienced simultaneously" (Coates et al, 2018).

In other words, race based on color is a social construct. It is a non-scientific belief system, or as Lewin put, "wrong concept," even though it has been and continues to be held dogmatically as "the truth" by many.

While writing this, Whoopie Goldberg caused a stir by saying the holo-caust wasn't about racism. Part of Whoopi's confusion, which is wide-spread, is that she apparently believes race is a fact and that you can tell what it is by physical appearances. Since "all white people look alike" (or so I've heard), she thinks racism is only between "whites" and blacks. She didn't say this that I am aware of, but she probably thinks it is only a one-way street, whites being racist to blacks, and not the other way around. She apparently didn't know, at least prior to her remarks, that race is socially constructed, as is racism. She believed the lie created to divide us that there are races based on scientific physiological differences (more to come on the history of this lie in Chapter 5).

The holocaust is proof that race is in the eye of the beholder (a social construct). The Nazis then (and white supremacists now) do not consider Jews "white," even though many people do. The Nazis considered the Jews to be an "inferior race."

Oppression based on the social construct of race has been very real. Overcoming that oppression deserves recognition and applause. Denying that color has played a role in oppression is a good example of the defense mechanism of denial and an insult to people who have been categorized by skin color for the purpose of oppression. Denying that other character-istics have been used to divide and categorize people by race (such as being Jewish) is also inaccurate.

There will be ample exploration of these basic yet important concepts as we build this framework. Meanwhile, let us turn back to Lewin, who was not afraid to apply his own social science to understanding the social con-struction of race: "Definite answers to such questions can be supplied only by an 'experimental cultural anthropology'..." (Lewin, 1943, 1997, p. 35). Lewin oversaw many such experiments, including the following research by a graduate student named Horowitz, which indicated that prejudice was a social construct passed on from generation to generation:

> Horowitz found no prejudices against Negroes in white children under three years. The prejudices increased between four and six years. This increase was as great in New York as in the South. It was independent of the degree of acquaintance of the children with Negro children, and of the actual status of the Negro child in the class which the white child attended. The prejudices are, however, related to the attitude of the parents of the white child. This indicates that the prejudices against the Negroes are due

to an induction and gradual taking over of the culture of the parents by the child.

Lewin (1946, 1997, p. 375)

My grandson does a wonderful job of proving the point of "no prejudice thus far." Hopefully, the love and modeling in his immediate family will inoculate him against the prejudices in our larger society.

IMAGE 2.1
No prejudice so far!

In other words, as Nelson Mandela noted, no one is born racist or sexist. We are socialized into it. We can change that socialization for future generations, and we can change our own beliefs if we are properly challenged and motivated to do so. Lewin provides guidance on how to do that, as we shall see. Meanwhile we must continue laying the foundation.

DEMOCRATIC PRINCIPLES

I hold these unabashedly. Lewin's democratic principles are not about voting, although neither he nor I would want to live in a political system where we didn't have the right to vote. These democratic principles go much deeper than that.

Before explaining further, allow me to get on my soapbox. Another victim of the social poison that is colonialism and racism is the backlash against the imposition of cultural standards, especially if they originated in what is known as Western culture. We will explore those origins, which were horribly misrepresented in a DEI workshop I attended recently, more in Chapter 13. Meanwhile I stand by the democratic principle, yet to be realized in the US, that all individuals have certain unalienable rights. Furthermore, that those rights give us power, and as Spiderman's Uncle Ben reminds us, that "With that power comes great responsibilities." Real democracy is a collective approach to respecting the individual, and we will not achieve equality without democracy as a guiding principle. If we believe in democracy and equality, then we will have a conflict with cultures that are racist and/or sexist. If we don't believe in democracy and equality, what do we believe in?

Inequality is also socially constructed, and the pursuit of equality *is the imposition of a cultural value on others*. I will pursue it to the day I die and I will not apologize for doing so. It is hypocritical to claim one is against imposing values while relentlessly attempting to do so. Saying you are against imposing culture is in itself an attempt to impose your values on others. In other words, you are doing what you are saying you are against. Both the right and the left are living examples of that type of hypocrisy in the US. Like kids blaming each other in the schoolyard, it is not getting us anywhere. Taking a stand for certain values is not the problem. Being clear about what you stand for is part of the solution.

Lewin studied firsthand what went wrong with German democracy after WWI and concluded that Germany had confused democracy with the right to do anything, even the right to undermine the very democracy that allowed groups such as the Nazis to openly advocate hatred and bully their way into power. Lewin believed that for democracy to work, freedom has to have limits, and the leadership must enforce those limits: "A democratic world order does not require or even favor cultural uniformity all over the world. The parallel to democratic freedom for the individual is cultural pluralism for groups. But any democratic society has to safeguard against misuse of individual freedom by the gangster or – politically speaking – the 'intolerant.' Without establishing to some degree the principle of tolerance, of equality of rights, in every culture the 'intolerant' culture will always be endangering a democratic world organization. Intolerance against intolerant cultures is therefore a prerequisite to any organization of permanent peace" (Lewin, 1943, 1997, p. 36).

This is no weak vision of democracy. This is a democracy that takes a clear stand to protect those with less power and to actively resist sedition. It's a vision of society where individuals have maximum opportunity to influence but also must take responsibility as citizens to behave in a manner that supports democracy. It's a vision of a society where all are included and treated with respect unless they violate that inclusion by trying to undermine the rights of their fellow citizens with autocratic and antidemocratic speech and behavior.

This fight may never be done, but we can get a lot closer to the goal than we currently are.

Lewin's democratic principles have a side benefit. His research established time and again that leading with democratic values, whether in a society or in an organization, consistently results in high productivity and morale. Again, this is not to be confused with voting. This is about coming from a place of genuine respect for all. It is about balancing clear leadership with as much freedom as possible within the structure provided by that leadership. It is the antithesis of both authoritarianism and what Lewin called laissez-faire(passivity or the absence of leadership). We will explore Lewin's theory of leadership in detail in Chapter 12.

Lewin's democratic principles apply to situations large and small and are a guiding light for creating a more equitable society. We will continue to apply them throughout the remainder of this text.

FIELD THEORY

As noted, Lewin borrowed from the physical sciences to help us understand social phenomenon. One such concept is homeostasis (which he also called "quasi-stationary equilibria" to convey that everything is changing in small and subtle ways) or the tendency of systems to stay the same. Social systems aren't the same as biological and other physical systems, but this concept is amazingly useful when attempting change. Think in terms of forces that are holding a system in place (Figure 2.3).

FIGURE 2.3
Driving and restraining forces.

Pressure on the system, such as shaming individuals or excluding them, amounts to increasing a driving force. Increasing driving forces leads to increased tension in the system, which eventually erodes forward progress. As in physics, force is met with equal counterforce. Lewin put it this way: "For any type of social management, it is of great practical importance that levels of quasi-stationary equilibria can be changed in either of two ways: by adding forces in the desired direction or by diminishing opposing forces. If a change…is brought about by increasing the forces toward...the secondary effects should be different from the case where the same change of level is brought about by diminishing the opposing forces...

In the first case, the process...would be accomplished by a state of relatively high tension, in the second case, by a state of relatively low tension. Since increase of tension above a certain degree is likely to be paralleled by higher aggressiveness, higher emotionality, and lower constructiveness, it is clear that as a rule, the second method will be preferable to the high pressure method" (Lewin, 1999, p. 280).

Well-intentioned people who are unaware of these dynamics attempt to impose their will on others and then blame the others for responding with defensiveness and resistance. It's needless in most cases, it's tiresome, and it's ineffective. It predictably increases the strength of the homeostasis.

Instead, Lewin engaged group after group in identifying what was holding the system back (the restraining forces) and then helped them implement solutions to address the restraints. I have tested Lewin's work by doing the same throughout my organization development career. The beauty of this approach is that it immediately addresses a restraining force present in most situations, that of having solutions imposed on others. It also brings people together across roles and other boundaries. People are much more likely to get things done when they have been able to collaborate and yet think for themselves. One of the measures my father came up with for any force-field analysis-based planning is to have everyone rate at the end whether or not they had been free to influence. The ratings consistently average an 8 or 9 on a 10-point scale, even when there has been a long history of conflict prior to the process.

As we shall see, in his action research, Lewin diminished "the opposing forces" by engaging people in group dialogue. We must do the same.

Changing the field of forces however is not all that there is to Lewinian field theory. It is also a way to understand the social field we are in at any given moment and place, including the field of inequality. In that field we are all on the margin, trying to figure out how to fit in and what is causing what. Most importantly, we must figure out how to unfreeze the homeostasis of inequality, move to a new and better level of group relations, and freeze in that better level with clear democratic principles so that we do not slip back into the abyss of inequality ever again.

GROUP DYNAMICS

In Lewin's social science, everything is connected. Hence, we have already touched on many of the remaining concepts, including group dynamics. Likewise, one of the core principles underlying group dynamics is also vital to what Lewin called "re-education."[3] That principle is the power of group learning over individual learning.

In an effective group process, people are able to think for themselves and come to their own conclusions. That is the only way changes are likely to really stick. Peer influence is a key variable. If a critical mass within the group is against what is being taught, then the majority of individuals will more likely stay polarized against it. If a critical mass is open to what is being taught, then the odds of individuals shifting their thinking are high.

Lewin demonstrated this time and again through studies of food habits and other research on real-life change. If people were lectured at, they resisted. If people were allowed to talk among peers (even if they were strangers to each other) about what they had been presented by an expert, they were much more likely to integrate what they had been taught into their own thinking and behavior. Lecture, especially any type of "talking down to," doesn't work; dialogue does.

Figure 2.4 illustrates one of many studies in which Lewin tested and validated his group dynamics theories. Participants who were lectured to are on the right. The passive experience led to very little adaptation of new ideas and implementation of change. Participants who received the same information and then were invited to think for themselves through a facilitated dialogue are on the left. The participants in that group adapted new ideas and implemented them at a high rate of success.

Consistent results such as the above convinced Lewin that "...it is easier to change ideology or cultural habits by dealing with groups than with individuals" (Lewin, 1944, 1999, p. 289).

Lewin's definition of a group is simple and pragmatic. "The essence of a group is not the similarity or dissimilarity of its members, but their interdependence" (Lewin, 1940, 1997, p. 68). For example, a family is a group, even though the individual members may in many ways have more in common with people outside the group (other men, other women, and other children) than with those within. The same holds true for any other

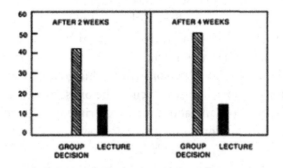

PERCENTAGE OF MOTHERS RE-
PORTING AN INCREASE IN THE CON-
SUMPTION OF FRESH MILK

Percentage of mothers reporting an increase in the consumption of fresh milk after group decision and after lecture.

FIGURE 2.4
Group dynamics.

type of group, such as work teams, sports teams, political parties, ethnic groups, etc.. To belong, the individual must mesh their own aspirations with those of the group. As Lewin put it, "The effect of group belongingness on the behavior of an individual can be viewed as the result of an overlapping situation: One situation corresponds to the person's own needs and goals: the other to the goals, rules, and values which exist for him as a group member. Adaptation of an individual to the group depends upon the avoidance of too great a conflict between the two sets of forces" (Lewin, 1946, 1997, p. 360).

The group dynamic of "peer pressure" is a powerful force on the individual. Buck peer pressure in a work setting by working too hard or not hard enough and you will be pushed and pulled back into place. Think differently than your primary groups on significant issues, and the same pressures will occur. As Lewin puts it: "An individual P may differ in his personal level of conduct (LP) from the level which represents group standards (LGr) by a certain amount n(LGr LP=n). Such a difference is permitted or encouraged in different cultures to different degrees. If the individual should try to diverge 'too much' from group standards he will find himself in increasing difficulties.

He will be ridiculed, treated severely, and finally ousted from the group. Most individuals, therefore, stay pretty close to the standard of the groups they belong to or wish to belong to" (Lewin, 1947, 1997, p. 328).

Lewin's research thus indicates that individual change (or the lack thereof) is a *systems issue*. That is, beliefs and behaviors are products of the effect of the social environment on the individual, more than the other way around: "How high a person will set his goal is deeply affected by the standards of the group to which he belongs, as well as by the standards of groups below and above him. Experiments with college students prove that, if the standards of a group are low, an individual will slacken his efforts and set his goals far below those he could reach. He will, on the other hand, raise his goals if the group standards are raised. In other words, both the ideals and the action of an individual depend upon the group to which he belongs and upon the goals and expectations of that group. That the problem of individual morale is to a large extent a social psychological problem of group goals and group standards is thus clear, even in those fields where the person seems to follow individual rather than group goals" (Lewin, 1942, 1997, p. 87).

Lewin's action research (a concept that concludes this chapter) provides strong evidence that group processes that genuinely engage people generally result in the increased willingness of individuals to consider new perspectives and adapt new behavior for the good of the group. Says Lewin, "…group decision provides a background of motivation where the individual is ready to cooperate as a member of the group more or less independent of his personal inclinations" (Lewin, 1944, 1999, p. 289). *This shift of group dynamics from a restraining force to a driving force is the critical lever needed to sustain changes in beliefs or behavior.* "Only by anchoring his own conduct in something as large, substantial, and superindividual as the culture of a group can the individual stabilize his new beliefs sufficiently to keep them immune from the day-by-day fluctuations of moods and influences to which he, as an individual, is subject" (Lewin, 1945, 1997, p. 50).

In other words, trying to change individuals without changing the social environment within which they live is like building one's house on sand. The group is the foundation that must be addressed, and even a group formed simply for a workshop can hold the field of influence necessary for individual change. "Perhaps one might expect single individuals to be more pliable than groups of like-minded individuals. However, experience in leadership training, in changing of food habits, work production, criminality, alcoholism, prejudices – all seem to indicate that it is usually easier to change individuals formed into a group than to change any one of them separately. As long as group values are unchanged the individual will resist changes more strongly the further he is to depart from group standards. If the group standard itself is changed, the resistance which is due to the relation between individual and group standard is eliminated" (Lewin, 1947, 1997, p. 329).

Group dynamics are the most reliable path to change. We shall learn more about how and why as we explore Lewin's approach to "re-education." But first, we examine prejudice.

PREJUDICE AS A FALSE HYPOTHESIS

Lewin viewed prejudice through the lens of science: "Incorrect stereotypes (prejudices) are functionally equivalent to wrong concepts (theories)" (Lewin, 1945, 1997, p. 52). If you accept this hypothesis, which is thoroughly consistent with what has already been said about the social construction of race, then to the degree that you are aware of them, you can challenge your own prejudices and those held by others. Awareness is tricky and certainly not guaranteed. Nonetheless, *the individual's awareness of their own awareness* deserves more respect than it is given by some DEI trainers. We'll say more about that in Chapter 3.

If it makes sense to you to do so, you can let go of prejudices. It can happen in a flash, it can take persistence, and it can take a lifetime. Whatever the timing, to truly let go of a deeply held prejudice requires a relatively open mind, and at the societal level, that requires creating conditions that encourage openness, not unlike the reconstruction of Germany (which Lewin indirectly, i.e., posthumously, influenced[4]).

Most humans, if they get that they hold a belief that is fundamentally flawed (such as Santa Claus is real) will eventually be less attached to that belief. As noted, that is especially likely if people they respect are also letting go of the belief. They may stay attached to affiliations, such as their ethnic group (and there is no reason not to), but they will be more capable of shedding false socially constructed beliefs such as that their ethnic group, gender, or generation is somehow inherently superior or that oppression is necessary, in their best interests, or justified.

———————

EDUCATION

Lewin's approach to education gets right to the heart of what is needed in DEI learning. It is non-polarizing and effective, and it means we don't have to make this stuff up from scratch. Lewin spent decades developing and testing his thinking and theories, and his writing guides us on what works and what doesn't work.[5] We will explore his methods here and apply them as a model for DEI education in Chapter 13.

One principle is that even though we play different roles in different settings, including roles of formal authority, we all are equals in our basic humanity and want to be treated as such. With this in mind, any Lewinian change effort depends on the conduct of the social scientist, by which I mean anyone who is leading, teaching, or influencing. Consistent with his democratic values, *anyone can be in the role* of social scientist. Lewin's methods were intended for all, not just for experts. A critical variable, then, is how the social scientist (amateur or professional, boss or peer) relates to the people in the intervention. *In Lewin's mind, they must guide the process, but also engage as human peers.* Holding oneself above or separate from the group can actually become a restraining force when conducting change. To influence a group, the social scientist must actually, even if only temporarily, become a peer with the group: "The normal gap between teacher and student, doctor and patient…can…be a real obstacle to acceptance of the advocated conduct. In other words, in spite of whatever status differences there might be between them, the teacher and the student have to feel as members of one group in matters involving their sense of values.

The chances for re-education[6] seem to increase whenever a strong we-feeling is created" (Lewin, 1945, 1997, p. 55).

And why not? Whether or not one recognizes it, by joining the group in pursuit of the goals of the particular intervention, the social scientist truly is an interdependent member of the group in terms of whether the goals will be realized. By relating as a human being and not just as a role, the successful development of the "we-feeling" diminishes a restraining force (fear of the social scientist, the consultant, the stranger, the authority figure, etc.). Part of creating this "we-feeling" in Lewin's process is another democratic principle, *freedom of expression:*

> When re-education involves the relinquishment of standards which are contrary to the standards of society at large (as in the case of delinquency,

minority prejudices, alcoholism), the feeling of group belongingness seems to be greatly heightened if the members feel free to express openly the very sentiments which are to be dislodged through re-education. This might be viewed as another example of the seeming contradictions inherent in the process of re-education: Expression of prejudices against minorities or the breaking of rules of parliamentary procedures may in themselves be contrary to the desired goal. Yet a feeling of complete freedom and a heightened group identification are frequently more important at a particular stage of reeducation than learning not to break specific rules.

Lewin (1945, 1997, p. 55)

Humility by the leader and freedom of expression both fly in the face of much DEI practice. This brings us back to the downside of Robin DiAngelo. DiAngelo, and those who take a similar approach, are there to "teach" not to listen. If you are white and you differ with her, she repeatedly ponders out loud, "...why people who identify as white are so difficult in conversations regarding race?" (DiAngelo, 2018, p. XVII). She reveals no apparent awareness that how she leads the conversations might have something to do with the persistent defensiveness she encounters. The message to white participants is that if they do or say what she considers the wrong thing (such as crying if you are a white woman or getting angry if you are a white man), they will be "called out" as racist in front of the entire audience, which often consists of their coworkers! It's hard to imagine any "we-feeling" emerging. "Openness" is only supported if it aligns with dogma. Such an "the expert is always right" approach supported by public humiliation is a formula for more *us versus them*, the very thing that got us into this mess in the first place.

In similar fashion, the two facilitators in a six-module DEI workshop I recently attended talked about openness but then rejected all feedback that didn't align with their behavior and their point of view. They attempted to keep their own thoughts and feelings to themselves, instead focusing on probing and reacting to whatever the participants did and said. They called it "Realizing another conversation exists." I thought that meant that they believed a different kind of conversation was needed, as I do. Instead, when I asked early on what they meant, they claimed they had "no expectations" of us or even of the outcome of the process. On the other hand, despite their claims of "no agenda," they consistently only supported certain types of behavior (like contrition on the part of white participants). While I experienced "we-feeling" with most of the other participants, regardless of race or gender, I increasingly felt separated from and judged by the facilitators. This held true in spite of the fact that we shared values like social equity and despite my sincere attempts from beginning to end to relate openly with them. When openness included any differing with what the facilitators did or said, the response was at best awkward and, as the process grinded on, increasingly unpleasant.

Lewin's hypothesis is that pressuring people out of saying what they really think is not likely to bring sustained change and may actually have the opposite effect. This does not mean that anything goes, but it does mean that if the primary responsibility for thinking about what one is saying lies outside the individual, real change has not occurred. This brings us back to the importance of the group's role in the social construction and re-construction of reality. No matter how tempting it is to try and force people into being the way you want them to be, it is only by allowing people to think for themselves and among themselves that real and sustainable change reliably occurs.

As Lewin puts it in his paper entitled *Conduct, Knowledge, and Acceptance of New Values*: "This principle of in-grouping makes understandable why complete acceptance of previously rejected facts can be achieved best through the discovery of these facts by the group members themselves. Then, and frequently only then, do the facts become really *their* facts (as against other people's facts). An individual will believe facts he himself has discovered in the same way that he believes in himself or in his group. The importance of this fact-finding process for the group by the group itself has been recently emphasized with reference to re-education in several fields. It can be surmised that the extent to which social research is translated into social action depends on the degree to which those who carry out this action are made a part of the fact-finding on which the action is to be based" (Lewin, 1945, 1997, p. 55).

Lewin goes on to say, "We are slowly coming to realize that all education is group work" (Lewin, 1943, 1999, p. 334). Certainly, that is true in primary education, most types of effective training, and in what Lewin termed "re-education," which is the process of helping individuals change how they think and behave in relation to issues such as race and role, including the roles of effectively leading and effectively following.

Lewin saw education as a reflection of the broader culture in which it resides and as an influence in promulgating or changing that culture.

> Education is in itself a social process…Education tends to develop certain types of behavior, certain kinds of attitudes…there exists a general cultural atmosphere…Those who have had the opportunity to observe closely enough the behavior of school teachers (for instance, in Germany between 1917 and 1933, especially in the period 1931–1933) could easily see how even small changes in the general political situation affected, almost from day to day, not only the ideals which they taught, but also the educational methods which they employed (such as the type and frequency of punishment, the amount of drill, and the degree of freedom and independence in learning). Times of political change show very impressively the high degree to which education, in nearly all of its aspects, depends upon the social structure of the group. *It seems to be easier for society to change education than for education to change society.*
>
> **Lewin (1936, 1997, p. 16)**

In other words, how you teach is one of the most important lessons you are teaching, in many ways more important than the subject matter itself. It certainly plays a huge role in whether you learn to think for yourself or you simply learn how to meet the teacher's expectations. The implications are clear both for DEI training and for our broader educational system. If we want a robust democracy that can foster and sustain real equity, where people are taking responsibility and thinking for themselves, we need dialogue, not compliance.

In Lewin's eyes,[7] the process of teaching either reinforces democratic principles (active engagement and influence) or it does not: "…for educating future citizens, no talk about democratic ideals can substitute for a democratic atmosphere in the school. The character and the cultural habits of the growing citizen are not so much determined by what he says as by what he lives (Lewin, 1944, 1999, p. 290)." Lewin's research clearly differentiated between active and passive participation, with active participation consistently yielding superior results. When he was in a teaching or group leadership role, he walked his own talk, encouraging his students into active dialogue even while at the stodgy University of Berlin, where such behavior was far out of the norm: "Lecturing is a procedure by which the audience is chiefly passive. The discussion, if conducted correctly, is likely to lead to a much higher degree of involvement" (Lewin, 1948, 1999, p. 271).

Through group dynamics, Lewin found that the social construction of reality could be shifted, and hence individual beliefs and values could be opened to influence. Active group participation, shifting the group from being a restraining force to a driving force, was essential to the difficult goals of re-education: "The re-educative process affects the individual in three ways. It changes his *cognitive structure*, the way he sees the physical and social world, including all his facts, concepts, beliefs, and expectations. It modifies his *valances and values,* and these embrace both his attractions and aversions to groups and group standards, his feelings in regard to status differences, and his reactions to sources of approval or disapproval. And it affects *motoric action,* involving the degree of the individual's control over his physical and social movements" (Lewin, 1945, 1997, p. 50).

Through a process of unlearning and learning, Lewin was a pioneer in the reduction and elimination of strongly held beliefs, such as prejudice, and to instilling democratic principles in leaders and their subordinates.

In Lewin's mind, what he called "experiential" learning became critical. That is, learning through an active experience that impacts the *cognitive structure, valences and values,* and *motoric action* and through facilitated reflection on that experience. Turning again to his paper *Conduct, Knowledge, and Acceptance of New Values,* we see that Lewin made it clear that random experience is not enough to assure learning and hence is not the same thing as "experiential learning":

> The difficulties encountered in efforts to reduce prejudices or otherwise to change the social outlook of the individual have led to a realization that re-education cannot be merely a rational process. We know that lectures or other similarly abstract methods of transmitting knowledge are of little avail in changing his subsequent outlook and knowledge. We might be tempted, therefore, to think that what is lacking in these methods is first-hand experience…
>
> *Even extensive first-hand experience does not automatically create correct concepts (knowledge).*
>
> For thousands of years man's everyday experience with falling objects did not suffice to bring him to a correct theory of gravity. A sequence of very unusual, man-made experiences, so-called experiments, which grew out of the systematic search for the truth were necessary to bring about a change from less adequate to more adequate concepts. To assume that first-hand experience in the social world would automatically lead to the

formation of correct concepts or to the creation of adequate stereotypes seems therefore unjustifiable.

Lewin (1945, 1997, p. 48)

Apples had been falling since the dawn of time. It took the accumulated knowledge of humanity up to the right moment, combined with the inspiration of Sir Isaac Newton, to formulate a scientifically valid theory of gravity.

We don't have that much time! Racism is continuing to deeply poison us at a time when we have many challenges we must face collectively! DEI re-education must work relatively fast! It must also reach deep within the individual. To do so and to have it last requires a process in which the individual willingly rethinks their own beliefs and behaviors. The individual must reach a point of taking responsibility for their own learning. If behavior is only enforced from outside, re-education has failed. As Lewin put it: "Re-education is frequently in danger of only reaching the official system of values, the level of verbal expression and not of conduct; it may result in merely heightening the discrepancy between the super-ego (the way I ought to feel) and the ego (the way I really feel), and thus give the individual a bad conscience. Such a discrepancy leads to a state of high emotional tension, but seldom to correct conduct. It may postpone transgressions, but it is likely to make the transgressions more violent when they occur.

A factor of great importance in bringing about a change in sentiment is the degree to which the individual becomes actively involved in the problem. Lacking this involvement, no objective fact is likely to reach the status of a fact for the individual concerned and therefore influence his social conduct" (Lewin, 1945, 1997, p. 52).

If people are simply lectured at, told "thou shalt" and "thou shalt not" by a critical authority figure, then all they are likely to learn is to watch what they say around the authorities. Such approaches increase polarization instead of decreasing it. Conflict goes underground and into polarized subgroups of the larger society, where it simmers and/or turns into counteraction. To foster real and lasting change, the individual, in concert with the group, must be invited into doing what Lewin called action research (our next and final topic in this section) on themselves. They must be a willing participant in testing beliefs, old and new, and testing new behaviors through dialogue and interaction.

The good news is that besides potentially unlearning bad cognitive habits such as prejudice, the participants in such learning gain emotional intelligence, leadership and followership skills, and increased capacity to learn from subsequent experiences. The downside of such learning for the individual is virtually nil, and the upside is priceless. We will return to Lewin in Chapter 13 and apply his methods to DEI learning.

ACTION RESEARCH

The basic elements of Lewin's planned change included "...action, research, and training as a triangle" (Lewin, 1946, 1997, p. 149).

Such training–action–research (as Lewin's student and colleague Dr. Ronald Lippitt more correctly put it in his 1949 book), more commonly referred to as "action research," is to be conducted at multiple levels. Most important to addressing the immediate situation is *participant* action research; action research by the people facing the problem: "The laws (of social science) don't do the job of diagnosis which has to be done locally. Neither do laws prescribe the strategy for change" (Lewin, 1946, 1997, p. 150).

A corresponding "law of social science" is that solutions are much more likely to be implemented by the people who come up with them. Imposed solutions are much more likely to flounder. By engaging the people facing the problem, the social scientist is already shifting a potential restraining force (trying to hand off or impose the solution) into a driving force. This bears repeating: "It can be surmised that the extent to which social research is translated into social action depends on the degree to which those who carry out this action are made a part of the fact-finding on which the action is to be based" (Lewin, 1945, 1997, p. 55). The people involved are also being trained to take a more scientific approach to any and all challenges facing them now and in the future. An important part of the training in Lewin's action research triangle was the transfer of knowledge so that anyone, independent of experts and regardless of role, could apply social science methods to solving problems and building a better world.

Going where no one had gone before, and where we still need to continue going, Lewin set out to do action research to better understand discrimination and prejudice, and to eradicate it. From the time that he launched what was known as the Commission for Community Interrelations (CCI) until the time of his death, Lewin and his staff "handled more than fifty separate different projects involving all four varieties of action research" (Marrow, 1969, p. 203). The following are a few examples documented by Lewin's biographer Marrow and elsewhere.

In one of his bolder studies, Lewin pondered the effects of segregation versus integration in public housing and how to effectively bring ethnic groups together. Interracial housing was a new concept in post-World War II America. Lewin's study offered two types of occupancy, segregated housing in a checkerboard pattern, or integrated buildings "filled on a first come first serve basis, without regard of color…The results disclosed a sharp contrast in attitudes…in the segregated projects resentments towards Negroes were much sharper and anti-negro prejudice stronger; indeed the white residents expressed strong preference for even greater segregation. On the other hand, where whites came to know Negroes as next door neighbors, they shared a growing sense of common humanity which relaxed the tensions they had brought with them and replaced antagonism with friendliness. The change was expressed (among other responses) by their preference for more and more integrated housing. Group cohesiveness and morale were higher in the integrated than in the segregated projects. White residents in integrated housing, despite initial forebodings, came to like living in them and many of them expressed pride in their building's 'democracy'" (Marrow, 1969, p. 209).

The experiment above and Lewin's other work consistently demonstrated that separation is a restraining force holding fear and prejudice in place. A wise workshop design begins with as much safety and inclusion for all participants as possible, in contrast to starting out with confrontation. The leaders must set the tone for this. We will explore that further in Chapters 13 and 14.

Likewise, and true to his theories of group dynamics, Lewin's experiments were systemic, not just focused on changing individuals. For example, CCI helped the town of Coney Island address gang behavior not only by building a successful relationship between a CCI staff member and the gang (which began in exchange for waiving legal charges after an attack on Jewish youth) but also by "providing more and better housing, building recreational centers… improving transportation" (Marrow, 1969, p. 204). The study achieved three of its goals. The gang "learned to behave in a way more acceptable to the community" (which meant less fighting among other criteria). The gang's energies were "redirected towards more constructive activities." Based on the CCI research, "the changes endured after the consultant was withdrawn" (Marrow, 1969, p. 204).

Another project took the form of legal action to combat discrimination. "Conferring with Lewin …," the American Jewish Congress, the funding body for the CCI, sued the Medical School of Columbia University over their restrictive "quota for Jews." Columbia denied any such quota system and refused to turn over their selection system records. They instead settled out of court, agreed to establish a transparent system, and stated publicly that "applicants would be judged without regard for race or religion." The victory "…resulted in a revision of discriminatory policies by leading schools of higher learning throughout the country" (Marrow, 1969, p. 206).

In another study, department stores were unwilling to hire African Americans as sales clerks because, "…as the store management put it, our customers wouldn't stand for it." CCI's research concluded that a large percentage of shoppers who admitted to racial prejudice in a survey kept shopping at their preferred store even when they were waited on by African Americans. The study concluded that the "…fear that sales would be hurt was not supported by the evidence" (Marrow, 1969, p. 206).

Yet another study examined how to respond to bigoted statements in public places such as a crowded elevator. Out of 513 participants, 80% "strongly preferred any answer at all to silence" (Marrow, 1969, p. 218). It was agreed that silence could be mistaken as consent. More on this important behavior is discussed in Chapter 14.

In 1946, just prior to his death, Lewin was involved in perhaps his most ambitious action research project to decrease racial tensions in the State of Connecticut. One notable outcome was that people who attended the workshop in groups (from a community or organization) were more likely to implement actions after the workshop, in contrast to individuals who attended on their own. This further reinforced Lewin's faith in group dynamics. Sadly, Lewin's death in early 1947 interrupted his usual documentation and research on outcomes.

Something else happened in Connecticut. To borrow from Stanley Kubrick, "something wonderful." The realization that encouraging workshop participants to discuss their individual experiences from moment to moment during the workshop led to powerful insights while also creating a fertile ground for experiments in behavior. Lewin named this type of group process, where the primary focus is on what is happening within and between the participants in the here and now, a T-group (or training group). My father experienced his first T-group in 1953. I've been involved in applying them to change in organizations since 1984. Despite searching far and wide, I have found no other learning method that gets straight to the heart of re-education so effectively and so fast.

In 2021, the 75th anniversary of the invention of the T-group, I went to the campus in Connecticut where the 1946 workshop was held and took the following photograph:

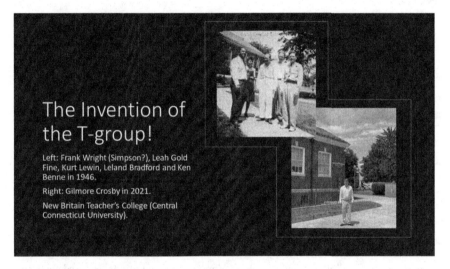

The Invention of the T-group!

Left: Frank Wright (Simpson?), Leah Gold Fine, Kurt Lewin, Leland Bradford and Ken Benne in 1946.

Right: Gilmore Crosby in 2021.

New Britain Teacher's College (Central Connecticut University).

IMAGE 2.2
75th Anniversary of the T-group.

I'd like to think that the 100th anniversary will be more widely celebrated. No one on the campus knew anything about the event! It was lonely out there! If this event is more widely celebrated in the future, as it should be, it will be because we have made great changes based on Lewin's social science in the time between now and then. Surely, with awareness, application will spread.

Not that all DEI work needs to be T-group work, nor should it be. People who are not trained should not try to lead T-groups![8] On the other hand, T-group learning, which *is* inclusive, reliable, and based on group dynamics, and the DEI framework in this book or something similar, is an unbeatable combination for creating DEI dialogue and real change.

Combined with social action, for example, rooting out and ending documented inequities such as unfair lending practices, we *can* make this a better world. We must change individuals and society if we are ever to achieve real democracy and equity.

To do so, we need the power of reason when we think about people and interactions. That brings us to the next layer in our DEI framework foundation, *The Interpersonal Gap*.

NOTES

1. Significant portions of this chapter are adapted with permission from Crosby (2021a). *Planned Change:Why Kurt Lewin's Social Science is Still Best Practice for Business Results, Change Management, and Human Progress*. Boca Raton, FL. Taylor & Francis Group.
2. Lewin experimented with anything and everything that seemed relevant, including using mapmaking methods to depict sociological situations!
3. Lewinian "re-education" is a process to open minds. He used the term first, and it is the polar opposite of the "re-education" brainwashing used later by oppressive regimes.
4. Although there is no known direct documentation of Lewin's influence on the construction of a new democracy in Germany following WWII, he was heavily involved with the state department in the years prior to his death in 1947. He wrote extensively about the failings of democracy in post-WWI Germany, German culture, and on how to go about implementing the reconstruction of Germany.
5. My own career and my father's before me have further proven the reliability and validity of Lewin's methods.
6. As noted, Lewinian "re-education" is a process to open minds. He used the term first, and it is the polar opposite of the "re-education" brainwashing used later by oppressive regimes.
7. Much like his contemporary, John Dewey.
8. As demonstrated by the expansion and contraction of the "T-group movement" in the 1960s and 1970s, documented in Art Kleiner's *The Age of Heretics*.

3

The Interpersonal Gap, *Microaggressions, and Defensiveness*[1]

Between stimulus and response there is a space. In that space is our power to choose our response. In our response lies our growth and our freedom.

Viktor Frankl (1949)

It is the hypothesis of this book that inequality complicates the ambiguity that is inherent to human interaction. False certainty and creeping doubts poison the atmosphere. Only by relentlessly working toward systemic equality will we ever truly eliminate the confusion and tension of inequality. In the meantime, we can use science to better understand our interactions and decrease needless drama. This is where a model called *The Interpersonal Gap*, by social scientist John Wallen (1918–2001), becomes an important asset in the *training* that needs to go with making a critical mass of us more effective at working toward equity.

Wallen's model is unique in its clarity that we are each responsible when sending and *receiving* interpersonal communication. Many DEI sources are hypercritical about how "white people" send and receive, and much less concerned with how minority individuals put things and take things. Even if this allows for short-term gains in self-esteem for minorities, such an imbalanced approach ultimately increases tension instead of decreasing it and does not lead to sustained dialogue. We will soon explore that imbalance and its consequences further. First, however, we must set the stage for that conversation by exploring Wallen's *Interpersonal Gap* (Figure 3.1).

To do so I find it helpful to integrate the Mayan wisdom of don Miguel Ruiz from his books *The Four Agreements* and *The Fifth Agreement*. This,

DOI: 10.4324/9781003335689-4

however, brings up another source of tension loosely banded about in DEI circles, the debate over whether sources are primarily "Western" and hence dominated by "white" males (a characterization which is ironic when it includes sources like Lewin, who was persecuted as "non-white," and still would be today by many who perceive themselves as "white"), or whether other voices are heard. We will closely examine that debate in Chapter 5.

Meanwhile, on to *The Interpersonal Gap*. Although they never met, John Wallen and don Miguel Ruiz are clearly kindred spirits. With their writing, they both illuminate the power that subjective perception holds over our emotional lives. Wallen drew the process this way:

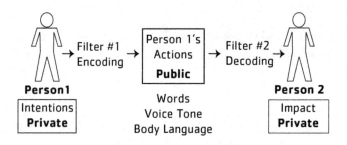

FIGURE 3.1
The Interpersonal Gap.

A difference between intent and impact equals a "gap."

Filter #1: Sender's beliefs and habits regarding how to translate intentions into words and actions.

Filter #2: Receiver's interpretation/judgment (beliefs/theories/stories) about what sender's behavior really means.

In short, Wallen's theory is that each of us has intentions in every interaction (we intend a certain impact), we translate (or encode) our intentions into words and actions, the people we are interacting with translate (decode) our words and actions, and the decoding by the receiver determines the initial emotional impact on the receiver. Our perception of the other(s) is creating our emotional response!

What is perception? Perception, in this sense, is cognitive and relies on words. We use words to describe ourselves, and we use words to describe others. This is true even if we keep the words to ourselves by thinking them but not speaking them. We create our subjective reality through words, and, so the first agreement of the Toltec Mayans according to don

Miguel Ruiz is to "Be impeccable with your word." As Ruiz puts it, to be impeccable: "You never use the words of gossip about yourself or just spread emotional poison by gossiping about other people. Gossiping is the main form of communication in human society…When we are children, we hear the adults around us gossiping about themselves, and giving their opinions about other people, including people they don't even know. But now you are aware that our opinions are not the truth; They are just a point of view" (Ruiz, 2010, p. 38)

As a reminder, this framework relies on Kendi's definition of racism as "…any concept that regards one racial group as inferior or superior to another racial group in any way" (Kendi, 2016, p. 5). By this definition, any gossip about racially defined groups *is* racism.

When we are troubled by someone because of our biases about how they look, or because of our reaction to what they have done or said, it is easy to forget that our perceptions "are just a point of view." We tend to believe and get attached to our perceptions and share them with others as if they were facts (which is the poison known as gossip). If the people we gossip to agree with us, it is even easier to believe our perceptions as if they are objective facts. "So and so disrespected me!" "You can't trust so and so!" "They are different than us!" In family systems theory, which we apply in Chapter 10, this fusion of negative judgments, secrets, and indirectness is called triangulation. Triangulation happens whenever two people talk about another instead of talking to the other. Of course, that is more damaging when the perceptions of the person (or group) being talked about are negative. Triangulation fuels separateness and homeostasis in the system. As Lewin's research demonstrated, staying separate will never bring us together.

Back to perception. The process of perception (or interpretation, or judgment, or assumption) occurs constantly, and in nanoseconds. It is the micro-moment in a macro-tapestry of interactions and beliefs. I react to you, and in that moment you are already reacting to my reactions. To further complicate things, our filters are complex and ever-changing. Our history together, our separate life experiences, our culture, and the nature of our relationship (i.e., roles such as white person and black person, teacher and student, parent and child, salesperson and customer, etc.), all impact our immediate filters about each other.

Face it, as soon as you see someone (or are seen), you have certain beliefs about them based on age, gender, skin pigmentation, and even more subtle superficial characteristics such as the overall body shape and the shape of features such as the eyes, lips, and nose. All of this information is saying at the most basic level of the brain that this person is like me or not like me and that this person is like this set of people and not like that set. I fit in here or I don't fit in. This person is a stranger or we have a past history. Even if you are not sighted, you quickly fill in these gaps with the information available, such as the sound of their voice. Bombarded by all that instantaneous information, relating to the other as they are in this moment in terms of their real thoughts, feelings, and aspirations takes extraordinary presence. Being truly present begins with setting aside preconceptions, not with being free of them. Claiming you don't notice differences such as age, gender, or skin pigmentation is denial, not awareness. The same is true of any superficial or preconceived beliefs about the other. The highest aspiration is not to be blind to differences but rather to not be blinded by them.

The lens of perception guides us, so we don't have to start from scratch in each encounter, and the lens of perception clouds what we see and believe. This is especially true if there is additional tension added by something as emotional as inequality.

Under even the best of circumstances, there is ample potential for misunderstanding at any step in the process (beginning with the formidable task of understanding yourself). Such misunderstandings are what Wallen refers to as a "gap." As he puts it, "The interpersonal gap refers to the degree of congruence between one person's intentions and the effect produced in the other. If the effect is what is intended, the gap has been bridged. If the effect is the opposite of what was intended, the gap has become greater."

Wallen goes on to say, "We see our own actions in the light of our own intentions, but we see the other's actions not in the light of the other person's intentions but in the effect on us."

In other words, we usually know what we intended, especially when we believe we've been misunderstood. It is easy to notice Wallen's gap in those moments. This awareness is the first vital step in potentially clearing up misunderstandings, as long as you don't just blame the other for the misunderstanding. It's more problematic when the shoe is on the other foot, when you interpret another's words and actions in a manner that has an undesired effect on you. That's when it is easy to forget how easy it is to be misunderstood and hence to misunderstand, and to believe the negative story you are making up about them as if it were the objective truth.

Understanding the power your interpretations have on your own reactions is the starting point for increasing your objectivity and becoming less of a victim of your own interpretations. For example, a person who gives you "close supervision" (an interpretation in itself) may be decoded/interpreted as a) "not trusting your work" or b) "being committed to you" (or c, or d, etc.). A person who conveys anger may be decoded/interpreted as a) "a troublemaker" or b) "passionate." The same behaviors, decoded differently, evoke different reactions in you (emotions, beliefs, etc.).

Simple – but hard to remember – when the subject matter is loaded and the (emotional) heat is on. This is especially true when your circle of friends or colleagues agree with your negative interpretations, lending what seems like validity to your judgments about the other person or group. And the subtle tension fueled by such negative beliefs makes it likely that future interactions will further reinforce the same outcomes.

Does this mean that you should never have "negative" judgments of others? Of course not. Besides the fact that such a suspension of interpretation would be virtually unachievable, it would be undesirable as well. If we held no negative judgments, we would not be fighting against racism. To put it a different way, without reservation, I judge racism as negative. This is, in my eyes, a "positive" negative judgment. Judging others in both positive and negative terms is necessary for relating to people and society. One must rely on their own judgment and the judgments of trusted others. The skill lies in both trusting our judgment and questioning it.

Let's turn back to don Miguel Ruiz and consider the second Mayan agreement, "Don't Take Anything Personally." In this way of thinking, not only are we constantly interpreting others but we are also constantly interpreting ourselves and making up a story about who we are. We have begun writing that story since birth. Ruiz calls the story we make up "dreaming."

"People live in their own world, in their own movie, in their own story. They invest all their faith in that story, and that story is truth for them, but it's a relative truth, because it's not truth for you. Now you can see that all their opinions about you really concerned the character who lives in their movie, not in yours. The one who they are judging in your name is a character they create. Whatever people think of you is really about the image they have of you, and that image isn't you…

Now it's easy to understand why there is so much conflict between humans. The world is populated by billions of dreamers who aren't aware that people are living in their own world, dreaming their own dream. For the point of view of the main character which, which is their only point of view, everything is all about them when the secondary characters say something that doesn't agree with their point of view, they get angry, and try to defend their position. They want the secondary characters to be the way they want them to be, and if they are not, they feel very hurt. They take everything personally. With this awareness you can also understand the solution, and it's something so simple and logical: *don't take anything personally*" (Ruiz and Ruiz, 2010, p. 52).

The story we are telling about ourselves and others is seductive. It seems like reality, but it is not. The stories are just words in our heads (and our mouths), which symbolize reality, a symbolization of reality we are constructing. Everyone else is doing the same. When they are upset with you, they are upset with you based on their own story (or dream).

The family systems concept of fusion is equivalent to taking everything personally, bouncing like a pinball from one reactive moment to the next. The reactive survival behaviors of fight (which in relationships often take the form of oppositional thinking instead of actual violence) or flight (which in relationships mostly take the form of "walking on eggshells") become the only options. The family systems concept of differentiation, explored further in Chapter 10 but relevant here, allows one to be in relationship and to care about impact on self and on others without swallowing and wallowing in drama.

Not taking it personally in Wallen's model means to not get too reactive to other people's interpretation of you and to not get too attached to your interpretation of others. It means staying as open-minded as possible even when tension goes up. It is the opposite of being sure you are right and that the other is wrong. If you are being objective, you will understand that your initial interpretation of someone's words and actions may be very different than what they meant. Your interpretation is coming from your own "dream." The third Mayan agreement, "Don't Make Assumptions," addresses interpretations this way: "Making assumptions is just looking for trouble because most assumptions are not the truth; they're fiction" (Ruiz and Ruiz, 2010, p. 67).

In more crass terms, you have likely heard the wise saying that "the word assume makes an ass out of you and of me." The good news is, you have the ability to reconsider your own assumptions, and that is a critical step for breaking any patterns of misunderstanding that are needlessly complicating interactions. This is especially important in the increased ambiguity caused by inequality.

Wallen states: "I know myself by my intentions; I know others by _____."

How would you finish the sentence? Think of your response, and then continue reading.

If you said, "I know others by their actions," your answer reflects the dominant cultural perspective of our times (which is a good example of a false hypothesis woven into the social construction of reality). In other words, most people would give that answer. It is part of the subtle *victim mentality* prevalent in contemporary culture. The solution is seen as being located outside of the self. "I know them by their behavior; for things to be different, their behavior has to be different." It follows that one's efforts will be on analyzing others and trying to change them (or getting rid of them). This is how dysfunctional DEI workshops are run. And since most people are operating in the same cultural mode (answering the question the same way), this seems to validate your perspective. "Don't talk crazy. Everyone knows the world is flat!" But is it?

Wallen's completion of that sentence is a radical shift. "I know myself by my intentions. I know others by my interpretations." I know you by the stories I *make up* about what I believe your words and actions *really* mean. I know you by the dream I am dreaming about what is real.

This leads to an empowering possibility. If I change my stories, I change my reaction. In other words, I create my own reactions. A subtle shift, but radically different than popular belief. "You made me angry!" Nope. "I interpreted your words and actions as an attack, as an attempt to thwart what I want, and my thoughts aroused anger within me." And if one is really objective, they might add, "And frankly, there's a good chance I misunderstood what you meant to convey, especially in the confusing social context of inequality."

"I know you by my interpretations" is both a sobering and calming perspective. Rather than believing, defending, and reacting to your own interpretations, if you maintain awareness of the possibility of misunderstanding (an awareness that will have a grounding effect), you open the door to more rational relationships – in neuroscience terms, you will calm the limbic survival reactions in your brain and put the prefrontal cortex more in charge.

Now let's look at *The Interpersonal Gap* from yet another angle. To understand your own reactions and convey useful feedback to another, it's important to be as clear as you can about what "action" you are interpreting. When you are conversing with someone, what sort of behavior are you taking in?

For our purposes, there are three primary sources of behavioral information: words, body language, and tone of voice. Words are what the person is saying and what you are hearing them say (which may be two different things!). Body language is constantly happening and includes the powerful information conveyed by facial expression. Are they smiling? Frowning? Looking at you? Leaning toward you? Leaning back? Tensing their muscles? Slumped in their posture? Folding their arms? All body language provides information about the sender of the message and is open to interpretation by the receiver. Last but not necessarily least, does the tone of voice match the words being conveyed? Think of the various tones that could be used with the words "Thanks a lot." As you can probably surmise, very different messages can be conveyed, depending on the tone.

A famous study by Dr. Albert Mehrabian assessed where the receiver tuned in for understanding when the messages from these three aspects of behavior (body, tone, and words) were inconsistent. Mehrabian's research breaks them down into percentages. What percentage do you think you get the message from when there are mixed messages from the sender? Take your best guess and then turn the page:

Body Language: _____%
Words: _____%
Tone: _____%

In Dr. Mehrabian's research, these were the percentages:

Body Language: 55%
Tone: 38%
Words: 7%

If you answered differently, that doesn't invalidate your answer. You may be getting more of your information from one or two of these sources than did the people in the study, or you may be closer to the study's numbers than you realize. Either way, your ability to be specific about what you are reacting to will increase your own clarity about your reactions and improve the clarity of the feedback you give to others. For example, when you believe you are receiving a mixed message, you could think or say something like this: "when you said you were happy, you were frowning, so I didn't believe it." Compare that type of feedback to somebody being affected by the same behavior and thinking or saying, "liar."

Feedback that primarily conveys specific behavior is generally less inflammatory than feedback that primarily or solely conveys judgments (interpretations). It's also more likely that the receiver and the sender can learn from and act on behaviorally specific feedback. The ability to give behaviorally specific feedback, free of interpretations, is essential at both work and in personal life if you want less fighting and more understanding. Frankly, if you can't be behaviorally specific, you are better off not saying anything at all. How you put things and what you focus on does matter.

You can also pay attention to the alignment of these three variables in your own communication. How aware are you of your own facial expressions? Do you smile when you are anxious or delivering a serious message? Many people smile because they are afraid of how the message will be received. Others cover their inner state by never varying their expression. Unfortunately, either behavior is likely to be confusing to the person on the receiving end. Neither behavior protects you from conveying *something* and sometimes conveying messages very different than what you intend. Ironically, people who have a more or less consistently blank facial expression, especially if they are in positions of authority, are often misinterpreted more. People have less to go on and are filling in the blanks with their own imaginations. With authority figures, they often imagine the worst.

If you want people to get a clear message, try smiling when you like what's happening and looking serious when you feel serious. Family Therapist

Virginia Satir calls this match between your inner experience and your outer expression "congruency." You started life that way. When you were happy you looked happy, when you were sad you looked sad, and so on. If you have ever been around an infant, you know this to be true. From that point on, we all learned habits of what to show and what not to show. This emotional learning is another aspect of the social construction of reality. Through persistent intentional effort, you can unlearn those habits which are no longer serving you well, and relearn how to be congruent when you want to be. Lewin's methods of education help with that type of learning.

The same is true of tone, and of words. As the Toltec Mayans have known for thousands of years, your words are powerful. Endeavor to say what you mean, and mean what you say. Be kind with your words, to yourself (in your head) and about others. Be impeccable with your words.

Wallen identified four skills that help close interpersonal gaps (which are covered in detail in Appendix B). The first is "behavior description," which is feedback that sticks with what Wallen defines as behavior (as described above). Behavior description increases the ability to be as factual as a human can be and decreases the likelihood of misunderstanding and emotional escalation. The second is "feeling description," which means using a word to describe your own emotions. The third, "paraphrasing," is saying what you think the other means. The fourth tool, "perception check," consists of verbalizing your hunch about what someone else is feeling. For example, you might say "you seem (sad, mad, glad, afraid)" or any variation thereof.

All four skills are most likely to close gaps when you are acting out of the fourth Mayan agreement, "Always Do Your Best" (Ruiz and Ruiz, 2010, p. 83). If your intent is really to understand, to be understood, to be compassionate, Wallen's skills will help you and will be great grounding techniques as well. Mindful focus on any of these behaviors *with the intent of doing your best* will decrease your own emotional intensity and likely have a calming effect on others. All four skills help wipe the lens of perception as clean as possible, thus decreasing needless drama.

When you do your best, even if things don't turn out the way you hoped, the words of Reed Richards (Mr. Fantastic) to Ben Grimm (the Thing) will ring true: "You did your best. That's all that anyone can ever do."

The fifth and final agreement is "Be Skeptical, but Learn to Listen" (Ruiz and Ruiz, 2010, p. 97). Be skeptical of your own stories. Be skeptical of stories from others about you or others. Actively listen. Learn what you can. Be open but take nothing personally.

Hopefully, you are already seeing the implications of *The Interpersonal Gap* for all interactions, including interactions related to equity and diversity. This model is vital now more than ever because a concept present in many DEI conversations seems to be the notion that having spent their lives in a racist system all minorities are victims of trauma. That makes some sense, but some, yes, like DiAngelo, appear to be leaping to the implication that most minority individuals are too wounded to be held responsible for their own behavior during interactions. They must be treated with kid gloves if they say something judgmental or if they feel offended. In other words, if a minority person feels offended, it is the fault of "the offender" regardless of their intentions or whether they were misunderstood, and it is insensitive to interpret what is happening any other way. As John McWhorter puts it, critiquing the impact of Robin DiAngelo on this "blacks as victims" mentality, "DiAngelo's outlook rests upon a depiction of Black people as endlessly delicate poster children…" (McWhorter, 2020, p. 6). The result, clearly on display during the DEI workshop I attended, is that how you *send* if you are not a minority is under a microscope, and how you receive if you are a minority is not to be examined.

We will not create a healthy equity through such an imbalanced view.

It's understandable for this dysfunction to creep into DEI interactions because most in our larger society blame others for interpersonal conflict. People are far more likely to say (or think) "you made me mad" than they are to say (or think) "I made myself mad based on how I interpreted what you said, and I realize I may have misunderstood you." As mentioned, most think that they know others based on the other's actions, not on their interpretations of the actions. The root cause of problems in that framework is all attributed to the other. Things will not be different unless *they* change. If they do, everything will be fine. Tossed into the ambiguity of inequality, this faulty hypothesis increases tension and defensiveness.

For dialogue that brings us together, each person must take as much responsibility as they can manage for how they react to others and how they understand what others mean. This takes humility on both parts. It also takes the ability, as is indicated in the DEI Framework and by Lewin's concept of "living on the margin," to look at interactions and events through the frame of isms, such as racism, but also to look at them without that frame. Sometimes it *is* about race. Sometimes it *isn't* about race. We will have that conversation in the chapters ahead.

A related concept, "microaggressions" (first introduced by Harvard Psychologist Chester Pierce in 1970), could be useful if applied with the same recognition of ambiguity. Sociologist Dr. Rodney Coates and his colleagues define microaggressions this way: "Intentional or unintentional brief insults to a person or group; these may be verbal, nonverbal, or behavioral" (Coates et al, 2022, p. 490). Using *The Interpersonal Gap* as a frame, the term microaggression is a judgment that a person's words and actions are in a subtle way reinforcing prejudice and inequality. Examples include negative comments or rules about black hair, backhanded compliments such as "he is so well-spoken for a black person," sexist comments such as characterizing strong women as "b_tch_s" (while admiring men who express anger as "strong"), "you people" (which can be dismissive of any group and of any individual based on associating them with a group), using the word "gay" derogatively, and so on.

A big reason baseball great Roberto Clemente came to mind as an inspiration for this book was that he overcame countless microaggressions. Pittsburgh sports writers called him "Bob" even though he repeatedly told them that he preferred his actual name. The same writers accused him of faking injuries. Clemente was deeply insulted by such allegations. He prided himself for going all out on every play. He slammed into walls making catches and fearlessly ran the bases. Consequently, he was plagued by injuries, but played through the pain. Instead of the respect he deserved, he was criticized by many of the same people who would later idolize him when he almost single-handedly secured the Pirates a World Series victory in 1971, the second championship of his storied career. Some might have been demoralized by the treatment he received. For Roberto, the effect was a simmering anger that drove him to relentlessly strive for excellence.

The value of the concept, then, is that it can help us be mindful from the minority perspective of the negative impact we may have. With or without the concept, we should challenge what we consider to be bigoted statements by others (more on that in Chapter 14). This doesn't, however, negate the dynamics of *The Interpersonal Gap*. Assuming it does is a false hypothesis and can have negative unintended consequences, such as a chilling effect on dialogue.

The topic of microaggressions is currently so volatile that the subjective and socially constructed nature of communication bears further exploration. Words are subjective, whether we are sending or receiving. When you think of the word "cat," is the word an actual cat? Of course not. The word "cat" is a symbol. The same is true of all words. Only the sender knows what they mean by their words (and even the sender isn't going to be precisely clear about their own intended meaning much of the time). The receiver is only guessing what was meant through their own filters. Like a game of horseshoes, most of the time this matching of intended meaning and perceived meaning is good enough. Despite this ambiguity, we can predict the impact of certain words, especially in a context such as systemic racism. Despite some predictability, how specifically they will be perceived, and even more importantly, how they will be handled is highly variable. No statement, behavior, or circumstance always has the same impact. Victor Frankl demonstrated that by finding hope while being a prisoner in a Nazi concentration camp when others (understandably) found only despair. No matter how comforting it would be to have a rule book and to be the referee in charge, it is a false hypothesis to try and categorize words and experiences as always meaning one thing or having one response. Would you have told Viktor Frankl, "Stop feeling hope! You are a Jewish prisoner in a Nazi concentration camp! You can only be feeling despair!" Of course not.

And yet ascribing a fixed meaning and impact is what some try to do with the concept of microaggressions. Psychologist Darold Wing Sue, a leading voice on the subject, has created tables with examples of microaggressions and their impacts. Unfortunately, the ambiguity illustrated by *The Interpersonal Gap* is not reflected in the table, lending credence to the idea that certain statements can only be interpreted in certain ways. Such thinking cannot withstand a thoughtful examination. Take one of Sue's examples, "There is only one race, the human race." That is actually an accurate scientific fact, yet Sue identifies it as a microaggression. What's missing is context, intent, etc. On the one hand, if it was said in the context of dismissing that racism exists, then it is understandable to interpret it as a microaggression. On the other hand, if the speaker acknowledges that racism has and does exist, and yet according to science, we are one race, that is a factual perspective that needs to be spread. Policing that statement as an alleged microaggression could inadvertently impede progress toward the sense of universal connection necessary to creating true equity.

Resist bigoted statements (see Chapter 14!) but don't turn microaggressions into dogma!

Other examples from Sue's table have similar problems. "Where are you from?" and "Where were you born?" are on the list, with the microaggression implication being that anyone non-white doesn't belong here in the US (Sue and Spanierman, 2020, p. 45). If that was intended, or if it was taken that way, it certainly would cause tension. However, the same words can be part of a friendly and respectful exchange between people from all walks of life. Are we never to say those words? Beyond extreme examples, which *should* be challenged as bigoted, there is simply a limit to the validity and usefulness of claiming that certain words always have the same impact and must be avoided.

It doesn't take research to make that argument. Application of the logic of *The Interpersonal Gap* is enough. Nonetheless, there is a growing body of research debating the claim that one can define microaggressions in a fixed manner and predict their intent and impact. One 2021 report concludes that it is clear that "…at this point, nobody – neither diversity administers, academics, or journalists – should take currently propagated lists of microaggressions as representative of anything meaningful" (Cantu and Jussim, 2021, p. 44). Another critic, Psychologist Scott O. Lilienfeld, comes to this conclusion: "The microaggression concept has recently galvanized public discussion and spread to numerous college campuses and businesses. I argue that the microaggression research program (MRP) rests on five core premises, namely, that microaggressions (1) are operationalized with sufficient clarity and consensus to afford rigorous scientific investigation; (2) are interpreted negatively by most or all minority group members; (3) reflect implicitly prejudicial and implicitly aggressive motives; (4) can be validly assessed using only respondents' subjective reports; and (5) exert an adverse impact on recipients' mental health. A review of the literature reveals negligible support for all five suppositions…Although the MRP has been fruitful in drawing the field's attention to subtle forms of prejudice, it is far too underdeveloped on the conceptual and methodological fronts to warrant real-world application. I conclude with 18 suggestions for advancing the scientific status of the MRP, recommend abandonment of the term "microaggression," and call for a moratorium on microaggression training programs and publicly distributed microaggression lists pending research to address the MRP's scientific limitations" (Lilienfeld, 2017, p. 1).

Other research claims to support microaggressions as a valid and reliable psychological concept. There is actually quite a fight going on in the academic community over this with one scholar posting that the concept is weak, another saying they are wrong, the first refuting the second, and so on. Psychologists Monnica Williams and Lilienfeld have produced a tit-for-tat series of articles in response to each other. Williams fired off this response to the above: "I show that, in contrast to the claim that the concept of microaggressions is vague and inconsistent, the term is well defined and can be decisively linked to individual prejudice in offenders and mental-health outcomes in targets. I explain how the concept of microaggressions is connected to pathological stereotypes, power structures, structural racism, and multiple forms of racial prejudice. Also described are recent research advances that address some of Lilienfeld's original critiques. Further, this article highlights potentially problematic attitudes, assumptions, and approaches embedded in Lilienfeld's analysis that are common to the field of psychology as a whole. It is important for all academics to acknowledge and question their own biases and perspectives when conducting scientific research" (Williams, 2019, p. 1).

Lilienfeld's first response to Williams can be summed up like so: "Nevertheless, because she appears to misconstrue many of my arguments regarding the MRP, many of her rebuttals are not relevant to my criticisms. Furthermore, her assertions notwithstanding, Williams does not effectively address my concerns regarding the (a) excessively fuzzy boundaries of the microaggression construct, (b) psychometric hazards of relying exclusively on subjective reports when detecting microaggressions, and (c) hypothesized causal impact of microaggressions on mental health…I conclude with a discussion of areas of potential common ground in microaggression research and application" (Lilienfeld, 2019, p. 1). They continue in other articles (without, as such debates often go, having any apparent influence on one another).

There are many voices engaged in this debate. It would be exciting to put them all in one room, with a referee and a play-by-play announcer: "Your constructs are invalid!" "Your research methodology is flawed!" "Oh my goodness! There are multiple flags on the field! It looks like the last two participants to speak are heading to the penalty box where they will have to review Appendix B of *Diversity Without Dogma* before returning to play!"

Admittedly, in this case, I trust the skepticism more than the attempted defense. The allusions in Williams' last two sentences about Lilienfeld's and the field of psychology's implicit bias seem like a low blow, all too common in DEI conflicts. If she started with herself and her own biases, her judgments about others would hold more weight, at least with me. "Start with yourself" is and will remain one of my biases. Furthermore, starting with yourself by "revealing" that you have already done a bunch of soul-searching, as I have heard DEI trainers claim, doesn't cut it. If you want to talk about bias, lead by example by starting with the biases you hold now. More on this in Chapter 13.

Despite the shortcomings and the messy public debate ensuing, the concept of microaggressions expresses something important. Just because people make the mistake of wielding it like a hammer and/or claiming it is above the dynamics of interpersonal communication does not invalidate the concept. Clemente *did* suffer "a thousand small cuts" from comments while he endured being one of the first black (he was a dark-skinned Puerto Rican) players permitted to play baseball with whites. And as Robin DiAngelo correctly points out, it wasn't because of lack of talent that there were no blacks in the major leagues. It was overt societal and institutional racism.

The following excerpt (with small adaptations) from *Planned Change*, my book on the work of Kurt Lewin (Crosby, 2021a, p. 119), explores the concept further:

> The cumulative effect of real or perceived micro-aggressions can put a person on high alert for life, damage their self-esteem, and make them a nervous wreck. Some micro-aggressions are intentional. Others are not intentional as when my wife, a dark-skinned Jamaican, had a Hispanic co-worker tell her, "To me you're not black. You're white." The co-worker seemed oblivious of the inherent racism in her intended compliment.
>
> Long before the term was coined, Lewin spoke of the effect of micro-aggressions and of the understandable difficulty facing the minority individual as they tried to distinguish between what is real discrimination and what is imagined. His words bear repeating: "*Unclearness* as to whether, in a given case, a set-back is due to the individual's lack of ability or due to anti-Semitism. If the young Jew is refused a job, is not invited to a birthday party, is not asked to join a club, he is usually not fully clear as to whether he himself is to blame or whether he is being discriminated against. A person who knows that his own shortcomings have caused his failure may do something to overcome them, or, if that is not possible, he can decide to apply his efforts in other directions.
>
> If he knows that his being refused has nothing to do with his own abilities he will not blame himself, and instead may try to change the social reality. However, if he is in doubt as to whether his own shortcomings are the cause of his experience, he will be disorientated. He will intermittently blame himself and refuse responsibility, blame the others and be apologetic. In other words, this unclearness necessarily leads to a disorganized emotional behavior on the area of self-esteem which is so important for adjustment and personality development (Lewin, 1941, 1999, p329)."
>
> The issue of real or perceived slights is confusing for the majority and the minority, and as such is potentially a further restraining force in overcoming prejudice. This recognition of ambiguity is missing from most of the literature on micro-aggressions. As long as there is sexism, the same unclearness will infect gender relationships as well. For those who have been in a group that has suffered discrimination, it's understandable to

suspect racism, sexism, or any other "ism" in any unsatisfactory inter-actions. My wife wondered about it in many interactions when she first migrated to the US; less so as time has gone by. On the other hand, it is easy for those that have been in power to deny the validity of any such fears, and to be blind to such dynamics even when they are genuinely happening.

The confusion in US society about these dynamics reared its head in an experience two of my colleagues, both white males, had recently. They were teaching *The Interpersonal Gap* in a T-group based workshop. A young African American woman took offense to the model and claimed that if a person (the receiver...her in this case) felt harmed by something someone else (the sender) did or said it was 100% the responsibility of the sender and they should apologize. When my colleagues stuck with their belief that how one receives messages is also important, and that it is easy to misunderstand on the receiving end, they were confronted as racist based on the young woman's understanding of the "microaggression" training she had recently received.

In personal correspondence about this incident, Dr. Rodney Coates (the author of *The Matrix of Race*) had this to say: "One word – well 2 – bs... that's called playing the race card...and makes any kind of real work and progress impossible. Look...whites are not guilty by virtue of being white; neither are blacks victims by virtue of being black. The problem with the victim shame blame game is that we don't get anywhere. That's why I favor restorative and not retributive justice.

Let me clarify if I can. A couple years ago I'm in my office talking to a black student, and a colleague passed by, saw me in the office, and said "boy, did you see that." The student looking aghast said "He just called you boy." I said, "No its an expression..." We filter things through layers of experiences, trauma, stress, pain and joy. And oftentimes when there is no trust we misread what is being said. It means we must listen even more carefully...we must extend trust that bridges across the valleys of distrust.

(That is) why micro-aggression and blind spots are the wrong way to start conversations about diversity. For if there are these deep-seated hostilities, biases, micro-aggression and blind spots then there should also be a corollary set of deep seated, fundamental values of good will that extends to all, regardless of identities. Conversations that begin and end with the former, and not the latter...only tell one side of the story.

Coates (2018)[2]

Lewin's research concurs that DEI conversations need to start with inclusion if we are to break free of polarization and make real progress. The DEI framework proposed in these pages can help build inclusion and common ground. Without such a framework, there is less objectivity and more like-lihood of imbalance. Without balance, if a minority person believes there is a microaggression, they and others are likely to believe that their belief is all that matters, and others are likely to be polarized in opposition to such an imbalanced belief.

As a member of an online discussion between organization development professionals, I experienced this firsthand. A member from Nepal posted something, which got four responses. Soon after, another colleague won-dered whether the "lack of response" was a microaggression, and the orig-inal member added, "…micro-invalidation of a brown-skinned Indian by the West." We will say more about attempts to contrast "East" and "West" in Chapter 13. Meanwhile, this assertion about microaggression struck me as a moment where the here-and-now interpersonal and the broader social context was fused. On the one hand, I admired my colleague for raising the issue. The voices of women and minorities have absolutely been underrepresented historically, and by no means have we leveled that play-ing field yet (as we shall explore further in Chapter 6). The wounds caused by that run deep. Nonetheless, this doesn't mean every such moment is about prejudice.

With no shared framework, I knew I was on shaky grounds if I chal-lenged the assertion that the lack of response to the post was a microag-gression. On the other hand, to avoid the topic, in a group of professionals whose life work is to help people hold difficult conversations, seemed hyp-ocritical. I put my toe in the water. As I feared, my toe suffered (metaphor-ical) lacerations. The reaction didn't change what I believed, but eventually (as Lewin predicts when the change method is based on pressure), I chose to patch the relationship and let the conversation go.

To make a long story short, what I wrote in response was that I didn't think this was a solid example of a microaggression. My reasoning was that I had posted many times in the group and gotten zero responses whereas the post in question received several responses, and the individ-ual had often gotten responses in the past. I also knew that personally I hadn't read any posts the past week, which is why I hadn't responded to the post in question or anyone else's. It was a false hypothesis to interpret my absence and lack of response to everyone as proof of bias. Finally, I added my concern that concepts like microaggression will become mean-ingless, or at least polarized into ineffectiveness, if they aren't held to some sort of rigor. As they say, if all you have is a hammer, everything will look like a nail. This could be true of the concept "microaggression" (or any other concept).

I may not have been as clear as possible in the moment. I own that. I tried to be, but my posts still led to one misunderstanding after another. The white males on the list went silent or supported me privately (neither behavior which I really appreciated). I eventually gave up, which is how a lot of polarized conversations end, which is another example of why we need common ground or a framework.

As decades of conflict work has shown me, *The Interpersonal Gap* model can play an important role in finding that common ground. If each party knows they may have misunderstood what someone did or said and that they might be misunderstood, they may also get it that only humility on their part and the part of others gives us a chance at overcoming misunderstandings.

Perception and misperception are so big in this drama that they deserve a closer look. The DEI workshop I participated in started with viewing a video during which I and most of the other participants focused on something that was unimportant and missed what was truly important. The obvious point was that perception is biased. We only see what we expect to see. No further lesson was attempted by the trainers. I think they wanted us to get it that we might be biased but unaware. Unfortunately, they were determined to stick to their story that they had no preconceived notions, so what they intended can, to this day, only be guessed at.

Here is the lesson as I see it. Human perception is selective. It has to be. If we didn't know how to focus, we would go crazy. There is too much information in front of us at any given moment competing for our attention. If we don't know how to ignore most of it and focus, we would be overwhelmed. Unfortunately, this means we filter out a lot and miss other possibilities. Not only that, we are prone to confirmation bias, which means that we only see and interpret in the way that we expect to. If you mistrust someone, you will be hyperalert to evidence that supports your mistrust. It's part of our primitive brain survival reflex. Likewise, if you trust someone, you'll tend to interpret their actions as further proof of the worthiness of the trust.

Our perception is further influenced by the social construction of reality we grew up in and live in today. As don Miguel Ruiz puts it, "We are dreaming our own dreams" and mistaking them for reality.

The subjective nature of perception validates *The Interpersonal Gap*. Think of the political party you support. Think of them saying or doing anything. Now think of someone in the other party doing the exact same behavior. Which are you likely to mistrust and which are you likely to give a break to? The same can easily go with ethnicity, gender, and other similarities and differences. Perceptual bias, then, is a real and important part of the human condition. Our judgment of others is necessary. It also limits us.

My DEI instructors didn't explain any of that. My interpretation of their message throughout the workshop, not just based on that video, was that bias is bad. What is ironic about that, if that is what they meant, is the bias in that message. It's more scientific to note that bias is part of being human, and the challenge is to know as much as one can about their own perceptual biases so one is as open-minded as possible. I am biased toward equity, for example. That's my story and I'm sticking to it. I'm also biased toward transparency in DEI work, and yes, that is a shot across the bow of anyone leading DEI work who thinks they have to hide what they think. Some of what you think is obvious, like equity is better than racism, so why hide it? And how can one teach people to explore their own biases if they are not openly exploring along with the participants? Lewin had it right. "We feeling" with the instructor or leader is essential to learning, and that doesn't come from staying distant.

That "we feeling" also comes from leaders' soliciting and being open to feedback. Participant feedback to the faculty was a critical moment in Lewin's aforementioned 1946 Connecticut race relations workshop, is critical in T-group learning, and is also critical in DEI work. Wallen sets the standard for effective feedback, emphasizing behavior specifics (what did the person receiving the feedback actually do and/or say) over judgments (which, if negative, are likely to induce defensiveness). The sender and the receiver both have the task of seeking clarity about behavior and taking responsibility for their own reactions.

The feedback interaction can be illustrated by yet another model, known as the Johari Window. Created by psychologists Joseph Luft (1916–2014) and Harrington Ingham (1916–1995) in 1955, this simple visual can help balance their awareness and behavior (Figure 3.2).

The model is simple and yet potentially elucidating. Starting with the blind spot, that is what others "know" about you that you are unaware of. "Know" should be put in quotations, or taken with a grain of salt, because "knowing" includes interpretations, and even if others believe them to be

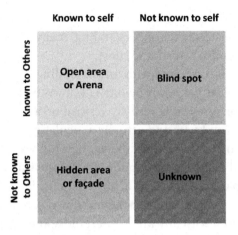

FIGURE 3.2
The Johari window.

facts that does not make them facts. What is factual is that others will at times have judgments about what you say and do that you are unaware of.

The façade is the opposite. That is, the facade is what you think, feel, and want of others that you are doing your best not to reveal.

Some of both of those quadrants are inevitable and even desirable. If you have ever seen the movie "Liar Liar" with Jim Carey, then you can imagine what life would be like if there was no façade and if most of what came to mind was immediately spoken (in Carey's character's case, what popped to mind were mostly insults). It's important to not reveal everything, and on the flip side, it is just as well not to know everything.

Nonetheless, there are probably things that each of us habitually hide that would be helpful for others to know, and there *is* information others hold that would be helpful to hear. Increasing the flow of information requires lowering the façade so as to reveal more and decreasing the blind spot by seeking feedback. Having the perspective and skills of *The Interpersonal Gap* model increases the likelihood that the feedback will be behavioral and that the ability to receive it will be less defensive. On the receiving end, taking a deep breath and making sure you understand the behavior specifics of the feedback ("what did I do or say") will make it far less likely that you will get reactive to any judgments and that you will be experienced as someone who is safe to give feedback to. If all you do is fight back, then the odds that the other will take the risk of giving you feedback go way down.

You don't have to agree with the feedback, but if you don't even understand it and demonstrate that understanding, many are likely to conclude that giving it to you isn't worth the effort.

Feedback given and received with understanding expands the arena or open area. Now what is known by one is known by the other. This can only be known for sure if it is verbally verified or, as Wallen put it, made public. Thinking you know and actually articulating what you know are two different things, and articulation is the only way to openly verify. Paraphrasing and behavior description, two of the skills in Appendix B, are critical to expanding the arena of any relationship.

The larger the arena, the smaller the unknown. Some things, however, are beyond knowing with any kind of certainty, and so the bottom right quadrant will always be there to some degree. This is part of the ambiguity of life, which one might as well embrace.

The Johari Window was presented early in the DEI workshop that I have been mentioning. The facilitators covered it quickly and only explained the blind spot. Whatever their intentions were stayed hidden behind the façade. My assumption was they meant that the blind spot was most important because we might reveal our biases to others, even if we are unaware of them. We had just taken a bias test, which we will explore later in Chapter 13. They made no overt attempt to explain the relationship between the four quadrants, nor did they attempt to create a model for feedback. Whenever I tried to give feedback, they got upset with me. I don't know how prevalent this is in DEI work, but it was more evidence to me that the leaders must walk the talk of what they are trying to teach. Such a sensitive topic needs helpful frameworks for difficult moments. The Johari Window is one such framework, or model, especially if it is embedded in the interpersonal communication clarity of *The Interpersonal Gap*.

Feedback is essential to knowing oneself. Knowing oneself is essential to starting with yourself. Starting with yourself is essential to walking the talk of Gandhi's wise advice to "Be the change you want to see in the world." As the Christian mystic Thomas Merton put it, "Finally I am coming to the conclusion that my highest ambition is to be what I already am. That I will never fulfill my obligation to surpass myself unless I first accept myself – and, if I accept myself fully in the right way, I will already have surpassed myself. For it is the unaccepted self that stands in my way – and will continue to do so as long as it is not accepted. When it is accepted it is my own stepping stone to what is above me" (Merton, 2004).

ASSUMPTIONS ABOUT MEANING AND DEFENSIVENESS

Let us further explore the theme of feedback. According to Robin DiAngelo, every time she tells an audience of "white people" that "All white people are invested in and collude with racism," she gets a defensive response (DiAngelo, 2018, p. 116). She calls her message giving feedback. Her oft-repeated hypothesis is that the defensive response is evidence that the white people in the audience are racist.

There are several problems with this approach.[3] One is that it is a circular argument. She is getting a response that is predictable whenever one delivers negative judgments about others and insists the judgments are "the truth." Her own behavior and the behavior of the trainers in the workshop I attended are at least part of the cause of the effect, and yet, all three claim the effect is proof of their theory about the others (although the trainers also claimed they had no theories). This is a false hypothesis, no matter what judgment is being used. *People feeling defensive does not invalidate their response or prove that the accusation is valid.*

Please make a note of that last sentence. I'll make this blanket judgment: everyone gets defensive. It happens whenever one thinks they have been misunderstood in a negative way and/or thinks they are being attacked. Explaining oneself is behavioral evidence of the emotional state. If someone says, "I agree but…," the word "but" is a clue that they are probably disagreeing. If they are disagreeing with what they perceived as a criticism of their own thinking or behavior, they are probably feeling defensive. Here's the deal. That's ok. Feel what you feel and *choose* what you do. This requires the emotional intelligence (EQ) skill of noticing what you are feeling. We'll spend more time on that in Chapter 10. At times it is wise to explain oneself and to defend oneself. This doesn't mean you are a "defensive person." Feelings, including defensiveness, come and go. They don't define who we are. On the other hand, feelings can cause problems. If a feeling is persistent, and especially if a person is persistently unaware they are feeling it, then that will be tiresome for them and for others. It will cause gaps and inhibit feedback.

Unfortunately, it is now a habit in many DEI sessions to accuse others, mostly white people, of being defensive. This predictably elicits the exact emotional response it is implying is bad. You may be feeling defensive as you read this, but face it, if you have the habit of judging others as defensive, you probably don't mean it as a compliment. Ironically, as the best defense is a good offense, labeling others as defensive often has the effect of putting them on the defense and protecting you, the sender, from being judged for your own behavior. Now anything the other says can be invalidated as further proof of defensiveness.

DiAngelo actually offers a list of statements (she calls them "claims") from white people that she automatically invalidates as defensive. As a critic of DiAngelo, John McWhorter, puts it:

> If you object to any of the "feedback" that DiAngelo offers you about your racism, you are engaging in a type of bullying "whose function is to obscure racism, protect white dominance, and regain white equilibrium."
> ...Namely, thou shalt not utter:
>
> > I know people of color.
> > I marched in the sixties.
> > You are judging me.
> > You don't know me.
> > You are generalizing.
> > I disagree.
> > The real oppression is class.
> > I just said one little innocent thing.
> > Some people find offense where there is none.
> > You hurt my feelings.
> > I can't say anything right.
>
> This is an abridgment of a list DiAngelo offers in Chapter 9 (of her book); its result is to silence people. Whites aren't even allowed to say, "I don't feel safe." Only Black people can say that. If you are white, you are solely to listen as DiAngelo tars you as morally stained. "Now breathe," she counsels to keep you relaxed as you undergo this.
>
> **McWhorter (2020, p. 13)**

Let us reason together. A person could be feeling defensive when they say any of the above. If so, exploring that defensiveness instead of judging it as a character flaw might be fruitful. It may also hold lessons for the person who is being defended against (the perceived attacker). It takes two to tango! Also, only the person saying the words knows for sure what they mean and what they are feeling. Even knowing that is not easy! No words automatically prove anything about what is going on inside another. If you think you can always know someone by their actions, you are operating on a false hypothesis. Do Not Pass Go and Do Not Collect $200! Reread this chapter from the beginning! If you have succumbed to the socially constructed habit of accusing people of defensiveness, stop. Start with yourself instead. What are you feeling? You must be feeling some kind of distress to be compelled to attack someone else with a judgment. As Jesus put it, "First take the plank out of your eye, and then you will see clearly to remove the speck from your brother's eye" (Luke 6:41–42). Own your own issues and work on yourself. Make sure you understand the other. Give them a break if they do feel defensive. Hopefully, people will treat you with the same kindness. Turning again to the New Testament for wisdom, it would profit us all to heed "the golden rule": "Do unto others as you would have them do unto you" (Mathew 7:12). Build bridges, not walls. "Be the change you want to see in the world."

In sum, blanket judgments completely disregard any standards of effective feedback. "All white people are invested in and collude with racism" is not effective feedback; it is a blanket judgment about an entire group. Thus it is, in Kendi's definition, racist. In contrast, effective feedback is behaviorally specific. One could say that all people who are regarded as white in the US are living in a racist system that favors them based on the pale color of their skin, and then go over the information in Chapters 5 and 6 as specifics to back that up. One could also say that what someone just did or said is racist, although that is still asking for a fight unless you have the patience and skill to shift toward dialogue. Better to stick to behavior specifics (such as actual quotes of the other) and to describe and own the impact on you. The conversation will still be difficult. Those are the skills everyone should have in any DEI workshop.

Let's be frank. Calling individuals or groups a judgment without behavior specifics is sloppy, and is predictably going to lead toward fight (defensiveness) or flight (avoidance). This framework (or something like it) is needed precisely so we can do better than that.

Now on to the first of the polarities in the proposed framework. *Sometimes it is about race* (or other isms).

NOTES

1. This chapter draws heavily on excerpts used with permission from Chapter 8 of my last book, *Spirituality and Emotional Intelligence*.
2. End of the excerpt.
3. This is feedback, something which DiAngelo says she welcomes. I hope that is true. That seems doubtful though since when the audience gives her feedback by getting defensive (which *is* a form of feedback), she dismisses it as all about them and not about her.

Section II

Racism and Other "Isms" Are Real

4

Institutional and Individual "Isms" Are All Too Often Real

Individual prejudice and institutional/systemic prejudice both exist, and often intersect. If you don't believe that, take a closer look.

Besides reams of data, some of which we will cover here, my own closer look has come from experiences with coworkers and with two marriages. Having been married twice, the first time for 22 years to a white woman and the second time for 9 plus years (at the time of this writing) to a black woman, has given me a unique vantage point for viewing institutional racism and sexism intersecting at the level of the individual. My current wife, who always dresses with a keen fashion sense, has drawn the attention of store security on numerous occasions during our relatively short marriage. On one of those occasions, the security at our local pharmacy insisted on checking the contents of her purse before allowing her to leave the store. Her purse of course had no stolen goods. She would never dream of shoplifting and felt offended at the implications.

I've never been confronted in such a way, and neither has my ex.

On another occasion, my current wife went into our bank branch to deposit a check. We have used that branch for almost a decade. The person had filled the check out with my wife's informal first name instead of the formal spelling. My full first name, for example, is Gilmore. I have cashed many checks made out to "Gil" without a problem.

A friendly young teller, who was also black, was trying to figure out a solution when another teller, a middle-aged white woman, overheard and went and got the acting manager, a middle-aged white male. He called the teller over and took my wife's id and her debit and savings account cards from the teller. He then came out of his office, never saying anything like

DOI: 10.4324/9781003335689-6

"hello," "how are you," or "how can I help?" He didn't offer to have her come in and sit in his office or do anything remotely friendly like that. Instead, the manager treated my wife as if she was a problem, jumping right into asserting that the branch couldn't accept the check. As my wife puts it, "I didn't feel like he wanted me there." Nonetheless, as confirmed by everyone who was present, she asked him politely, "what else can I do?" The manager didn't bother to check her accounts and simply said, "There's nothing else you can do. Go back and have them rewrite the check." She said, still politely, "That's ridiculous. I've cashed these here before." The manager replied, "They shouldn't have done it for you" and turned his back to my wife and went back into his office. End of conversation.

He certainly was better behaved when I, a 60ish white male, showed up complaining about how he had treated my wife. He practically fell over himself, fawning in my presence. At first he tried to give me the same line that the only solution was to drive all the way back to the person who had issued the check and have them rewrite it. I was unimpressed. Then it dawned on him that she could sign the check over to me. That's how we handled it even though he said, "You are doing this at your own risk," to which I responded, "$80.00 isn't a risk." If he had checked, he would have seen that we had ample funds in our combined personal, business, and joint checking accounts to cover such a small amount, even if the check bounced. Besides which we knew it wouldn't. It wasn't until I had mentioned that we had plenty in our accounts, and that we might switch them to another bank, that he came up with the simple and obvious solution. If he had calmly and politely talked it through with my wife, he could have told her the same, i.e., "This is easy…just sign it over to your husband and he can cash it." Or if he had trusted her and/or confirmed the accounts, he probably could have cashed it like it was.

All of the above are examples of microaggressions, the concept discussed in the last chapter wherein small moments of real or potential racism (or sexism, or any prejudice) accumulate over time and can easily keep one on edge while doing the simple things that others take for granted. The well-documented increased risk for black drivers during routine traffic stops is a good example. Whether the traffic stop has anything to do with racism or racial profiling, the black driver has good reason to fear escalation that could possibly become life-threatening. In contrast, as a white driver, all I have feared throughout my life is that the officer might write me a ticket. More on that later.

Back to our story. The bank manager called to apologize, "even though he had done nothing wrong," and another bank official wrote to explain that "even though the bank had handled the situation well," she also apologized. Neither said anything about how my wife was treated, except that "the branch made an exception" in eventually depositing the check.

The letter claimed that all associates involved have been "educated and further coached." The letter concluded by saying they have "shared" our "experience" with the Diversity & Inclusion committee. You may draw a different conclusion, but in my eyes the bank's response seemed canned, one-sided, and more concerned with closing the incident and covering themselves than with genuine exploration and possible change. One imagines that after a sigh of relief over dodging the potential legal and public relations bullet, the institution returned to business as usual. They had defended the behavior instead of admitting it at least looked bad and might have something to do with their culture.

In this case, they were dealing with a white male social scientist who responded to their responses in a series of correspondence and phone calls. Imagine how quickly they shrug off the average customer.

The incident is a good example of how possible racism, possible sexism, and possible ageism can converge. Fear of litigation makes the conversations even murkier. Nobody wanted to admit that if I had been the customer that day, the branch would have probably just deposited my check, or at least would have done so after briefly considering how to proceed. Because that is what had always happened, it is a safe bet that is what would have happened.

On the other hand, it's a mistake to forget that there is ambiguity in most interactions. The best we can do is non-defensively try to challenge, understand, and alter behaviors that appear biased against one group or the other, especially where there are documented patterns of bias.

Ironically, the banking industry is one of the arenas where bias *is* a documented pattern. This isn't history (that's next chapter). Unless a miracle has occurred by the time this is published, it is happening now. Discriminatory lending practices have been documented as recently as during the pandemic. As pointed out in The New York Times, "From the very start of the Paycheck Protection Program last year, it was clear that minority entrepreneurs, especially Black business owners, struggled more than white borrowers to find a willing lender. A new research project indicates that the problem was particularly pronounced at smaller banks – and human bias appears to be the main reason" (Cowley, 2021, pp 1). Research found that lenders who used automation to vet and process loans, such as large banks and "financial technology companies" (or "fintechs"), were much more likely to lend to minority applicants than were small banks that used much more personal processing. This was true even for long-standing minority customers of the small banks, even though the PPP loans were completely risk free for the lending institutions. If you were black and you were handled through a personal transaction, it was harder to get a loan. The same trend wasn't evident for other minorities, such as Asians and Hispanics (more on those racial classifications in Chapter 5).

Did some vast network get organized to tell everyone in those banks to be wary of black business owners seeking a PPP loan? Of course not. This institutional racism was instead a cumulative effect of individual bias and lack of oversight committed to assure fair lending. It is evidence of how much individual bias in the form of racism against blacks exists today, right now, in the United States.

This bias by lenders is nothing new. Astonishingly, the homeownership gap is bigger between blacks and whites now than it was during segregation. Some of this is rooted in historical practices that have since been illegalized, such as the "redlining" policy of the US Government Home Owners Loan Corporation during the Great Depression, which intentionally prevented lending to "neighborhoods infiltrated by negroes." Meanwhile more than a million white families received low-interest loans. Recent research found that lenders denied black applicants with the exact same financial histories at an 80% higher rate than white applicants. If you are an African American making $100,000 per year, you are likely to be put into a subprime loan and receive the same high interest as a white person making less than 35k (CNN…black in America). Hard to believe, but outrageous and true.

Don't take my word for it. If you are skeptical and/or curious, there is plenty of data available. Hopefully whatever your ethnicity or gender, you *are* curious and will take a look at your own profession and organizations with a commitment to find and root out discriminatory practices. If you are part of a profession that has a clearly tainted history, you have no excuse for not being all over this stuff. If not now, when?

I mentioned my coworkers earlier. I traveled extensively with a particular female colleague for years, and there was no mistaking a pattern of "micro-invalidations" that emerged. My colleague would be ignored by clerks in one hotel after another as well as in other customer service situations. As soon as I would walk up, the same people were practically falling all over each other trying to serve me. The same thing happens with my current wife. I don't know how much race has to do with it (my coworker was also white) but sexism was present enough in one interaction after another to create a clear and predictable pattern.

The point is, institutional and individual racism, sexism, and other biases do exist, and must be recognized and eradicated. If you don't believe that, you are sticking your head in the sand. That doesn't mean that each and every suspicious thing that happens is institutional racism. Ambiguity is also real. Pretending the isms don't exist or that the ambiguity doesn't exist creates additional trouble. No one said this would be easy. To make real progress, it is essential to be intolerant of what appears to be discrimination, and yet simultaneously humble when interpreting individual interactions.

The same must be said for understanding history, and we turn our focus there now.

5

Accuracy about History:
Denial Is Poison

Family systems therapy (the focus of Chapter 10) teaches us that secrets in families are poison. The same applies to societies. Denial keeps us stuck. Acceptance helps us move forward. It is time to stop debating history and historical figures as all good or all bad, and instead, as objectively as possible, scrutinize each as, to varying degrees, representing both the best and the worst of being human. This chapter is a brief attempt at such with a focus on the history of racism and an even briefer look at the history of sexism and all oppression.

Acknowledging different views is as close as we can get to accuracy. Take religion, for example. Judged by the misdeeds of the followers, most faiths are awful. As a Christian, I cringe at the role the church played in encouraging colonialism and slavery, for example. On the other hand, judged by the good deeds of the faithful, most religions are wonderful. The same is true for many historical figures and events. Here we will try to judge them by both the good and the bad.

Please note there is too much ground to cover to possibly explore it all in one book, let alone one chapter. The more research I did, the more material I found, and so, I had to cut off the process in the interests of getting this written. This will necessarily only be a sample from the growing body of quality information that could be explored. On the other hand, this small chapter will hopefully provide a significant contribution to summarizing the history of racism.

Please also note that I am not officially a historian, just a lover of history and an enemy of prejudice. I have tried to be as accurate and objective as I can be. Some will no doubt take offense to some or all of the following.

DOI: 10.4324/9781003335689-7

If you have only viewed the history of the United States as all good, you will find much of what is written here troubling. The opposite is also true. If you disagree with any of this and you have documentation that indicates another view, I welcome that information.

EARLY HUMANITY

Briefly, according to the Smithsonian Institute,

> The species that you and all other living human beings on this planet belong to is *Homo sapiens*. During a time of dramatic climate change 300,000 years ago, *Homo sapiens* evolved in Africa. Like other early humans that were living at this time, they gathered and hunted food, and evolved behaviors that helped them respond to the challenges of survival in unstable environments...
> For millions of years all humans, early and modern alike, had to find their own food. They spent a large part of each day gathering plants and hunting or scavenging animals. By 164,000 years ago modern humans were collecting and cooking shellfish and by 90,000 years ago modern humans had begun making special fishing tools. Then, within just the past 12,000 years, our species, *Homo sapiens*, made the transition to producing food and changing our surroundings. Humans found they could control the growth and breeding of certain plants and animals. This discovery led to farming and herding animals, activities that transformed Earth's natural landscapes – first locally, then globally. As humans invested more time in producing food, they settled down. Villages became towns, and towns became cities.
>
> **Smithsonian Institute**

We are one species. All the evidence indicates that we started in Africa. Both assertions are confirmed by genetic science. According to J. Craig Venter, one of the heads of the human genome project, "Race is a social concept, not a scientific one. We all evolved in the last 100,000 years from the same small number of tribes that migrated out of Africa and colonized the world" (Painter, 2010, p. 474). Historian Nell Irvin Painter summarizes the implications of the genome project in her meticulous, *The History of White People*, this way: "Each person shares 99.99 percent of the genetic material of every other human being. In terms of variation, people from the same race can be more different than people from different races.

And in the genetic sense, all people – and all Americans – are African descended" (Painter, 2010, p. 475). She goes on to quote President Clinton during the unveiling of the genome project at the White House in 2000: "In genetic terms all human beings, regardless of race, are more than 99.9 percent the same. What that means is that modern science has confirmed what we first learned from ancient faiths. The most important fact of life on this earth is our common humanity."

Recent research concludes that the first major migration out of Africa, caused by climate change approximately 55,000 years ago, happened through Egypt (Gray, 2015, pp. 1) (Figure 5.1).

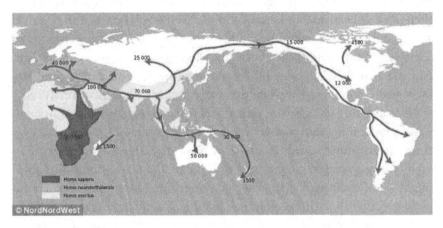

FIGURE 5.1
Migration of early humanity. (Source: © GoGraph. Used with Permission)

One thing that is clear is that those who stayed near the equator developed darker pigmentation and more melanin due to exposure to sunlight, and those who migrated north developed various shades of lighter pigmentation due to less sunlight. In Painter's words, "Skin color is a by-product of two kinds of melanin: red to yellow pheomelanin and dark brown to black eumelanin in reaction to sunlight. And several genes interact to make people light or dark, reddish, brownish, or yellowish. Ancient scholars were wiser than they knew when they related skin color to climate. Today's biologists concur. Sunny climates do make people dark-skinned, and dark, cold climates make people light-skinned. How much of which sort of melanin people have in their skin – and to what degree it is expressed – depends entirely over time on exposure to the sun's ultraviolet (UV) radiation" (Painter, 2010, p. 477).

The culture was also influenced by heat and cold, with those in the colder climates becoming much more driven by the seasonal rhythms of planting and harvesting while those in more stable climates enjoyed a less time-driven bounty.

What we also know, based on studies of the people who live the lifestyle closest to our prehistoric ancestors, is that early culture was almost certainly very egalitarian and collective. Everyone participated in the work of gathering, which is how most sustenance was acquired. The cartoon image of big guys thumping things with clubs while the women stayed home and minded the cave is almost entirely fiction. Contrary to the myth of "man the hunter," hunting among "hunter-gatherers," while important, was often done collectively and provided only an irregular part of the diet. A more accurate name would be "gatherer-hunters." As anthropologist Lila Leibowitz put it, "The above review of field observations of...non-human primates reveals that male and female foraging activities are essentially alike, and forces us to conclude that early hominids...were not naturally prone to dividing tasks by sex. Other data from biology provide additional reasons for coming to this conclusion. Short life spans, a relatively late age of sexual maturation, and rates of population growth which suggests that fertility levels were low combined to indicate that early hominid populations were composed primarily of young...members. Species survival could not, then, have hinged on the subsistence activities of the few adults in the group, but must have depended on the development of cooperative production by all and for all" (Coontz and Henderson, 1986, p. 55). Everyone forging, everyone sharing the fruits of their labors, was the surest method of survival. Only later in time did we start differentiating the tasks of the males and females and of the adults and children in any significant way. It was even later on, with the accumulation of wealth that came from early agriculture, that one group started having advantages over the others.

It is now well-documented that male anthropologists, dominating the early days of the field, believed or at least projected the socially constructed patriarchal myths they grew up with, including male domination, onto the cultures they documented. As Leibowitz notes, "Inevitably what a social or behavioral scientist sees and reports is colored and shaped by what he or she expects to see, knows about, and is encouraged or required to write about. Like everybody else, social scientists are subject to the traditions in which they grow up" (Leibowitz, 1978, p. 119).

However we look back, the same challenge faces us, of projecting our bias onto the past and onto different cultures. We must also sift through the bias present in much of the documentation of history if we want to be as objective as possible. And why wouldn't we want to be?

What we know now of cultures such as the Kalahari bush people is that sexism, racism, and power dynamics such as class warfare and even concepts like personal property simply don't apply. Neither do our sex role stereotypes. Men, for example, are active in child-rearing. There is no significant separation between work and life, between young and old, between men and women. Life was in many ways hard, and short, but the social harmony is remarkable. We also know that "primitive" humans are and were just as intelligent as "modern" humans. Their knowledge base is different, but their brains are just as sharp. If you doubt that, go to the Kalahari and see how long you last without help from the bush people.

While radically different than what I was taught about prehistory as a kid, these claims are not just wishful thinking (another form of bias). This is a reasonable understanding of prehistory, drawing on the available documentation of the bush people and similar cultures who are or were living as close as we can tell to our early conditions.

It *does* imply that we are capable of living without social diseases such as racism and sexism. Whether we ever will again remain to be seen.

INDIGENOUS PEOPLES

The indigenous peoples of the world have a rich history. No matter how one tries to justify it, and the majority culture in the US and elsewhere has tried hard to do so, the treatment of indigenous peoples in the last few hundred years has been nothing short of criminal. Racism on an enormous scale toward indigenous groups continues even as we speak, and a fundamental part of this DEI framework is that any prejudice begets more prejudice (see Chapter 7). We must be consistent in seeking equity for all, or we risk undermining equity for any.

Having said that, it's important to recognize history and current conditions while at the same time not idealizing everything non-European, as some DEI practitioners do (more on that in Chapter 13). While it would be an upgrade on the social construction of reality, in my opinion, if we all adapted the commitment of many tribes,[1] that one should always consider the impact of one's action on the next seven generations to come; not every aspect of indigenous thinking is uniform or so lofty. One needs to look no further than the Aztecs to find some of the worst traits of humanity, such as brutal exploitation and oppression of their neighbors. An important element in the victory of the unbelievably outnumbered Spaniards (800 facing an empire with a capital city inhabited by 200,000 people) was the help rendered by the vast network of oppressed indigenous peoples nearby, numbering some 370 city-states, who desperately hoped that the Aztecs would be defeated.

Historian Victor Hanson paints this picture of conditions in Central America when the Spaniards first arrived:

> The Mesoamericans fought the Aztecs not because they were enamored of the Spanish-indeed for much of 1519 and early 1520 they tried to exterminate Cortes-but because they met an unexpected and powerful enemy who could be unleashed on their even greater adversary, Tenochtitlan, which had systematically butchered their own women and children in a most gruesome and hideous fashion. The near constant wars of the past century with the Aztecs had left most Mesoamerican peoples between the interior and the coast-the Tlaxcalans especially-under either an oppressive subjugation that stripped their fields and often their population for material and human tribute, or a state of siege for as much as six months out of the year to ward off Aztec depredations.

Hanson (2001, p. 212)

The point is, it's a mistake to idealize indigenous culture as all good, just as it is a mistake to look down on them as all bad or "primitive." Where people *did* live together in relative peace and harmony, and there are plenty of examples of that, one certainly has to be pretty biased to call that "primitive." However, in case you do hold that bias, perhaps these words written in 1852 to the President of the United States by one such "primitive" will shift your thinking:

> The president in Washington sends word that he wishes to buy our land. But how can you buy or sell the Sky? The land? The idea is strange to us. If we do not own the freshness of the air and the sparkle of the water, how can you buy them?

Every part of this earth is sacred to my people. Every shining pine needle, every sandy shore, every mist in the dark woods, every meadow, every humming insect. All are holy in the memory and experience of my people.

We know the sap which courses through the trees as we know the blood that courses through our veins. We are part of the earth and it is part of us. The perfumed flowers are our sisters. The bear, the deer, the great eagle, these are our brothers. The rocky crests, the juices in the meadow, the body heat of the pony, and man, all belong to the same family.

The shining water that moves in the streams and rivers is not just water, but the blood of our ancestors. If we sell you our land, you must remember that it is sacred. Each ghostly reflection in the clear waters of the lake tells of events and memories in the life of my people. The water's murmur is the voice of my father's father.

The rivers are our brothers. They quench our thirst. They carry our canoes and feed our children. So you must give to the rivers the kindness you would give any brother.

If we sell you our land remember that the air is precious to us, that the air shares its spirit with all the life it supports. The wind that gave our grandfather his first breath also receives his last sigh. The wind also gives our children the spirit of life. So if we sell you our land, you must keep it apart and sacred, as a place where man can go to taste the wind that is sweetened by the meadow flowers.

Will you teach your children what we have taught our children? That the earth is our mother? What befalls the earth befalls all the sons of the earth.

This we know: the earth does not belong to man, man belongs to the earth. All things are connected like the blood that unites us all. Man did not weave the web of life, he is merely a strand in it. Whatever he does to the web, he does to himself.

One thing we know: our God is also your God. The earth is precious to him and to harm the earth is to heap contempt on its creator.

Your destiny is a mystery to us. What will happen when the Buffalo are all slaughtered? The wild horses tamed? What will happen when the secret corners of the forest are heavy with the scent of many men and the view of the ripe hills is blotted by talking wires? Where will the thickets be? Gone! Where will the eagle be? Gone! And what is to say goodbye to the swift pony and the hunt? The end of living and the beginning of survival.

When the last Red Man has vanished with his wilderness and his memory is only the shadow of a cloud moving across the prairie, will these shores and forest still be here? Will there be any of the spirit of my people left?

We love this earth as a newborn loves its mother's heartbeat. So, if we sell you our land, love it as we have loved it. Care for it as we have cared for it. Hold in your mind the memory of the land as it is when you receive it. Preserve the land for all children and love it, as God loves us all.

As we are part of the land, you too are part of the land. This earth is precious to us. It is also precious to you. One thing we know: there is only one God. No man, be he Red Man or White Man, can be apart. We *are* brothers after all.

Chief Seattle (Campbell, 1988, p. 34)

It's hard for me to imagine anyone reading that and thinking it is "primitive" or in any way inferior to the culture it was resisting.

Another mistake, besides thinking one's group is actually superior, is to think of any vast and widespread groups of people as being one group. The diversity of so-called indigenous cultures is virtually endless and would take a lifetime to study.

The same is true of any US government-designated racial groups, such as "Asians," "Hispanics," "African Americans," and "Whites," even though the designations have slowly sunk into our collective consciousness as if they describe a homogenous group. Most people hold a more specific cultural identity than that, especially in the "Asian" and "Hispanic" groupings, even if they are getting used to checking that box on a form. My wife is a US citizen, but she identifies herself as Jamaican, not "African American." Try to convince her otherwise and see how that works out for you. Try telling anyone designated "Asian" that they are exactly the same as every other ethnic group from Asia and you will be taking on an equally nonsensical and futile task. More on the history of racial designations and their role in racism lies ahead.

Meanwhile, however you judge the various indigenous groups, there is no denying that they have mostly been wiped out, brutally forced off their land and out of their lifestyle, and largely disrespected and exploited to this very day.

Part of the social construction of history that people in the US have been raised on is the notion of brave and moral cowboys fighting savage "Indians." The media depiction in print, film, and television, at least until recently, can only be considered as one-sided as a Nazi propaganda campaign. The theme song, to one of my favorite characters, tells it all. "Daniel Boone was a man, he was a real man. And he fought for America to keep all Americans free." One of my happiest Christmas memories was getting a coonskin cap and a Daniel Boone rifle so I could go out and kill some imaginary "bad guys." My father, a tireless crusader against racism and other forms of injustice, bought me that.[2] People I love, like Walt Disney, pumped that material out. While some must have known it was a distortion of the truth, others no doubt did not. Let ye who are without bias cast the first stone. But we can be critical nonetheless, and we can present more factual depictions of the past.

Daniel Boone *was* a man. He was an actual man. What constitutes being a real man, of course, is open to debate. That line actually reflects the socially constructed myth of patriarchy, in case it isn't obvious. Noting that isn't about bashing men. It *is* about giving the same respect to women, and also to men who have characteristics besides those attributed to the mythic figure of Boone.

Oddly, I don't actually know much about the real Daniel Boone. I do understand from reliable sources, however, that other "frontiersmen," like Davy Crockett and Sam Huston, were lifelong friends of the Native Americans and lived near them in harmony during the years between the War of 1812 and the forced removal known as the "Trail of Tears" by the administration of Andrew Jackson (Zinn, 1980, p. 135). Whatever the case with my childhood hero, it is a safe bet Daniel Boone didn't "fight to keep all Americans free." Did he resist slavery? That would have been a Quixotian task and certainly would have made the headlines. Clearly, however, he felt about it; he didn't lead an uprising against slavery nor fight the US government to resist the oppression of the Native Americans, so that line in the song is a fairy tale.

The question is, like when we learn that Santa Clause isn't real, can we grow up about history and at least see it from different angles? I think we must if we are going to have any sensible conversations about it, and as the saying goes, "if you can't learn from history…"

A prime example of distorted history involving the indigenous peoples of North America is Thanksgiving. Like most Americans, I was taught that the Native Americans helped the Pilgrims survive harsh conditions, and in return, the Pilgrims invited the Native Americans to a feast of thanksgiving, celebrated in modern times on November 27 every year.

Here are the facts as we know it: New England had been settled for nearly 12,000 years when the Pilgrims arrived. The Wampanoags who lived there had a sophisticated way of life which included summer dwellings near the shore and winter villages further inland. The Pilgrims came upon and immediately desecrated burial grounds, storage pits, homes, and other property. There was a system of roadways marked so that travelers could learn and recall the history of the region as they moved along the roads. These were not hunters and gatherers but rather people who had developed a system of horticulture as their main means of subsistence. As with the people of the Kalahari, these were people who were no less intelligent than any others.

There was an estimated 21,000–24,000 Wampanoags in the region, and many more indigenous people nearby, organized into a vast political structure wherein tribute was paid to the most powerful "sachem" or leader, who would handle diplomacy, warfare, trade, etc.

The Wampanoags didn't choose to make contact with the Pilgrims until March 1621, almost a full year after the arrival of the English. Small wonder, as years of trade, often ending in bloodshed and abductions of Native Americans by European ships, had been occurring in the region since 1524. We know from the story of Tisquantum, or Squanto for short, that when his party of Wampanoags went aboard an English merchant ship to trade in 1614, the Captain, Thomas Hunt, seized 20 of the men and took them to Spain, where he sold them as slaves. Squanto, through luck (a group of friars blocked his sale) and persistence, made his way to London. Eventually, by becoming an interpreter and guide, he was able to make the long journey home. In 1619, he returned with a trading expedition, only to find his people had been nearly wiped out by an epidemic (one of many such epidemics to come).

The story is complex. His Captain, Dermer, secures the release of two Frenchmen who had been held prisoner by the Wampanoags. Sailing on to another area, where unbeknownst to the English, a bitter fight between the locals and the French had occurred a few years prior, Dermer is first taken prisoner and then manages to escape and take two sachems prisoner. An exchange is made, and Dermer sails on. As historian David Silverman puts it, "Just a year and a half later, the Mayflower landed thirty-five miles to the north at the edge of what had effectively become a war zone between the Wampanoags and one ship crew after another" (Silverman, 2019, p. 69). Hardly the image I held as a child of the Pilgrim's arrival in America.

Dermer, meanwhile, sailed on, next landing in Martha's Vineyard, where, to his surprise, a Wampanoag named Epenow greeted him in English. Epenow had been taken by the English years earlier, had returned on a similar journey, had hailed his people in his native language and talked them into surrounding the ship and pummeling the crew with arrows, and had managed to jump overboard and make his escape. Epenow held no apparent love for the English. To make matters worse, unbeknownst to Captain Dermer, another English trading "...vessel had anchored off Pokanoket, invited 'many' of the people aboard" and then slaughtered them for no apparent reason (Silverman, 2019, p. 70). Epenow led Dermer into a trap, and he and his crew were wiped out. Fortunately for Squanto, he had somehow managed to stay behind with his people and not accompany Captain Dermer to his doom.

Into this war zone sailed the Mayflower, carrying a new type of visitor to the "new world": people determined to stay. The Mayflower party was funded by the Virginia Company, the same profit-seeking entity behind the Jamestown colony. The Virginia Company was only willing to fund the journey if they would reap the lion's share of profit from the colony for several years, and on the condition that they could send along laborers to assure such profit. The laborers, in turn, hoped to improve their lot in life through grants of land and reward for their labors. This awkward mixture of fervently religious "separatist" Pilgrims, who were determined to separate from the Church of England, and "strangers" loyal to the Church of England but seeking a better life, endured a hellish journey that included the loss of a second ship, The Speedwell. The near rebellion of the strangers led to the "Mayflower pact." Bonded together sufficiently to avert disaster and crowded together in misery on the Mayflower, they landed on November 11, 1620, in Provincetown Harbor, far later in the year than they had intended.

They spotted the Wampanoags within days, and no doubt the English were spotted by the Wampanoags even sooner. The natives, weighing decades of painful experience with the Europeans, kept their distance. The colonists, meanwhile, went about the business of "exploring," breaking into structures, taking stores of corn and grains, and desecrating graves. According to their own journals, having already dug around in one gravesite, they came upon another a few days later and noted one grave was "...much bigger and longer than any we had yet seen. It was also covered with boards, so we mused what it should be...(and) resolved to dig it up" (Silverman, 2019, p. 136). This behavior led to hostilities with the locals (small wonder!), and the colony had to relocate to another harbor, which they named Plymouth. Whether because of the already long history, because of their behavior upon arrival, or both, the colony had to struggle on its own through its first winter. Over half of the 102 colonists perished, and the others only barely survived.

Contrary to the story I was taught, no help was offered during that winter unless you count the Wampanoags choosing not to wipe out the colony as "help." Instead, after considering his options, the most powerful local sachem, Ousamequin, set out to cautiously forge an alliance with the English. Ousamequin wanted help against his enemies, the Narragansetts to the north, who were trading partners with the French. He knew the French and English were enemies. He knew the English wanted furs to send back to England, and he wanted English goods, including weaponry. In short the evidence is that Ousamequin was well-informed and effective with his political maneuvering. Far from the simple and welcoming people portrayed in grade school plays, neither Ousamequin nor his people were naive as they pondered the risks and benefits of dealing with the Pilgrims.

The Pilgrims were astonished when an English-speaking emissary named Samoset walked boldly into the colony with a small group of warriors on March 16, 1621, and "saluted us in English and bade us welcome" (Silverman, 2019, p. 145). After several days of tentative interactions and exchanges, Squanto reappears on the scene, announcing the arrival of Ousamequin who "…appeared atop a nearby hill accompanied by sixty armed men. The sachem was dressed no differently from the others except that he wore 'a great chain of white bone [or shell] beads about his neck' to represent light, truth, and peace" (Silverman, 2019, p. 149). A tenuous alliance was formed, based on trade and mutual promises of security.

In late November 1621, a celebration did indeed occur. The Pilgrims had much to give thanks for. They had survived the horrors of the first winter. They had a bountiful harvest and a functioning alliance with the most powerful local sachem. The colony's leaders agreed that once the harvest was in, it was time to "rejoice together." "Recreations," which included feasting and drinking beer, "strong water," and possibly wine, also consisted of "militia drill and target practice" (Silverman, 2019, p. 168). During this revelry, and much to the Pilgrim's surprise, Ousamequin and 90 armed men appeared at the gates. According to the Wampanoag version of history, they came because they heard the gunfire and were worried that their English allies were under attack. Instead, after some tense moments, the Wampanoags joined the celebration, which went on for three days. Although the meal almost certainly involved no pies, consisting instead of wild game (including turkey) and seafood, the event really happened, just not the way we have been told.

Why does the telling matter? Because for many years, Thanksgiving was portrayed not as two cultures coming together in a complex relationship but as proof that the early colonists were good white protestant Christians and that the Native Americans (usually clad erroneously in the garments of the great plains) were basically props in the march of history. It's a fairy tale version of history that ignores many facts, not the least being that many contemporary Native Americans consider it a day of mourning. Once it was over, there is no evidence the Pilgrims or the Wampanoags gave the event any further thought. They certainly didn't make it an annual celebration. It was not celebrated in any organized way until 1863 when President Lincoln declared during the civil war that the last Thursday in November should be held as a national day of Thanksgiving. Meanwhile, beginning in 1769, the civic leaders of Plymouth had been promoting "… the once obscure Pilgrims as the symbolic founders of New England and even the United States by virtue of their religious ideals, commitment to democracy, and resolve to build their colony in the face of adversity" (Silverman, 2019, p. 5). It wasn't until President Franklin Delano Roosevelt made it into a national holiday that the image of the Protestant Pilgrims and the Native Americans sitting down to a feast started to stick.

The Pilgrims and the Wampanoags managed to forge an alliance that lasted until the Pequot War of 1636–1637, followed by another 40 years of peace culminating in the bloody King Phillip's War of 1675–1676. Both wars were justified by alleged "criminal behavior" by the Wampanoags, a pattern that would be repeated across the continent. It was an alliance then that lasted for generations (life spans were shorter back then) but one that could not last forever, as the growing colonies became more powerful and remained convinced of their racial, religious, and cultural superiority. We will explore that mindset shortly.

The history of the indigenous peoples of the Americas is a stark reminder that history has often been presented in a one-sided way by many with good intentions and by others, like Joseph Goebbels, Hitler's propaganda chief, with more cynical intent. We must be willing to sort through the facts to the extent that they are available, not cling to the stories we were told as children, and not cast one side as "all good" and the other as "all bad." It rarely works that way. We can continue to gather and give thanks while being mindful that the same historical event was the beginning of the near-genocide of the indigenous peoples of North America. There is much to mourn and to celebrate, and there is no reason we can't do both.

EUROPEAN COLONIZATION AND THE INSTITUTIONALIZATION OF RACISM

Race and its twin, racism, are recognized by historians and sociologists to be relatively recent social constructs (in other words, stuff we made up, as discussed in Chapter 2). The roots of labeling one group better than another are far older, tracing back to prehistory. The aforementioned Aztecs are an example, lording over their neighbors through the use of force and through the belief that they and their rulers were divinely favored. In most corners of the globe and throughout time, those with power have justified their domination of others as ordained by higher powers and by virtue of their group "superiority." Patriarchy, in all its varied forms, is an example of the same type of thinking, or as Lewin would put it, the same false hypothesis.

Like other ancient peoples, the Greeks, even as they championed the use of logic, were seduced by just such scientifically invalid thinking. As historian Ibram Kendi notes, "Aristotle labeled Africans 'burnt faces' — the original meaning in Greek of 'Ethiopian' — and viewed the 'ugly' extremes of pale or dark skins as the effect of the extreme cold or hot climates. All of this was in the interest of normalizing Greek slaveholding practices and Greece's rule over the western Mediterranean. Aristotle situated the Greeks, in their supreme, intermediate climate, as the most beautifully endowed superior rulers and enslavers of the world. 'Humanity is divided into two: the masters and the slaves; or, if one prefers it, the Greeks and the Barbarians, those who have the right to command; and those who are born to obey,' Aristotle said. For him, the enslaved peoples were 'by nature incapable of reasoning and live a life of pure sensation, like certain tribes on the borders of the civilized world, or like people who are diseased through the onset of illnesses like epilepsy or madness" (Kendi, 2016, p. 17).

Sounds like racism to me. The Greeks were clearly not alone in such prejudice. Their archenemies, the Persians, thought much the same of themselves. Thus did the first "East-West" culture clash arise, with Greek civilization being labeled "Western Civilization," a label that has been expanded to mean European culture including the United States. As previously mentioned, this East-West contrast is often presented as a loose concept that idealizes non-Western sources and favors them on the grounds that they have been given less respect historically. The same occurred in the DEI workshop I attended (where it was relabeled Indigenous-Western). While it is true that Western civilization has dominated much of recent history and has been biased in favor of itself in the process, rejecting Western concepts is simply more of the same faulty thinking. We can do better by seeking an objective understanding of the contrast between East, West, and Indigenous, and also the commonalities. If we seek to understand the different voices, we can think for ourselves and make more rational decisions about what to learn from, what to continue, and what to reject. We will explore this further in Chapter 13.

Meanwhile, with the roots of discrimination already spread far and wide, we come to the infamous papal decree of 1493. Some point to this as the beginning of racism as we know it today. Loosely paraphrased, the decree sanctioned the conquest of and dominion over the Americas, granting no rights to the indigenous people already dwelling there:

> Out of our own soul largesse and certain knowledge and out of the fullness of our apostolic power, by the authority of Almighty God conferred upon us in blessed Peter and of the vicarship of Jesus Christ, which we hold on earth, do by tenor of these presents, should any said islands have been found by your envoys and captains, give, grant, and assigned to you and your heirs and successors, kings of Castile and Leon, forever, together with all their dominions, cities, camps, places, and villages, and all rights, jurisdictions, and appurtenances, all islands and mainlands found and to be found, discovered and to be discovered towards the West and South, by drawing and establishing a line from the Arctic pole, namely the north, to the Antarctic pole, namely the south, no matter whether the said mainlands and islands are found and to be found in the direction of India or towards any other quarter, the said line to be distinct one hundred leagues towards the west and south from any of the islands commonly known as the Azores and Cape Verde. With this proviso however that none of the islands and mainlands, found and to be found, discovered and to be discovered, beyond that said line towards the west and south, be in the actual possession of any Christian king or prince up to the birthday of our Lord Jesus Christ just past from which the present year one thousand four hundred ninety-three begins. And we make, appoint, and depute you and your said heirs and successors lords of them with full and free power, authority, and jurisdiction of every kind. Pope Alexander VI (National Institute of Health).

The decree, named Inter Caetera, was written following the maiden voyage of Columbus, which every school child in the US knows from the following ditty of unknown origin:

> In fourteen hundred ninety-two
> Columbus sailed the ocean blue.
>
> He had three ships and left from Spain;
> He sailed through sunshine, wind and rain.
>
> He sailed by night; he sailed by day;
> He used the stars to find his way.
>
> A compass also helped him know
> How to find the way to go.
>
> Ninety sailors were on board;
> Some men worked while others snored.
>
> Then the workers went to sleep;
> And others watched the ocean deep.
>
> Day after day they looked for land;
> They dreamed of trees and rocks and sand.
>
> October 12 their dream came true,
> You never saw a happier crew!
>
> "Indians! Indians!" Columbus cried;
> His heart was filled with joyful pride.
>
> But "India" the land was not;
> It was the Bahamas, and it was hot.
>
> The Arakawa natives were very nice;
> They gave the sailors food and spice.
>
> Columbus sailed on to find some gold
> To bring back home, as he'd been told.
>
> He made the trip again and again,
> Trading gold to bring to Spain.
>
> The first American? No, not quite.
> But Columbus was brave, and he was bright.

I doubt the last two lines were there when I was a kid. Of course, what is also missing is the other side of the story. Columbus was, without doubt, a brave adventurer and a skilled navigator. The initial journey of 33 days must have seemed much longer, with no way to know when, where, and if landfall would be made. The three ships were amazingly tiny, the largest, the Santa Maria, being only 100 feet long. The combined fleet carried a modest crew of 90 men. I've seen a replica of the Nina, all 65 feet of it, and I cannot imagine crossing the Atlantic in that. The "discovery" of the Americas was an event of epic proportions. Funded by Spain, the Italian-born Columbus is revered by many in both cultures and in the United States to this day.

What wasn't taught and what was absolutely documented by eyewitnesses is that Columbus was ruthless in his treatment of the indigenous population. Besides gold, which was not as abundant as hoped for, Columbus sent slaves back to Spain until it became evident that the "very nice" Arawaks were more likely to die in the process, en route or in captivity. The arrival of Columbus is another day of mourning for Native Americans and their allies, many of whom have redubbed the holiday, "Indigenous People's Day." Far from a moment to celebrate, this understandable alternate perspective views the arrival of Columbus as the beginning of the unprecedented destruction of the indigenous population inhabiting two continents.

Columbus first set foot in the Bahamas. The Arawaks were indeed friendly, swimming out to meet the strangers. Columbus sailed on to Cuba and then to Hispaniola before returning to Spain to report on his findings and seek further support. His exaggerated report, which included promises of "… as much gold as they need…and as many slaves as they ask," resulted in his second of four expeditions, this one equipped with 17 ships and more than 1,200 men (Zinn, 1980, p. 3). The conquest had begun.

In his audience with Isabella and Ferdinand, Columbus described the Arawaks as "…so naive and so free with their possessions that no one who has not witnessed them would believe it. When you ask for something they have, they never say no. To the contrary, they offer to share with anyone" (Zinn, 1980, p. 3). Imagine if Columbus had genuinely returned the friendship or had not been "so naive" as to think that his way was better. Instead of spending his life desperately chasing gold, he could have learned a new way of living that most of us can only dream of. Columbus, unable to see anything as valuable unless it was gold, instead unleashed a reign of terror on the Caribbean.

During his second voyage in 1495, on the island of Haiti, when no gold worth mentioning was to be found, Columbus took 500 Arawaks as slaves to be sold in Spain. Of those, 200 died on the voyage. As Columbus wrote, "Let us in the name of the Holy Trinity go on sending all the slaves that can be sold" (Zinn, 1980, p. 4). Meanwhile, the hunt for gold intensified. Any Arawak 14 or older was to collect a certain amount of gold every three months. If they failed, the Spaniards chopped off their hands. As there was no gold to speak of on the island, this example of unspeakably cruel institutional racism led to the rapid genocide of the Arawaks. In two years, half of the 250,000 Arawaks in Haiti were dead. After giving up on the hunt for gold in Haiti, the Spaniards instead worked the Arawaks to death on huge estates, and by 1515, there were only 50,000 left. By 1550, there were only 500, and by 1650, there was not a trace of their once thriving population in what can only be regarded as one of the most heartless and criminal acts in history. If not, what is?

A young priest named Bartolome de las Casas bore witness to much of the Arawak genocide. In his *History of the Indies*, he writes, "Endless testimonies…prove the mild and pacific temperament of the natives…but our work was to exasperate, ravage, kill, mangle and destroy; small wonder, then, if they tried to kill one of us now and then…The admiral, it is true, was blind as those who came after him, and he was so anxious to please the King that he committed irreparable crimes against the Indians…" (Zinn, 1980, p. 6). La Casa documents many of those crimes. In a sick twist of Christianity, Columbus had the dead Arawaks hung in groups of 13 "…in memory of our Redeemer and his twelve apostles" (Dyson, 1991, p. 190). The men under Columbus "… thought nothing of knifing Indians by 10s and 20s and of cutting slices off them to test the sharpness of their blades" (Zinn, 1980, p. 6). "Two of these so called Christians met two Indian boys one day, each carrying a parrot; they took the parrots and for fun beheaded the boys" (Zinn, 1980, p. 6). The desperate Arawaks repeatedly rebelled and were defeated.

The first successful indigenous rebellion occurred on the island of Haiti, where, following his maiden voyage, Columbus had left 39 soldiers behind. The soldiers were wiped out after they roamed the island, killing and raping the natives. Haiti later became the only revolt by African slaves to result in an independent nation, as they threw off the yolk of the French (1791–1804). Ironically, the Haitian revolt was influenced by the French revolution of 1789. However, instead of respecting this event as a triumph against tyranny, the other European powers and the US, despite their own animosity toward Napoleon and the French, regarded it as a threat and began an isolation of the fledgling nation that has had repercussions to this very day. In the eyes of most historians to date, revolutions of the era were considered "progress" as long as they weren't blacks revolting against whites. Unless you identify more with oppressors than the oppressed, the Haitian revolution deserves more widespread respect than it has received.

By then, the Arawaks were long gone. While the population shrank, the men toiled under the lash in mines searching for the gold Columbus so desperately sought. The women were kept separate and forced to dig mounds for cassava plants. In his early notes, the surprisingly unjudgmental La Casas described the Arawak way of life: "Marriage laws are nonexistent; men and women alike choose their mates and leave them as they please, without offence, jealousy or anger. They multiply in great abundance; pregnant women work to the last minute and give birth almost painlessly; up the next day, they bathe in the river and are as clean and healthy as before giving birth. If they tire of their men, they give themselves abortions with herbs that force stillbirths, covering their shameful parts with leaves or cotton cloth; although on the whole Indian men and women look upon total nakedness with as much casualness as we look upon a man's head or at his hands...They're extremely generous with their possessions and by the same token covet the possessions of their friends and expect the same degree of liberality..." (Zinn, 1980, p. 5).

In contrast, under the Spaniards, "...husbands and wives were together only once every eight or ten months and when they met they were so exhausted and depressed on both sides...they ceased to procreate. As for the newly born, they died early because their mothers, overworked and famished, had no milk to nurse them, and for this reason, while I was in Cuba, 7000 children died in three months. Some mothers even drowned their babies from sheer desperation...in this way, husbands died in the mines, wives died at work and children died from lack of milk...and in a short time this land which was so great, so powerful and fertile...was depopulated...My eyes have seen these acts so foreign to human nature, and now I tremble as I write...Who in future generations will believe this? I myself writing it as a knowledgeable eyewitness can hardly believe it..." (Zinn, 1980, p. 7).

Who indeed? Although this isn't my first reading, I weep as I compile this history. I hope the reader understands that the current animosity toward celebrating Columbus isn't simply because he represents the arrival of Europeans on these shores, but because he also represents the racist and sadistic brutality that he directed, participated in, and encouraged.

Such are the complexities of history.

Armed with the same beliefs expressed in the Papal decree of 1493, the British arrived in Virginia. They were also armed with centuries of British class warfare. The Virginia colony was not, by the way, an example of people seeking religious or political freedom. They arrived as representatives of the crown and of the Church of England, which were one and the same. They came in competition with the other European powers in search of wealth and territory to claim for themselves and the King.

From this cultural mix, combined with the influence of the growing African slave trade, Virginia holds the dubious historical distinction of being the place where the social construction of race and racism was institutionalized for the first time based on skin pigmentation. The seeds for that moment were planted in the history of England, to which we must briefly turn.

Here, we rely on the work of historian Theodore Allen, who documents how the upper classes in England persistently used the power of the state to drive small landholders off their land, until the industrial revolution images found in Dickins of vast hordes of poverty-stricken unemployed came to be. Once upon a time, there was a golden age for English peasants. The Peasant Revolt of 1381 had put an end to the old feudal order, and "...the self-employed laboring peasant, as freeholder, leaseholder, or copyholder, held ascendancy in English agriculture" (Allen, 2012, p. 30). What followed was a relentless attempt to strip these relatively affluent peasants of their rights and their land, and the peasants fought back with major revolts in 1536, 1549, 1554, 1569, and 1607. Allen cites original sources that stated the conflicts "at intervals between 1530 and 1560 set half the counties of England in a blaze" (Allen, 2012, p. 31). To make a long story short, the peasants worked "common lands," and the upper classes methodically took those lands away. At the end of the 15th century, the majority of the laboring population in England were small landowners. By the end of the 17th century, this system had been replaced by wage labor and a cycle of poverty, with a fourth of the population reduced to begging for at least a portion of each year.

Controlling the swelling masses of the poor was no small feat and was "solved" by the creation of a lower-middle-class layer that would be allowed to keep their land holdings and make a humble but steady wage in exchange for serving in militia and police functions. Sir Francis Bacon advocated in 1625 a ruling-class strategy of "…dividing and breaking of all factions and combinations that are adverse to the state, and setting them at distance, or at least distrust among themselves" (Allen, 2012, p. 326). The upper classes were receptive to this strategy of dividing and conquering the lower classes, a strategy one could argue is still employed by politicians to this very day. The system created portends the London of Dickins: "The successful day-to-day operation of the social order depended upon the supervisory and enforcement functions performed at the parish level by yeoman constables, churchwardens, Overseers of the Poor, jailers, directors of houses of correction, etc. They were charged with serving legal orders and enforcing warrants issued by magistrates or higher courts. They arrested vagrants, administered the prescribed whippings on these vagrants' naked backs, and conveyed them to the boundary of the next parish, enforcing their return to their home parishes. As Overseers of the Poor, they ordered unemployed men and women to the workhouses and apprenticed poor children without their parents' leave. Trial juries were generally composed of yeoman, and they largely constituted the foot soldiers of the militia" (Allen, 2012, p. 35).

Laws were enacted that only represented the upper classes. Most wage earners, for example, had to sign contracts stipulating that they would work for a prescribed period of time during which they could not seek other employment. Breaking such a contract meant jail time and fines and possibly being reduced to the status of vagrancy, which essentially meant house arrest and working for no wages besides such room and board as was deemed fit. Any male between 10 and 18 could be made a "husbandry apprentice" by any land-owning farmer and forced to do whatever labor was assigned. They could not marry without permission. Again, imprisonment was the punishment for resisting any such involuntary "apprenticeship."

As if those laws weren't oppressive enough, a "Slave Law" was enacted in 1547 that made any unemployed person the property of whoever scooped them up. This law increased the intensity of the lower class rebellions and troubled the conscience of many in the upper classes, and so it was repelled after three years.

The lot of lower-class women in England was worse. The men, no matter how lowly in the order of things, were "lord and master" over their wives. If unmarried and able-bodied, "...any woman of the laboring class was compelled to serve by the year, week, or day in any 'reasonable' sort of work and at such wage rates as any two magistrates or alderman, or the mayor, having local jurisdiction might assign for her. Upon refusal so to serve, the woman was to be held in jail 'until she shall be bounded to serve'" (Allen, 2012, p. 41). Corporal punishment for the women and the children was at the man's discretion.

The homeostasis in the system, tense though it was, was maintained by letting the lower middle classes lord it over the poor, and the men lord it over the women. The stage was set for a race-based system of oppression in the colonies.

And now, it's time to throw the Irish into the equation. Being "thrown in" is an apt way to put it. The English treatment of the Irish was even worse than their treatment of the English poor. The final British conquest of Ireland took place in the Tyrone War (1594–1603). The Irish, stripped of their land and rights, created a new crisis of poverty in the British Isles, and part of the "solution" was to bring Irish labor to the colonies. In 1653, the Commonwealth of Virginia authorized a merchant from Bristol "... to export one hundred Irish...who were to be sold as slaves in Virginia" (Allen, 2012, p. 460). This type of slavery, most commonly referred to as "bonded servitude," was imported along with the rest of the British culture of the times.

An astonishingly large amount of the colonists were forced to the new world. It is estimated by historian Abbott Smith that "between ten and twenty thousand kidnapped British laborers were brought to the colonies throughout the colonial period" (Allen, 2012, p. 461). Some were just tricked with promises of land ownership and opportunity that never materialized. The treatment of the lower classes was brutal, and the mortality rate was higher than 50%. During 1619–1625, half of the Virginia colony perished, but only one in six of the newly "immigrated" survived. Small wonder, as the wealthy feasted, the laboring classes survived on crumbs. Besides being ill-fed, "The laborers were, like other colonists, subject to the severities of 'Laws Divine, Moral, and Martial.' Offences against the code could bring down on a worker the harsh cruelty of the military camp such as pillorying, cutting off of the ears, boring through of the tongue, whipping of offenders through the town tied to a cart, banishment from the colony to the wilderness, and inducement of the premature birth and death of an infant by the whipping of a pregnant woman, for offenses such as speaking ill of a master or official, stealing food from a master's store, and failure to complete a work task" (Allen, 2012, p. 79). Not officially slavery, but not far from it.

The system of law institutionalized the oppression. The jurors were all from the ruling class. "In 1666 a New England court accused a couple of the death of a servant after the mistress had cut off the servant's toes. The jury voted acquittal. In Virginia in the 1660s, a master was convicted of raping two women servants. He also was known to beat his own wife and children. He had whipped and chained another servant until he died. The master was berated by the court, but specifically cleared on the rape charge despite overwhelming evidence" (Zinn, 1980, p. 44).

Unlike Columbus, many of these servant-class Europeans eyed the Native American lifestyle with envy and those that could make a dash to the "wilderness" did so in such numbers that death was invoked as a legal penalty.

The contrast between rich and poor was not so stark in 1607 when the colony was founded. It couldn't be when survival was the primary focus and interdependence was high. Indeed the original charter assured that all colonists "...shall have and enjoy all liberties, franchises and immunities of free denizens and natural subjects,...to all intents and purposes as if they had been abiding and born within this our Realm of England" (Allen, 2012, p. 74). Perhaps that last part should have been considered by the poorest members as a catch. Nonetheless, in the early period, servants were upgraded to freedom, land (taken from the Native Americans) was granted, and the number of the servant population relative to the total population was low.

Then came the cultivation of tobacco. Greed followed to such an extent that by 1618, the colony almost starved itself as more and more land was shifted from food production to growing the cash crop that Europe and the funders of the colony, the Virginia Company, craved. Streams of laborers soon followed, by hook or by crook. The result, according to historian Lerone Bennett Jr., was to create the social conditions for African slavery: "White servitude was the proving ground. The plantation pass system, the slave trade, the sexual exploitation of servant women, the whipping post and slave chain and branding iron, the overseer, the house servant, the Uncle Tom: all these mechanisms were tried out and perfected on white men and women" (Allen, 2012, p. 74).

The Virginia Colony leadership cast their eyes elsewhere for servants to work the fields. By 1619, a million Africans had been enslaved and brought to the Caribbean and South America. A little background is again necessary. Africa before colonization was a thriving continent with large urban centers, iron implements and agriculture, with a population of around 100 million. The stories of early European contact with the varied peoples of Africa are strikingly similar to what the Spaniards found in the Caribbean. In 1563, an Italian named Ramusio urged his countrymen to, "...go and do business with the King of Timbuktu and Mali and there is no doubt that they will be well received there with their ships and their goods and treated well, and granted the favors that they ask..." (Zinn, 1980, p. 26). The Dutch, the first to reap enormous profits off the African slave trade, were greeted with open arms and marveled at the civilization they had stumbled upon. A Dutch explorer describing the West African nation of Benin in 1602 wrote, "The town seemeth to be very great, when you enter it. You go into a great broad street, not paved, which seemeth to be seven or eight times broader than the Warmose Street in Amsterdam. The Houses in this Towne stand in good order, one close and even with the other, as the Houses in Holland stand" (Zinn, 1980, p. 26). Another explorer describes the people of the Guinea Coast as follows, "...very civil and good natured people, easy to be dealt with...and very ready to return double the presents we make them" (Zinn, 1980, p. 26).

These same welcoming people were soon to be heartlessly conquered and enslaved. We shall return to that travesty shortly.

Meanwhile, in 1619, in a moment that should live in infamy, a Dutch ship arrived at Jamestown carrying 20 African slaves. The slave trade to the colonies had begun.

While there is evidence that black servants in these early days were treated even worse than lower-class whites, there is also ample evidence suggesting that the white and black poor got along so well as to make the ruling classes nervous. There is nothing like a shared fate to pull people together, and the indentured servants and early African slaves had more in common than either had with their overlords. The result was rebellion. There were enough minor rebellions and threats thereof that the Virginia legislature (founded in the same year, 1619, as the arrival of the first African slaves) passed laws to punish rebels. The preamble to the law read: "Whereas many evil disposed servants in these late tymes of horrid rebellion taking advantage of the loosness and liberty of the tyme, did depart from their service, and followed the rebels in rebellion, wholy neglecting their masters imployment whereby the said masters have suffered great damage and injury" (Zinn, 1980, p. 45).

In 1676 Bacon's rebellion was so successful that the governor had to flee the burning capital of Jamestown, and England had to send troops to restore order. This uprising of "frontiersmen, slaves and servants" almost succeeded in overthrowing the ruling class in the colony, and shook their nerves to the bone. The class system had been cracking. Just prior to the rebellion Governor Berkley described his people as "...six parts of seaven at least are Poore Endebted Discontented and Armed" (Zinn, 1980, p. 40). In the British tradition, he undoubtedly blamed this condition on the character of the poor.

Bacon, also from the upper class, a landowner who was elected to the House of Burgess in the spring of 1676, originally wanted support from the governor to fight the nearby Pamunkey tribe. When he didn't get permission, he attacked the tribe anyway and was arrested. Two thousand Virginians descended on the capital in support of Bacon. He was released and went about the business of again attacking the Pamunkeys, killing eight of them. Bacon then published a "declaration of the people" full of grievances to the governor, and the rebellion began.

In a colony of 40,000, Bacon's rebellion numbered more than 6,000 European and 2,000 African servants. They stormed West Point, where they took over the arsenal. Tobacco production was disrupted for 14 months. The rebellion was serious.

A royal commons report described Bacon's activity this way: "He seduced the Vulgar and most ignorant people to believe (two thirds of each county being of that Sort) Soe that their whole hearts and hopes were set now upon Bacon. Next he charges the governour as negligent and wicked, treacherous and incapable, the Laws and Taxes as unjust and oppressive and cryes up absolute necessity of redress. Thus Bacon encouraged the Tumult and as the unquiet crowd follow and adhere to him, he listeth them as they come in upon a large paper, writing their name circular wise, that their ringleaders might not be found out. Having connur'd them into this circle, given them Brandy to wind up the charme, and enjoyned them by an oath to stick fast together and to him and the oath being administered, he went and infected New Kent County ripe for rebellion" (Zinn, 1980, p. 39).

The rebellion began in July. In the fall, Bacon, only 29 years old, fell sick and died. The rebellion was soon crushed by the arriving British troops.

The legacy of the ruling class's response still lingers. Forming a buffer zone betwixt themselves and the poorest of the poor had "worked" from the perspective of the upper classes in England. Why not try it here? The tactic, made all the easier by the presence of the African slaves, distinguishable by ethnicity and by skin pigmentation from the European servant class, took a new and despicable twist. The strategy was clear: enlist the lower class of Europeans in the control of the Africans, thus elevating the pride of the Europeans and giving them a stake and a role in the maintenance of the social order. Not only did this pacify the lower-class Europeans but it also distanced them from the alliances that they had naturally formed with the African servant class and, to a large extent, transformed the Europeans from sources of rebellion to forces of "law and order."

And so, the word "white" began to appear in the laws of the Virginia colonies and soon began to spread. The first such language appeared in the "Act for suppressing outlying slaves," passed by the Virginia legislature in April 1691. Here, it is in its infamous entirety:

WHEREAS many times negroes, mulattoes, and other slaves unlawfully absent themselves from their masters' and mistresses' service, and lie hid and lurk in obscure places killing hoggs and committing other injuries to the inhabitants of this dominion, for the remedy whereof for the future, *Be it enacted by their majesties lieutenant governour, councell and burgesses of this present general assembly, and the authoritie thereof, and it is hereby enacted,* that in all such cases upon intelligence of any such negroes, mulattoes, or other slaves lying out, two of their majesties justices of the peace of that county, whereof one to be of the quorum, where such negroes, mulattoes or other slave shall be, shall be impowered and commanded, and are hereby impowered and commanded to issue out their warrants directed to the sherriffe of the same county to apprehend such negroes, mulattoes, and other slaves, which said sherriffe is hereby likewise required upon all such occasions to raise such and soe many forces from time to time as he shall think convenient and necessary for the effectual apprehending such negroes, mulattoes and other slaves, and in case any negroes, mulattoes or other slaves or slaves lying out as aforesaid shall resist, runaway, or refuse to deliver and surrender him or themselves to any person or persons that shall be by lawfull authority employed to apprehend and take such negroes, mulattoes or other slaves that in such cases it shall and may be lawfull for such person and persons to kill and distroy such negroes, mulattoes, and other slave or slaves by gunn or any otherwaise whatsoever.

Provided that where any negroe or mulattoe slave or slaves shall be killed in pursuance of this act, the owner or owners of such negro or mulatto slave shall be paid for such negro or mulatto slave four thousand pounds of tobacco by the publique. And for prevention of that abominable mixture and spurious issue which hereafter may encrease in this dominion, as well by negroes, mulattoes, and Indians intermarrying with English, or other white women, as by their unlawfull accompanying with one another, *Be it enacted by the authoritie aforesaid, and it is hereby enacted,* that for the time to come, whatsoever English or other white man or woman being free shall intermarry with a negroe, mulatto, or Indian man or woman bond or free shall within three months after such marriage be banished and removed from this dominion forever, and that the justices of each respective countie within this dominion make it their perticular care, that this act be put in effectuall execution. *And be it further enacted by the authoritie aforesaid, and it is hereby enacted,* That if any English woman being free shall have a bastard child by any negro or mulatto, she pay the sume of fifteen pounds sterling, within one moneth after such bastard child be born, to the Church wardens of the parish where she shall be delivered of such child, and in default of such payment she shall be taken into the possession of the said Church wardens and disposed of for five yeares, and the said fine of fifteen pounds, or whatever the woman shall be disposed of for, shall be paid, one third part to their majesties for and towards the support of the government and the contingent charges thereof, and one other third part to the use of the parish where the offence is committed, and the other third part to the informer, and that such bastard child be bound out as a servant by the said Church wardens untill he or she shall attaine the age of thirty yeares, and in case such English woman that shall have such bastard child be a servant, she shall be sold by the said church wardens, (after her time is expired that she ought by law to serve her master) for five yeares, and the money she shall be sold for divided as is before appointed, and the child to serve as aforesaid.

And forasmuch as great inconveniences may happen to this country by the setting of negroes and mulattoes free, by their either entertaining negro slaves from their masters service, or receiveing stolen goods, or being grown old bringing a charge upon the country; for prevention thereof, *Be it enacted by the authority aforesaid, and it is hereby enacted,* That no negro or mulatto be after the end of this present session of assembly set free by any person or persons whatsoever, unless such person or persons, their heires, executors or administrators pay for the transportation of such negro or negroes out of the countery within six moneths after such setting them free, upon penalty of paying of tenn pounds sterling to the Church wardens of the parish where such person shall dwell with, which money, or so much thereof as shall be necessary, the said Church wardens are to cause the said negro or mulatto to be transported out of the countery, and the remainder of the said money to imploy to the use of the poor of the parish.

General Assembly (1691)

And so with the stroke of a pen, the word "white" was introduced into colonial law. "Negroes" could no longer be freed within the "said county," sexual relations between the European and African poor became illegal, and whites could be rewarded for the capture or killing of "...any negroes, mulattoes or other slaves or slaves lying out as aforesaid shall resist, runaway, or refuse to deliver and surrender him or themselves." And that was only the beginning. The idea of and the advantages to be derived from "whites" being better than "Negroes" gained enough traction with the hitherto beaten down white servant class that the Virginia legislature poured it on. The revised Virginia code of 1705 removed the right to "whip a Christian white servant naked, without an order from the justice of the peace" (Allen, 2012, p. 328). Such was their lot that this was an improvement. Meanwhile, in the same legislation the war on African slaves was intensified, stripping them of what few rights they had. Their livestock was to be confiscated by the state, they were barred from holding any office of public trust, they could not be a witness in any case against a white person, they were subject to 30 lashes at the public whipping post for "lifting his or her hand" against a white person, they were barred from the armed militia, and they were forbidden from possessing "any gun, powder, shot, or any club, or any other weapon whatsoever, offensive or defensive" (Allen, 2012, p. 329). In an amazingly short period of time, Virginia not only created race-based racism they also institutionalized it into their laws. In a demented example of the then collaborative relationship between the church and state, the legislation mandated that the laws be read every spring and fall to every church congregation. Sheriffs were also to do the same outside the courthouse doors during the summer sessions of the court.

To make sure they got their point across, a 1723 Virginia law added that "...any white person found in company with any [illegally congregated] slaves" was to be fined or to "receive, on his, her, or their bare backs, for every such offense, twenty lashes well laid on" (Allen, 2012, p. 330).

The new buffer group included the Irish, prior victims of institutional racism on a massive scale at the hands of the English, now bequeathed overnight with a step up based on racial superiority. A half step, to be more accurate. As late as 1899, according to a widely held pseudoscientific theory, the "Iberian hypothesis," the Irish were said to be of "African descent" and hence a lower class of whites (Coates et al, 2018, p. 9). Once this system of race based on a loose confluence of skin pigmentation and ethnicity was established, this type of classification and transition from exclusion to inclusion became a pattern in US history, much to the general relief of the groups that got to "move up" in the system of racial profiling. The classification system (African American, White, Hispanic, Asian, Native American, etc.), which makes race seem "real," continues to be official US policy to this day.

The division of the poor through a system of racism was no accident. Governor Francis Nicholson of Maryland in 1698 warned of the possibility of "great disturbances" if the Irish bond-laborers would "confederate with the negros" (Allen, 2012, p. 321). In the spirit of Sir Francis Bacon, an intentional wedge was to be driven between the poorest of the poor. Viewed from the perspective of the upper classes, the strategy had the desired effect. "The only rebellions of white servants in the continental colonies came before the entrenchment of slavery" (Allen, 2012, p. 330). Poor whites not only had new status, they also had new jobs. A Virginia law in 1727 created special militia known as "the patrol" instituted to disperse "all unusual concourse of negros, or other slaves, and for preventing any dangerous combinations which may be made among them at such meetings" (Allen, 2012, p. 330). In South Carolina, the Assembly passed a law requiring any who owned "six negroes" or more to employ "one or more White person" to help manage the slaves (Allen, 2012, p. 331). A system of oversight through employment and other means grew and spread, attaching the lower-class whites more to the upper-class whites than to the African slaves over whom they now ruled.

Far from holding the high ideals lauded in the founding of our nation, the Governor of Virginia from 1710 to 1722, Alexander Spotswood, considered aspirations of freedom as the problem: "…we are not to depend on either their stupidity, or that babel of languages among 'em; freedom wears a cap which can, without a tongue, call together all these who long to shake off the fetters of slavery" (Allen, 2012, p. 321).

Such was the beginning of modern racism. What can only be regarded as a devil's bargain was struck. A pandemic of the heart and mind, if you will, eventually sticking deep in the collective consciousness of the nation, dividing those at the bottom, and continuing to divide us today.

AN ATTEMPT AT A MORE ACCURATE LOOK AT THE US AND SLAVERY

The approach in Virginia was in sharp contrast to the approach the British took in the Caribbean and elsewhere. The difference is part of the reason racism haunts the US so deeply. The British were no angels in the Caribbean, but they never attempted to strip free blacks of their rights, and there was a path to freedom. Slaves and all the lower classes were looked down on and treated like dirt, but people of African descent could be free. Once free, they could obtain an education, serve in the militia, hold other positions, and own land. People were, to some degree, treated more based on their current social status than on their ethnic background or skin pigmentation. The ability for some to rise within the system, although only granted to and accomplished by a very small minority, was an important part of the ruling-class strategy to reduce revolt. It had the additional effect of keeping prejudice based on race from playing as big a role as in the US system.

Indeed, prior to Bacon's rebellion and the laws of 1692, there are multiple records of free black landowners in the Virginia colony, similar to the practice in other parts of the empire, including the right to employ indentured "white" servants. Here is just one such example from historian Allen's documentation: "Patent on 100 acres bounded by lands owned by Anthony, Richard's father, and by brother John Johnson, granted by governor Richard Bennett to Richard Johnson, 'Negro,' for the transportation of two bond-laborers: William Ames and William Vincent (Virginia land patent book number 3, page 21 November 1654)" (Allen, 2012, p. 244).

Abolitionism was growing among the British and, with the 1688 *Germantown Petition against Slavery*, was taking root in colonial America as well. The *Petition* was the work of the Mennonites, who had fled brutal religious persecution in Central Europe. "There is a saying, that we shall doe to all men like as we will be done ourselves; making no difference of what generation, descent or colour they are" (Kendi, 2016, p. 52). The fight was on in the colonies between those who supported racism and those who opposed it. The supporters of racism nearly won in the early rounds by a knockout, but the fight isn't over.

The divergence between the practices in the rest of the British Empire and the practices in the colonies led to tensions within the governing classes. Attorney General Richard West put it this way in disagreeing with article 23 of the 1723 Virginia legislation, *An act directing the trial of slaves, committing capital crimes; and for the more effectual punishing conspiracies and insurrections of them; and for the better government of Negros, Mulattos, and Indians, bond or free*:

> I cannot see why one freeman should be used worse than another, merely upon account of his complexion...to vote at elections of officers, either for a county, or parish...is incident to every freeman, who is possessed of a certain proportion of property, and, therefore, when several negros have merited their freedom, and obtained it, and by their industry, have acquired that proportion of property, so that the above mentioned incidental rights of liberty are actually vested in them, for my own part, I am persuaded, that it cannot be just, by a general law, without any allegation of crime, or other demerit whatsoever, to strip all free persons, of a black complexion (some of whom may, perhaps be of considerable substance), from those rights, which are just so justly valuable to every freeman.

> **Allen, 2012, p. 317**

Attorney-General West was basing his argument on the precedent set through the rest of the empire. Other colonial powers took a similar approach, including the French in Louisiana. Governor William Gooch of Virginia dismissed West's objection in order intentionally "...to fix a perpetual brand upon Free Negros and Mulattos" (Allen, 2012, p. 317).

The contrast between the British system and the colonies was on unique display during the War of 1812. As Francis Scott Key witnessed the shelling of Fort McHenry, he was almost certainly aware of the British Corps of Colonial Marines composed entirely of freed slaves who "received the same training, uniforms, pay and pensions as their Royal Marine counterparts" participating in the assault (Anderson, 2013, pp. 1). Part of the pension was land, which was granted after the war in Trinidad. The British took advantage of the racism in the US, offering the same to any slaves who escaped and reached them. As many as 4,000 from Virginia and

Maryland managed to do so. Even if he was unaware of the presence of the Marines, Key, a member of a wealthy plantation family who is quoted as describing blacks as an "inferior race," was well aware of the British offer of freedom when he penned the following third stanza to what later became the national anthem (Brockell, 2020, pp. 13):

"And where is that band who so vauntingly swore, That the havoc of war and the battle's confusion, A home and a Country should leave us no more? Their blood has wash'd out their foul footstep's pollution. No refuge could save the hireling and slave, From the terror of flight or the gloom of the grave. And the star-spangled banner in triumph doth wave, O'er the land of the free and the home of the brave."

Key's brother-in-law, Roger Taney, later was appointed Chief Justice of the Supreme Court by President Andrew Jackson. In 1857, Taney broke the tie on a politically deadlocked supreme court and issued the infamous *Dred Scott* ruling. For many years, Scott had been the "personal servant" of a Dr. Emerson. When Emerson died in 1846, Scott sued for his freedom. "Negros," Taney wrote in the ruling, "... are so inferior that they have no rights which a white man was bound to respect" (Davis, 1990, p. 157). Taney added that Scott was not a citizen but instead was only property, no different than a mule or a horse, and property was protected by the Fifth Amendment in the Bill of Rights, and consequently that Congress had no rights to deprive citizens of their property (Davis, 1990, p. 158). In other words, Taney had used the Bill of Rights and the power of the US Supreme Court to protect slavery.

Into this uniquely twisted and prejudiced US system sailed the African slave trade. The horrors of this crime against humanity are well-documented elsewhere. For those readers who are unfamiliar, here is a quick overview from historian Howard Zinn: "They were captured in the interior (frequently by blacks caught up in the slave trade themselves), sold on the coast, then shoved into pens with blacks of other tribes, often speaking different languages..."

The marches to the coast, sometimes for 1,000 miles, with people shackled around the neck, under whip and gun, were death marches, in which two of every five blacks died. On the coast, they were kept in cages until they were picked and sold. A man named John Barbot, at the end of the 17th century, described these cages on the Gold Coast:

> As the slaves come down to Fida from the inland country, they are put into a booth or prison...near the beach, and when the Europeans are to receive

them, they are brought out into a large plain, where the ship's surgeons examine every part of every one of them, to the smallest member, men and women being stark naked...Such as are allowed good and sound are set on one side...marked on the breast with a red hot iron, imprinting the mark of the French, English, or Dutch companies...the branded slaves after this are returned to their former booths where they await shipment, sometimes 10–15 days...

Then, they were packed aboard the slave ships, in spaces not much bigger than coffins, chained together in the dark, wet slime of the ship's bottom, choking in the stench of their own excrement. Documents of the time described the conditions:

The height, sometimes, between decks, was only eighteen inches; so that the unfortunate human beings could not turn around, or even on their sides, the elevation being less than the breadth of their shoulders; And here they are usually chained to the decks by the neck and legs. In such a place, this sense of misery and suffocation is so great, that the Negros...are driven to frenzy.

On one occasion, hearing a great noise from below decks where the blacks were chained together, the sailors opened the hatches and found the slaves in different stages of suffocation, many dead, some having killed others in desperate attempts to breathe. Slaves often jumped overboard to drown rather than continue with their suffering. To one observer a slave-deck was "so covered with blood and mucus that it resembled a slaughterhouse."

Under these conditions, perhaps one of every three blacks transported overseas died, but the huge profits (often double the investment on one trip) made it worthwhile for the slave trader, and so the blacks were packed into the holds like fish.

First the Dutch, then the English, dominated the slave trade. (By 1795 Liverpool had more than a hundred ships carrying slaves and accounted for half of all the European slave trade). Some Americans in New England entered the business, and in 1637 the first American slave ship, the *Desire*, sailed from Marblehead...By 1800, 10 to 15 million blacks had been transported as slaves to the Americas, representing perhaps one-third of those originally seized in Africa. It is roughly estimated that Africa lost 50 million human beings to death and slavery in those centuries....

Zinn (1980, p. 28)

More Africans than Europeans arrived in the Americas between 1500 and 1800 (Allen, 2012, p. 23). The population of slaves exploded following Bacon's rebellion, growing from 6,000 in Virginia in 1700, one-twelfth of the population, to 170,000 by 1763 or one-half of the population. The need and opportunity for the white lower-class buffer layer grew just as fast.

Things were no better for the unlucky Africans upon their arrival, especially after the white-over-black laws passed beginning in 1691. The misery for a slave in the slave-holding states is mind-numbing and well-documented, so I will just touch on some nuances that are less well known. That region included New York up until 1830. According to the New York Historical Society, "In 1799, New York passed a Gradual Emancipation act that freed slave children born after July 4, 1799, but indentured them until they were young adults. In 1817 a new law passed that would free slaves born before 1799 but not until 1827. By the 1830 census there were only 75 slaves in New York and the 1840 census listed no slaves in New York City."

New York was actually the location of the first large-scale slave revolt in 1712. As historian Zinn tells it, "About twenty-five blacks and two Indians set fire to a building, then killed nine whites who came on the scene. They were captured by soldiers, put on trial, and twenty-one were executed. The governor's report to England said; 'Some were burnt, others were hanged, one broke on the wheel, and one hung alive in chains in the town...'" (Zinn, 1980, p. 35). Around this time, the Boston City Council ruled that any slaves who were gathered in groups of two or more were to be punished by whipping. Maryland passed a law in 1723 providing for cutting off the ears of blacks that struck whites (Zinn, 2012, p. 35). Attempted revolts and fear of revolts was a constant. As we have seen, fear that poor whites and poor blacks would join together in revolt, as indeed they did on numerous occasions, was part of the motivation for creating a system based on race that set poor whites against the black population. One such rebellion, Shay's rebellion in 1786, included black and white veterans of the Continental Army, now suffering in poverty. According to one source, up to 1,000 blacks served during the revolution from Massachusetts alone (Kaplan, 2008, p. 8). Army veteran Daniel Shay led a mostly white force of farmers and poor laborers which swelled to 1,000 members before being crushed by an army paid for by Boston's frightened merchants, including Sam Adams, the former revolutionary who now frowned on rebellion against his own republic (Davis, 1990, p. 83).

Although a casual glance at history might lead one to think that the North was antislavery and the South proslavery in the early years of the colonies and of the republic, the truth was far more muddled. Even as the North moved away from slavery, by the 1800s, the mills of the north, the banks of the north, and the wealthy of the north were making a killing on the cheap cotton produced by southern slaves. The growing working class was employed based on the same interdependent system, albeit for the most part with no rights, starvation wages, and horrid conditions. The economic exploitation of black labor continued after the civil war, as we shall see.

An abhorrent act of institutional racism took place in 1787 in the form of "The Great Compromise" by the Continental Congress. The northern states had larger populations. They wanted influence based on that. The south, with a smaller population, wanted influence to be equal between states. They also wanted slaves to be included in their census. The solution was the division of the government into the two chambers of the house, based on population, and the senate, where each state plays an equal role. That part of the compromise could have happened with or without slavery. What is astonishing was the further compromise that even though they had absolutely no rights whatsoever as human beings, each slave would be counted as three-fifths of a person in the census so as to swell the number of representatives designated from the slave-holding states. Insult (imagine being considered only three-fifths of a person) was added to injury, as the slave owners were able to increase their political power based on the head count of their slaves, even though they did not treat them as human beings, much less as citizens. The structure of our government today is still based on "the great compromise," granting representation and hence influence in the senate based on the number of states, instead of on the number of citizens. There are more conservative states, and so even though the population of the US leans more to the left of center, the senate leans more to the right. The legacy of the long fight over racism is embedded deep into the contemporary fabric of our nation.

Sometimes it is embedded in surprising ways. While writing this book, the American Psychological Association (APA) issued an "Apology to People of Color for APA's Role in Promoting, Perpetuating, and Failing to Challenge Racism, Racial Discrimination, and Human Hierarchy in U.S." The APA's statement is an action worthy of applause that should be a model for many others to do the same. The APA thus far, however, overlooked one of the ugliest contributions of "psychology" to the institutionalization of racism, namely, the work of Dr. Samuel Cartwright. In his 1851 book, *Diseases and Peculiarities of the Negro Race*, Cartwright lent the veneer of early psychology to the subjugation of slaves. According to Cartwright, slaves who tried to escape slavery had "Drapetomania," a mental illness. The cure was to cut off their big toes (Coates et al, 2018, p. 181). This is just one example of why many African Americans have a deep distrust of the medical profession. For a glimpse into the demented mind of Cartwright, and many others like him, here is his description of the illness:

DRAPETOMANIA, OR THE DISEASE CAUSING NEGROES TO RUN AWAY.

It is unknown to our medical authorities, although its diagnostic symptom, the absconding from service, is well known to our planters and overseers… In noticing a disease not heretofore classed among the long list of maladies that man is subject to, it was necessary to have a new term to express it. The cause in the most of cases, that induces the negro to run away from service, is as much a disease of the mind as any other species of mental alienation, and much more curable, as a general rule. With the advantages of proper medical advice, strictly followed, this troublesome practice that many negroes have of running away, can be almost entirely prevented, although the slaves be located on the borders of a free state, within a stone's throw of the abolitionists.

If the white man attempts to oppose the Deity's will, by trying to make the negro anything else than "the submissive knee-bender," (which the Almighty declared he should be) by trying to raise him to a level with himself, or by putting himself on an equality with the negro; or if he abuses the power which God has given him over his fellow-man, by being cruel to him, or punishing him in anger, or by neglecting to protect him from the wanton abuses of his fellow-servants and all others, or by denying him the usual comforts and necessaries of life, the negro will run away; but if he keeps him in the position that we learn from the Scriptures he was intended to occupy, that is, the position of submission; and if his master or overseer be kind and gracious in his hearing towards him, without condescension, and at the same time ministers to his physical wants, and protects him from abuses, the negro is spell-bound, and cannot run away.

According to my experience, the "genu flexit"–the awe and reverence, must be exacted from them, or they will despise their masters, become rude and ungovernable, and run away. On Mason and Dixon's line, two classes of persons were apt to lose their negroes: those who made themselves too familiar with them, treating them as equals, and making little or no distinction in regard to color; and, on the other hand, those who treated them cruelly, denied them the common necessaries of life, neglected to protect them against the abuses of others, or frightened them by a blustering manner of approach, when about to punish them for misdemeanors. Before the negroes run away, unless they are frightened or panic-struck, they become sulky and dissatisfied. The cause of this sulkiness and dissatisfaction should be inquired into and removed, or they are apt to run away or fall into the negro consumption. When sulky and dissatisfied without cause, the experience of those on the line and elsewhere, was decidedly in favor of whipping them out of it, as a preventive measure against absconding, or other bad conduct. It was called whipping the devil out of them.

If treated kindly, well fed and clothed, with fuel enough to keep a small fire burning all night–separated into families, each family having its own house–not permitted to run about at night to visit their neighbors, to receive visits or use intoxicating liquors, and not overworked or exposed too much to the weather, they are very easily governed–more so than any other people in the world. When all this is done, if any one of more of them, at any time, are inclined to raise their heads to a level with their master or overseer, humanity and their own good require that they should be punished until they fall into that submissive state which it was intended for them to occupy in all after-time, when their progenitor received the name of Canaan or "submissive knee-bender." They have only to be kept in that state and treated like children, with care, kindness, attention and humanity, to prevent and cure them from running away.

DYSAETHESIA AETHIOPICA, OR HEBETUDE OF MIND AND OBTUSE SENSIBILITY OF BODY–A DISEASE PECULIAR TO NEGROES–CALLED BY OVERSEERS, "RASCALITY."

Dysaesthesia Aethiopica is a disease peculiar to negroes, affecting both mind and body in a manner as well expressed by dysaesthesia, the name I have given it, as could be by a single term. There is both mind and sensibility, but both seem to be difficult to reach by impressions from without. There is a partial insensibility of the skin, and so great a hebetude of the intellectual faculties, as to be like a person half asleep, that is with difficulty aroused and kept awake. It differs from every other species of mental disease, as it is accompanied with physical signs or lesions of the body discoverable to the medical observer, which are always present and sufficient to account for the symptoms. It is much more prevalent among free negroes living in clusters by themselves, than among slaves on our plantations, and attacks only such slaves as live like free negroes in regard to diet, drinks, exercise, etc. It is not my purpose to treat of the complaint as it prevails among free negroes, nearly all of whom are more or less afflicted with it, that have not got some white person to direct and to take care of them. To narrate its symptoms and effects among them would be to write a history of the ruins and dilapidation of Hayti, and every spot of earth they have ever had uncontrolled possession over for any length of time. I propose only to describe its symptoms among slaves.

From the careless movements of the individuals affected with the complaint, they are apt to do much mischief, which appears as if intentional, but is mostly owing to the stupidness of mind and insensibility of the nerves induced by the disease. Thus, they break, waste and destroy everything they handle,–abuse horses and cattle,–tear, burn or rend their own clothing, and, paying no attention to the rights of property, steal others, to replace what they have destroyed. They wander about at night, and keep in a half nodding sleep during the day. They slight their work,–cut up corn, cane, cotton or tobacco when hoeing it, as if for pure mischief. They raise disturbances with their overseers and fellow-servants without cause or motive, and seem to be insensible to pain when subjected to punishment. The fact of the existence of such a complaint, making man like an automaton or senseless machine, having the above or similar symptoms, can be clearly established by the most direct and positive testimony. That it should have escaped the attention of the medical profession, can only be accounted for because its attention has not been sufficiently directed to the maladies of the negro race. Otherwise a complaint of so common an occurrence on badly-governed plantations, and so universal among free negroes, or those who are not governed at all,–a disease radicated in physical lesions and having its peculiar and well marked symptoms and its curative indications, would not have escaped the notice of the profession. The northern physicians and people have noticed the symptoms, but not the disease from which they spring. They ignorantly attribute the symptoms to the debasing influence of slavery on the mind without considering that those who have never been in slavery, or their fathers before them, are the most afflicted, and the latest from the slave-holding South the least. The disease is the natural offspring of negro liberty–the liberty to be idle, to wallow in filth, and to indulge in improper food and drinks.

Cartwright (1851, pp. 1–6)

While speaking of mental illness, Cartwright is only identified as a doctor in the sources I found. Hard to blame the APA for not claiming him.

Please note the infusion of Christianity into Cartwright's racist pseudoscience. In yet another twisted use of religion, reminiscent of the Papal

Decree of 1493, the twin claims that blacks were the descendants of Ham ordained for slavery in the Old Testament and that being meek was the only path to heaven were recited to slaves every chance the overseers got. Law, force, religion, and "science" were all brought to bear to control the population. Of course, not everybody listened. Howard Thurman recalls this story from his Grandmother, who was born a slave in 1840: "Once a year a black preacher was allowed to deliver the sermon. The rest of the year we had a white preacher who quoted again and again Ephesians 6:5, 'Slaves obey your earthly masters with fear and trembling.' But the black preacher, at the end of the sermon, would lean towards them and say, 'You are not a slave. You are not a nigger. You are a child of God.'"

Cartwright's writing clearly displays the racism built upon a deep morass of lies that was firmly in place. Whether they believed the lies or not, there was pay off for enough of the upper- and lower-class whites to maintain the system. There was plenty to dole out, as the cotton output grew from 1,000 tons in 1790 to a million tons in 1860. The slave population grew with it, from 500,000 to 4 million.

Congress had added a 20-year moratorium on new laws that might inhibit slavery as yet another despicable part of "the great compromise." On the upside, they also had secured the right to add three non-slave-holding states to the Union. In 1808, to their credit, congress banned the importation of slaves. On the other hand, the US Naturalization Law of 1790 further institutionalized racism by limiting citizenship to immigrants who were "free white persons of good character" (Coates et al, 2018, p. 232). Despite some resistance, racism was embedded deep in our institutions. As Mississippi senator Jefferson Davis openly put it on the floor of the US Senate on April 12, 1860 (objecting to a bill funding black education in Washington, D. C.): "This government was not founded by negroes for negroes," but rather "by white men for white men." He went on to add that the "inequality of the white and black races" was "stamped from the beginning" (Kendi, 2016, p. 3).

Not everyone held this view. Especially not the slaves. The pressure and tension kept building. As Frederick Douglas, who had been born a slave, put it in 1853:

> Let me give you a word of the philosophy of reforms. The whole history of the progress of human liberty shows that all concessions yet made to her august claims have been born of struggle...if there is no struggle there is no progress. Those who profess to favor freedom and yet deprecate agitation,

are men who want crops without plowing up the ground. They want rain without thunder and lightning. They want the ocean without the awful roar of its many waters. The struggle may be a moral one; or it may be a physical one; or it may be both moral and physical, but it must be a struggle. Power concedes nothing without a demand. It never did and it never will....

Zinn (1980, p. 179)

The British Emancipation Act of 1833 added to the internal pressure within the US by beginning a phased and relatively orderly ending of slavery throughout the empire (United Kingdom National Archives, pp. 10). Meanwhile, not only did the slaves in the US have an epidemic of Cartwright's "Drapetomania," whenever possible they arose in armed revolt. In 1811, near New Orleans, it took the US military to quell a rebellion of nearly 500 slaves. In 1831, Nat Turner led about 70 of his fellow slaves from plantation to plantation, managing to kill at least 55 men, women, and children. The South lived on edge and armed to the teeth, with the State of Virginia in 1831 during peacetime claiming 101,488 men in its militia out of a total population of just over a million (Zinn, 1980, p. 170).

When not rebelling, they were escaping. During the 1850s, nearly 1,000 slaves a year successfully got away, with many more trying despite the risks and punishments. Harriet Tubman, who personally led 19 trips on the underground railroad freeing more than 300 slaves, expressed the feelings of many this way: "There was one of two things I had a right to, liberty or death; if I could not have one, I would rather have the other; for no man should take me alive..." (Zinn, 1980, p. 171). By 1850, there were 200,000 free blacks in the North and a multitude of whites risking their lives to resist slavery.

Interestingly, the liberty bell was part of the abolitionist effort. It was known as the "Old Statehouse Bell" until the 1830s when a group of Boston abolitionist rechristened it "The Liberty Bell." Their message was clear: "Proclaim liberty throughout all the land unto all the inhabitants thereof" (Church, 2002, p. 29). That brings us more or less to the civil war, which has been written about amply elsewhere, and the events that followed, which deserve further examination.

First, however, let's attempt to explore history by taking an objective look at both sides of some prominent individuals. Brace yourself. If anything is likely to upset readers from all walks of life, this is probably it.

AN ATTEMPT AT A MORE ACCURATE LOOK AT SOME HISTORICAL FIGURES

Please remember, this chapter is about seeing through the lens of racism. History, of course, isn't all about racism, but a chapter about history here without that focus would not be relevant. Through the lens of racism, the British Empire, cruel as it was toward its "subjects" foreign and domestic, red as its own hands were with the blood of slavery, was a step above the young United States. Comparatively, the British system was based more on class than race and allowed more social mobility for former slaves. Consequently, the transition to emancipation and later to independence for nations like Jamaica was far smoother.

As immoral as colonial and later US treatment of indigenous people, poor Europeans, and African slaves was (with women always getting the worst of everything), the founding fathers at the time of the revolution were on the whole genuinely influenced and inspired by the Age of Enlightenment's hope of progress based on reason and democratic principles. The beginning words of the Declaration of Independence, though patriarchal, imperfectly implemented, and written by an imperfect man, still set an eloquent precedent for a truly democratic union:

> We hold these truths to be self-evident; that all men are created equal; that they are endowed by their creator with certain unalienable rights; that among these are life, liberty, and the pursuit of happiness; that to secure these rights, governments are instituted among men, deriving their just powers from the consent of the governed; that whenever any form of government becomes destructive of these ends, is the right of the people to alter or to abolish it, and to institute new government, laying its foundation on such principles, and organizing its powers in such form as to them shall seem most likely to affect their safety and happiness.

The author of those words, Thomas Jefferson, is as good a place to start as any in trying to be objective about historical figures. During the six-session DEI workshop I attended, the white male co-facilitator (his partner was an African American female) went on what I can only describe as a rant about Jefferson, basically asserting (loudly) that he was a rapist and a racist. This, of course, is based on Jefferson's relationship with a slave, Sally Hemmings, through which he sired six children. By that point in the workshop, I had learned to keep my mouth shut. No one else, to my recollection, said anything in response to the emotional speech by the facilitator, and so, we moved one with his one-sided judgments ringing in our ears.

Was Jefferson a slave holder? Absolutely. Did his relationship with Hemmings occur within an uneven power structure? Without a doubt. Did he rape Sally Hemmings? If you consider any master-slave relationship rape, then the answer is yes. The facilitator made that assertion, perhaps having read the same in a 2017 Washington Post article (Danielle, 2017, pp. 3). The article goes on to admit that there are no written accounts by Hemmings, and almost no information from Jefferson or any other sources.

So, there it is. Thomas Jefferson, crafter of the Declaration, third President of the United States (1801–1809), owned 607 slaves and had ongoing sexual relations with one of them (Danielle, 2017, pp. 9).

The question is, can we admire historical figures and stand against them on important matters at the same time? If not, more and more people and events will become taboo. We will not be able to learn from them or see ourselves in them as if we are above them and they have nothing to do with us now. History is crazy, but we risk being even crazier if we can't reconcile different aspects of the same people and events. For that reason, there are two Southern generals included in the following discussion. The debate about their place in history is among our most polarized topics. I considered adding women, Native Americans, and blacks but could think of none whom I regard with the same mixed views. In other words, many historical figures come to mind, such as Frederick Douglas, but my bias views them in only a favorable light. Hence, there is no compelling need for including them in this type of analysis. To that end, without claiming that my understanding is the only truth, I have built Table 5.1 regarding historical figures up until around the time of the civil war.

TABLE 5.1

The Good, the Ambiguous, and the Ugly of Historical Figures

Historical Figure	The Good	The Ambiguous	The Ugly
Christopher Columbus	Daring explorer, amazing navigator.	Leader of men both at sea (good) and on land (ugly), launched the European conquest of the Americas.	Personally oversaw and participated in genocide in the Caribbean.
Thomas Jefferson	Profound contributions to the American "creed," especially the Declaration of Independence.		Lived the hypocrisy of slave ownership while writing the words, "All men are created equal." Indulged in sexual relations based on slavery.
George Washington	Led the Continental Army to victory in the Revolutionary War. First President of the US. Freed his slaves in his will.		One of the largest slave holders in the nation.
James Madison	A key framer of the constitution and the 4th President of the US (1808–1817).		Bragged to a British visitor that for only $12 per year for each slave he could make $257 annually (Zinn, 1908, p33).
Andrew Jackson	Hero of the Battle of New Orleans, 1815, and 7th President of the US (1829–1837).	The first populist anti-establishment politician. Identified more with the white poor than with the upper classes.	Oversaw the forced removal and near genocide of the "Five Civilized Tribes" of the Southeast, culminating in the horrific "Trail of Tears.["]
Abraham Lincoln	Sixteenth US President (1861–1865). Oversaw the defeat of the Confederacy, the preservation of the Union, and the abolition of slavery. In 1863 issued the Emancipation Proclamation. Gifted writer and orator. Firmly committed to liberating southern slaves and recruiting them into the Union Army.[2]	Maintained a non-committal stance on ending slavery, instead emphasizing the preservation of the Union.[3] Even the Emancipation Proclamation only freed slaves in states "in rebellion against the United States (Zinn, 1980, p187)."	Ordered the largest mass execution in US history, sending 38 Dakota Indians to the gallows in 1862[4], and oversaw the removal of the Sioux and Winnebago from their lands in Minnesota (Wiener, 2012, pp7).

(Continued)

TABLE 5.1 *(Continued)*

The Good, the Ambiguous, and the Ugly of Historical Figures

Historical Figure	The Good	The Ambiguous	The Ugly
General Robert E. Lee (1870)	Skilled tactician, inspiring leader to his men.	Some will no doubt say, "How dare he include Robert E. Lee?" History is full of such leaders: Hannibal, Alexander, Napoleon, Rommel, Yamamoto. One can admire their skills and courage without agreeing with what they represented.	Fought on the side of slavery. Owned slaves. Quietly but clearly racist.[5] Refused to exchange black prisoners of war even though it meant not freeing his own men (Chernow, 2017, p450). Despite being treated graciously at Appomattox, refused to condemn violence and support reconstruction. Opposed reconstruction and military occupation of the South (Chernow, 2017, p622).
General Tecumseh Sherman	Helped end the war quickly through his bold march behind Southern lines to the sea, freeing thousands of slaves in the process.		
General James Longstreet	Stood by Grant and the US government in 1874 against "White Leaguers" in New Orleans, firing onto men he had once commanded and killing more than 20 of them (Chernow, 2017, p761).[6]		Fought on the side of slavery. Owned slaves.

1 In the works since 1835, and slowed by the Cherokee Nation appeal to the Supreme Court, who ruled against them, the actual forced removal and march of 15,000 to 17,000 Cherokees from Georgia, where they had long since adapted many of the ways of the Europeans surrounding them, occurred in 1838 soon after Jackson left office. Four thousand died along the route to Oklahoma in one of the cruelest racist episodes in US history (Davis, 1990, p122).

2 200,000 blacks served in the Union Army during the war, many of them escaped or emancipated salves. 38,000 blacks gave their lives (Zinn, 1980, p190).

3 To be clear about my biases, I unabashedly support both causes, the abolition of slavery and the preservation of the Union.

4 After careful deliberation Lincoln made the highly unpopular move of commuting the death sentence of another 265 members of the "uprising" (Wiener, 2012, pp6).

5 Wrote Lee, "…Blacks are immeasurably better off here than in Africa, morally, socially, & physically. The painful discipline they are undergoing, is necessary for their instruction as a race, & I hope will prepare and lead them to better things (Chernow, 2017, p368)."

6 Longstreet came to regard his former adversary Grant as "the soul of honor himself (Chernow, 2017, p728)."

THE US POST-SLAVERY

Longstreet's role in fighting the "White Leaguers" brings us to reconstruction. The nightmare for blacks in the South was far from over, and belief in race, belief in the superiority of the white race, and institutional racism were deeply embedded in the socially constructed reality of the US. As we shall see, they linger on to this day.

Regarded by many as the distant past, the opposite is equally true. These events were recent! My grandfather was born in 1896, and we will soon reach that date in our consideration of history. To lament that we should be "over it" is about as useful as telling a veteran that they should get over their Post Traumatic Stress Disorder (PTSD). This country has collective PTSD, and the most likely way to heal from it as much as we can is to do so by acknowledging and exploring the truth, something that has never happened in any significant way. Fighting that exploration and acknowledgment just keeps us stuck.

Any careful analysis can only consider the reconstruction of the South a failure. The very people who revolted were able to regain power and terrorize the black population without restraint. Whites who resisted were brutalized along with blacks. Northern politicians showed no will to do what was necessary and soon turned a blind eye to the region and the plight of the newly freed slaves.

Here is a brief recap of the post-war years:

Lincoln was reelected, in no small part due to the success of General Sherman's "March to the Sea" which gave hope to a war-weary North and crippled the Southern war effort. In his inauguration speech, in anticipation of the end of the war, he offered these words which are engraved on the Lincoln Memorial: "With malice toward none, with charity for all, with firmness in the right as God gives us to see the right, let us strive on to finish the work we are in, to bind up the nation's wounds, to care for him who shall have borne the battle and for his widow and his orphan-to do all which may achieve and cherish a just and lasting peace amongst ourselves and with all nations."

That work has arguably never been completed. The celebration of the end of the war, the emancipation of slavery, and the preservation of the Union were abruptly shaken on April 14, 1865, just five short days after Lee's surrender at Appomattox, by the assassination of Lincoln. A second assassin assaulted the Secretary of State, and attacks on General Grant and Vice

President Andrew Johnson were planned but not carried out (Davis, 1990, p. 182). Lincoln, who had clearly set a course of reconciliation, was replaced by Johnson. Johnson was a southern Democrat from Tennessee (although born in South Carolina) who was on the ticket with Lincoln because of his appeal to voters Lincoln could not reach. Meanwhile the South elected many of the same people who had led the confederacy back into Congress, barred blacks from participating in the political process, and enacted a series of "black codes," which forced blacks into labor camps, restricted their movement, and regulated their family lives. "If you call this freedom," a black veteran asked, "what do you call slavery?" (Kendi, 2016, p. 235).

Republicans, who still controlled Congress, responded with a Freedman's Bureau, to help the 4 million freed slaves, and the Civil Rights Act of 1866, which declared that blacks were citizens and protected their rights. Identifying more and more openly with the white ruling class of the South, Johnson attempted a veto, which was the first such presidential veto overridden in the history of the US. With violence growing against blacks, congress passed a series of Reconstruction Acts, the first of which put the South under martial law. The reconciliation hoped for by Lincoln, imperfect though it was (for example, in legislation signed by Lincoln, the property confiscated during the war reverted to the heirs of the confederate owners, instead of giving any of it in compensation to the slaves who had worked the land), died with him.

The shock of the nation over Lincoln's death was expressed at the time by Walt Whitman:

> O Captain! my Captain! our fearful trip is done.
> The ship has weather'd every rack, the prize we sought is won,
> The port is near, the bells I hear, the people all exulting,
> While follow eyes the steady keel, the vessel grim and daring;
> But O heart! heart! heart!
> O the bleeding drops of red,
> Where on the deck my Captain lies,
> Fallen cold and dead.

Lincoln's death and Johnson's ascension to the presidency couldn't have been a more dramatic turn of events for the nation. According to Historian Ron Chernow,

> No American president has ever held such openly racist views. "This is a country for white men," he declared unashamedly, "and by God, as long as

I am President, it shall be a government for white men." In one message to Congress, he contended that "negroes have shown less capacity for government than any other race of people." He privately referred to blacks as "niggers"…he wanted to ensure that the "poor, quiet, unoffending, harmless" whites of the South weren't "trodden underfoot to protect niggers." Not only did he think whites genetically superior to blacks but he refused to show the least respect to their most brilliant spokesman. When Frederick Douglass came to the White House with a black delegation, Johnson turned to his secretary afterward and sneered: "He's just like any nigger and would sooner cut a white man's throat than not."

Chernow (2017, p. 550)

Far from leading reconciliation, Johnson was a wrecking ball as president, becoming the first US president to be impeached. On face value, the charge was petty. Johnson had fired the war secretary without senate consent. But the conflict between President Johnson and the republican congress ran deep at a time when the nation was sorely in need of guidance.

Let's back up a little, first by looking forward. On June 19, 2021, following an astonishingly bipartisan unanimous vote in the Senate and a 415-14 vote in the House, President Biden signed into law the establishment of Juneteenth as a federal holiday, commemorating the official emancipation of slavery following the civil war. Celebrated by an ever-growing number since 1886, the date marks the moment, June 19, 1865, two months after Lee had surrendered at Appomattox, and nearly two and a half years after the Emancipation Proclamation, that Maj. Gen. Gordon Granger in Galveston, Texas, issued General Order No. 3: "The people of Texas are informed that, in accordance with a proclamation from the Executive of the United States, all slaves are free. This involves an absolute equality of personal rights and rights of property between former masters and slaves, and the connection heretofore existing between them becomes that between employer and hired labor. The freedmen are advised to remain quietly at their present homes and work for wages. They are informed that they will not be allowed to collect at military posts and that they will not be supported in idleness either there or elsewhere (United States National Archives)." That last part presaged the racist homeostasis that was to come.

Nonetheless, the ending of slavery was one of the greatest moments in the history of the United States. In the words of Suzie Melton, herself a slave,

I was a young girl, about 10 years old, and we done heard that Lincoln gonna turn the niggers free. Ol' missus say there wasn't nothin' to it. Then a Yankee soldier told someone in Williamsburg that Lincoln done signed the 'mancipation. Was wintertime and mighty cold that night, but everybody commenced getting ready to leave. Didn't care nothin' about missis-was going to the Union lines. And all that night the niggers danced and sang right out in the cold. Next morning at day break we all started out with blankets and clothes and pots and pans and chickens piled on our backs, 'cause missus said we couldn't take no horses or carts. And as the sun came up over the trees, the niggers started to singing:

> Sun, you be here and I'll be gone
> Sun, you be here and I'll be gone
> Sun, you be here and I'll be gone
> Bye, bye, don't grieve after me
> Won't give you my place, not for yours
> Bye, bye, don't grieve after me
> Cause you be here and I'll be gone

Zinn (1980, p. 1919)

Two other slaves, Anna Woods and Anne Mae Weathers, described the moments they heard the news this way: "We wasn't there in Texas long when the soldiers marched in to tell us that we were free...I remember one woman. She jumped on a barrel and she shouted. She jumped off and she shouted. She jumped back on again and shouted some more. She kept that up for a long time, just jumping on a barrel and back off again." "I remember hearing my paw say that when somebody came and hollered, 'You niggers is free at last,' he just dropped his hoe and said in a queer voice, 'Thank God for that'" (Zinn, 1980, p. 191).

Taking a step backward in time again, General Sherman, during the late stages of the war, having completed his march of destruction through Georgia to Savannah, met with 20 black ministers and church officials. A great multitude of freed slaves had followed and aided his army along the way, and the group of 20 spoke for them. They entreated Sherman that "The best way we can best take care of ourselves is to have land, and till it by our labor" (Zinn, 1980, p. 192). Sherman responded with "Special Field Order No. 15." Thirty miles of Southern coastline was designated to freed slaves, in lots of 40 acres per family. By June 1865, 40,000 former slaves had settled the land. In one of many low blows to come, President Johnson in August 1865 gave the land back to its former confederate owners who forced the blacks off the land and back into homeless poverty. Such was the beginning of reconstruction under an anti-reconstruction president.

Despite such setbacks, and in bitter resistance to them, the Republican Congress parried Johnson well enough that martial law and civil rights legislation progressed. The 13th Amendment ended slavery. The 14th Amendment established that, "All persons born or naturalized in the United States" were citizens and that, "No State shall make or enforce any law which shall abridge the privileges or immunities of citizens of the United States; nor shall any State deprive any person of life, liberty, or property, without due process of law; nor deny to any person within its jurisdiction the equal protection of the laws." The 15th Amendment, ratified on February 3, 1870, proclaimed: "The right of citizens of the United States to vote shall not be denied or abridged by the United States or by any State on account of race, color, or previous condition of servitude" (Zinn, 1980, p. 193). In an address to congress, the next president after Johnson, Ulysses S. Grant, declared it, "A measure which makes at once Four Millions of people heretofore declared by the highest tribunal in the land, not citizens of the United States, nor eligible to become so, voters in every part of the land, the right not to be abridged by any state, is indeed a measure of grander importance than any other one act of the kind from the foundation of our free government to the present day…The adoption of the 15th amendment constitutes…the most important event that has occurred since the nation came into life" (Chernow, 2017, p. 655). With the notable continuing exclusion of women from voting rights, the legal basis was set for black males to vote and for all citizens to be protected under the law.

Protected by Union troops, blacks participated in their first national election in 1868, casting over 700,000 votes. Ulysses S. Grant owed his victory directly to black voters, winning by a margin of 300,000. Grant served two terms and was an ardent supporter of a reconstruction that would defend the civil rights of black Americans, but the struggle required backbone and bloodshed, and support eroded steadily.[3]

Martial law proved necessary. As soon as the war was over, pockets of Southern whites began to behave badly. In Memphis, Tennessee, in May of 1866, a white crowd went on a rampage, killing 46 blacks, most of them being veterans of the Union Army, as well as two white sympathizers. Five black women were raped. Ninety homes, 12 schools, and 4 churches were burned. In New Orleans, in the summer of 1866, another riot killed 35 blacks along with a handful of their white friends (Zinn, 1980, p. 198). This violence was dampened by martial law but never stamped out.

Despite such threats, blacks seized the moment, voting in great numbers and getting elected in several Southern legislatures. They became the majority in one chamber of the government of South Carolina. Two blacks, both from Mississippi, were elected to the US Senate, and 20 to the House of Representatives. Between 1865 and 1873, the South Carolina legislature "introduced free public schools for the first time into that state. Not only were 70,000 Negro children going to school by 1876 where none had gone before, but 50,000 white children were going to school where only 20,000 had attended in 1860" (Zinn, 1980, p. 195).

Such progress was soon stamped out. Ignoring the civil rights legislation and the federal government, the Georgia legislature in 1868 expelled all black members, totaling 2 senators and 25 representatives. One of these elected officials, Henry MacNeal Turner, gave this speech to the collection of white men as they were brazenly overturning the democratic process:

> Mister Speaker…I wish the members of this House to understand the position that I take. I hold that I am a member of this body. Therefore, sir, I shall neither fawn or cringe before any party, nor stoop to beg them for my rights…I am here to demand my rights, and to hurl thunderbolts at the men who had dare to cross the threshold of my manhood…
>
> The scene presented in this House, today, is one unparalleled in the history of the world…Never, in the history of the world, has a man been arraigned before a body clothed with legislative, judicial or executive functions, charged with the offence of being of a darker hue than his fellowmen…It has remained for the state of Georgia, in the very heart of the nineteenth century, to call a man before the bar, and there charge him with an act for which he is no more responsible than for the head which he carries upon his shoulders. The Anglo-Saxon race, sir, is a most surprising one…I was not aware that there was in the character of that race so much cowardice, or so much pusillanimity…I tell you Sir, that this is a question which will not die today. This event shall be remembered by posterity for ages yet to come, and while the sun shall continue to climb the hills of heaven…
>
> We are told that if black men want to speak, they must speak through white trumpets; if black men want their sentiments expressed, they must be adulterated and sent through white messengers, who will quibble, and equivocate, and evade, as rapidly as the pendulum of a clock…

The great question, Sir is this: Am I man? If I am such, I claim the rights of a man...

Why, Sir, though we are not white, we have accomplished much. We have pioneered civilization here; we have built up your country; we have worked in your fields, and garnered your harvest, for two hundred and fifty years! And what do we ask of you in return? Do we ask you for compensation for the sweat our fathers bore for you-for the years tears you have caused, and the hearts you have broken, and the lives you have curtailed, and the blood you have spilled? Do we ask retaliation? We ask it not. We are willing to let the dead past bury its dead; But we ask you now for our RIGHTS....

Zinn (1980, p. 196)

The request fell on deaf ears. Along with the institutional racism of the Georgia government and others, violent acts by whites rose like the wave of a pandemic. The Ku Klux Klan, the White Leaguers, and other white supremacists consisting mostly of former confederate troops began a reign of terror. Here is a small sample of 116 crimes documented by the National Archives committed between 1867 and 1871 in Kentucky alone:

1. A mob visited Harrodsburg in Mercer County to take from jail a man named Robertson Nov 14, 1867...
2. Sam Davis hung by a mob in Harrodsburg, May 28, 1868.
3. W'm Pierce hung by a mob in Christian July 12, 1868.
4. Geo. Roger hung by a mob in Bradsfordville Martin County July 11, 1868.
5. Silas Woodford age 60 badly beaten by a disguised mob...
6. Negro killed by Ku Klux Klan in Hay County January 14, 1871.

Left to their own druthers, too many Southern whites were willing to continue the brutal racism of the past. When General Adelbert Ames took command of the Fourth Military District overseeing Arkansas and Mississippi, he found that "... the negroes who had been declared free by the United States were not free, in fact they were living under a code that made them worse than slaves; and I found that it was necessary, as commanding officer, to protect them, and I did" (Chernow, 2017, p. 655). Indeed, granted no property nor financial assistance by the federal government, blacks had little choice but to work for their former slave owners or to migrate elsewhere. Still at the bottom of the economic system, the effort to strip blacks of their newly won rights grew from a tide to a tidal wave. Ironically, now that blacks were full citizens instead of three-fifths a citizen, the South gained extra delegates in Congress and electoral votes, even while they robbed blacks of their right to participate in democracy.

The battle to resist reconstruction and re-enslave Southern blacks was relentless. As Governor William Holden of North Carolina reported in 1871, "Bands of these armed men ride at night through various neigh-borhoods, whipping and maltreating peaceable citizens, hanging some, burning churches, and breaking up schools which have been established for the colored people" (Chernow, 2017, p. 701). Attempts by local and federal authorities to bring justice were outmaneuvered, as witnesses were either too frightened to testify or were murdered with impunity. Governor Robert Scott of South Carolina witnessed citizens, "...at the dead hour of night dragged from their homes and lashed on their bare backs until the flayed flesh hung dripping in shreds, and seams were gaping in their mangled bodies large enough to put my finger in" (Chernow, 2017, p. 702).

Grant was swamped with pleas for help. Mrs. S. E. Lane of South Carolina wrote: "... Sir, we are in terror from Ku Klux threats & outrages... our nearest neighbor-a prominent Republican now lies dead-murdered, by a disguised Ruffian Band, which attacked his House at midnight a few nights since-his wife also was murdered...& a daughter is lying danger-ously ill from a shot-wound...my Husband's life is threatened...we are in constant fear & terror-our nights are sleepless, we are filled with anxiety & dismay" (Chernow, 2017, p. 702).

Meanwhile, in an echo of modern times, Grant's Republican Party got battered in the 1870 mid-terms, and he faced an increasingly hostile congress. Historic in the election of six black Southern candidates, White racism in the North reared its ugly head in response with one New York newspaper writing that Congress "will soon have its full proportion of darkey members" (Chernow, 2017, p. 703).

In Mississippi, the violence increased. As historian Ron Chernow reports: "...scores of black churches and schools were burned without prosecutions. In March 1871 three blacks in the small town of Meridian were brought up on charges of delivering 'incendiary' speeches. At the court hearing, the Republican judge and two black defendants were killed. The violence spilled over into gruesome riots in which 30 blacks were gunned down, including 'all the leading colored men of the town with one or two excep-tions'...nobody served a day for these crimes" (Chernow, 2017, p. 703).

Despite congress, Grant had heard enough. He sent troops to reestablish martial law in South Carolina. Klan members were arrested, federal attorneys prosecuted, and federal judges tried their cases to prevent local interference. Ignoring bitter opposition in the press and in Congress, on April 20, 1871, Grant signed the third of his reconstruction "Enforcement" acts, this one commonly called the "Ku Klux Klan" Act. The act outlines criminal penalties for depriving citizens of their rights and made it illegal, "to conspire together, or go in disguise upon the public highway…for the purpose…of depriving any person…of equal protection of the law" (Chernow, 2017, p. 706). Former Confederate General Nathan Bradford Forrest, the first Grand Wizard of the Ku Klux Klan, responded to Grant's actions with these words: "If they send the black men to hunt those confederate soldiers whom they call kuklux, then I say to you, 'go out and shoot the radicals'" (Chernow, 2017, p. 707).

While the fight for equality was far from over, the fight against the original Klan was victorious,[4] thanks to the tireless leadership of Grant and Attorney General Amos Ackerman. Again, we turn to Chernow to summarize: "By 1872, under Grant's leadership, the Ku Klux Klan had been smashed in the South. (Its later 20th century incarnation had no connection to the earlier group other than a common style and ideology.) He had employed forceful, no-holds-barred actions to loosen the Klan's grip. As southern violence subsided, southern Republicans regained confidence and cast votes with an assurance of their safety, and for southern blacks the changed mood was palpable. 'Peace has come to many places as never before,' wrote Frederick Douglass. 'The scourging and slaughter of our people have so far ceased'" (Chernow, 2017, p. 709). Convictions of KKK members went on for years, and prison terms resulted. It was one of the most necessary and remarkable enforcements of civil rights in history.

The dramatic quelling of violence helped propel Grant in 1872 to a second term. On the other hand, Northern patience with reconstruction progressively waned. Too many Northern whites identified with the whites of the South and did business with them, and the political willingness to continue reconstruction eroded. As one "American diplomat" put it, the North was increasingly tired of, "…this wornout cry of 'Southern outrages'!!! Hard times & heavy taxes make them wish the 'nigger,' 'everlasting, nigger,' were in…Africa" (Chernow, 2017, p. 762). With the end of Grant's second term in 1877, any meaningful resistance to racism by the

US government ended as well. The government instead became an active instrument of racism.

Even with Grant still in office, the Supreme Court helped pave the way for the resurgence of white supremacy in the South. In 1873, supporters of black Republican William Ward were attacked by White Leaguers, who killed at least 73 of them and possibly many more. A federal grand jury handed down 72 indictments, but only 3 were convicted. Their case went to the Supreme Court, and in the 1876 ruling of the *United States vs Cruikshank*, the court ruled that the 14th Amendment only applied to the actions of states, not to individuals. The perpetrators of the massacre were cleared of all charges. Said Grant to Congress: "Insufferable obstructions were thrown in the way of punishing these murderers, and the so-called conservative papers of the state not only justified the massacre, but denounced as federal tyranny and despotism the attempt of the United States officers to bring them to justice. Fierce denunciations rang through the country about office holding and election matters in Louisiana, while every one of the Colfax miscreants goes unwhipped of justice, and no way can be found in this boasted land of civilization and Christianity to punish the perpetrators of this bloody and monstrous crime" (Chernow, 2017, p. 760).

After the White League and former confederate soldiers took over New Orleans on September 14, 1874, Grant dispatched the military once again to restore order. General Sheridan, who took charge of Louisiana, estimated that more than 2,000 political murders had occurred in the state since 1866. Conditions were so desperate that a group of more than 200 blacks petitioned Grant to help them immigrate out of the country: "We cannot get upon a man's Steamboat and make a round trip but what Some of us are whipped or Beat or Killed or Driven ashore. if we Stand up as men for the protection of our Wives and our Daughters… these white men…says that we must die" (Chernow, 2017, p. 795). For the remainder of his days in office, pleas for help were constant, and the order was increasingly dependent on the reinsertion of troops. The age of Jim Crow, segregation, overt institutional racism, and economic oppression was beginning.

In 1883, the Supreme Court supported racism further by neutralizing the Civil Rights Act of 1875 by stating that, "Individual invasion of individual rights is not the subject matter of the amendment" (Zinn, 1980, p. 199). In 1896, in the case of *Plessy v. Ferguson*, the Court continued its series of shameful and racist rulings by concluding that a railroad could segregate blacks and whites. Louisiana had been doing so since 1890. When Homar Plessy, allegedly seven-eighths white but one-eighth black, tried to sit in the white car, he was arrested (Davis, 1990, p. 213). According to the Court: "The object of the amendment was undoubtedly to enforce the absolute equality of the two races before the law, but in the nature of things it could not have been intended to abolish distinctions based upon color, or to enforce social, as distinguished from political equality, or a commingling of the two races upon terms unsatisfactory to either" (Zinn, 1980, p. 200). What had been accomplished was swept away, the progress toward actual democracy was undone, and the brief period of hope and dignity for black men and women in the South was methodically destroyed.

Thomas Fortune, a young black editor of the *New York Globe*, testified before Congress in 1883 about the plight of blacks in the South: "The average wage of Negro farm laborers in the South was about fifty cents a day... He was usually paid in 'orders,' not money, which he could use only at a store controlled by the planter, 'a system of fraud.' The Negro farmer, to get the wherewithal to plant his crop, had to promise it to the store, and when everything was added up at the end of the year he was in debt, so his crop was constantly owed to someone, and he was tied to the land, with the records kept by the planter and storekeeper so that the Negros are 'swindled and kept forever in debt." Fortune continued, "...the penitentiary system of the South, with its infamous chain gang...the object being to terrorize the blacks and furnish victims for contractors, who purchased the labor of these wretches from the state for a song...the white man who shoots a negro always goes free, while the negro who steals a hog is sent to the chain gang for 10 years" (Zinn, 1980, p. 204).

In 1890, the state of Mississippi took things even further, instituting a literacy test at the polls. It was entirely up to the all-white registrars to determine whether a person had demonstrated understanding of a question about a portion of the Mississippi constitution. That practice, which quickly spread to all the Southern states, along with poll taxes, drove a final stake in the black man's ability to vote in the South.

Even with the relatively friendly Teddy Roosevelt in the White House (from 1901 to 1909), nothing really changed. Roosevelt embodied the myth of the "great white hope," believing that "The expansion of the peoples of white, or European, blood during the past four centuries...has been fraught with lasting benefit to most of the peoples already dwelling in the lands over which the expansion took place" (Blackmon, 2008, p. 163). He also naively believed most white people at the time were "good-natured" and would not stand in the way of efforts by blacks to improve their own circumstances. When he invited Booker T. Washington to dine at the White House, he was in for a rude awakening. As historian Douglas Blackmon tells it: "US senator Ben 'Pitchfork' Tillman of South Carolina sputtered: 'Now that Roosevelt has eaten with that nigger Washington, we shall have to kill a thousand niggers to get them back to their places.' The *Memphis Press-Scimitar* called the evening meal 'The most damnable outrage which has ever been perpetrated by any citizen of the United States.' The *Richmond News* declared that Roosevelt 'at one stroke and by one act has destroyed regard for him. He has put himself further from us than any man who has ever been in the White House.' The governor of Georgia, Allen Candler, said 'No southerner can respect any white men who would eat with a negro" (Blackmon, 2008, p. 166). Welcome, dear reader, to the 20th century.

Hated by Southern whites, Roosevelt managed to tarnish his reputation with blacks in 1906 when he ordered the dishonorable discharge (and loss of pensions) of 167 black soldiers of the black 25th Infantry Regiment due to charges over which the NY Times reported there was "not a particle of evidence" (Kendi, 2016, p. 296).

Things weren't much better for blacks in the North, who lived in slums and were lucky to get the worst jobs at the lowest wages. The two systems were intimately linked financially, as the wealthiest Northerners got even wealthier, and even the working classes in the Northern Steel mills unknowingly benefited from the abuse of blacks in the South. To be fair, the most horrific conditions were hidden from all but those who perpetuated them, suffered from them, or directly profited from them. The steel industry is a prime example, the most powerful cog in the economic engine of the nation at the time. The U.S. Steel Corporation on its own accounted for a 7th of the Gross Domestic Product (GDP) in 1901 (Blackmon, 2008, p. 171).

In case you are under the impression that the playing field was "even" after the civil war ended slavery, you might want to sit down and pour yourself a stiff drink (or some herbal tea) before you read this:

> On March 30th, 1908, Green Cottenham was arrested by the sheriff of Shelby County, Alabama, and charged with "vagrancy."

Cottenham had committed no true crime. Vagrancy, the offense of a person not being able to prove at a given moment that he or she is employed, was a new and flimsy concoction dredged up from legal obscurity at the end of the nineteenth century by the state legislatures of Alabama and other southern states. It was capriciously enforced by local sheriffs and constables, adjudicated by mayors and notaries public, recorded haphazardly or not at all in court records, and, most tellingly in a time of massive unemployment among all southern men, was reserved almost exclusively for black men. Cottenham's offense was blackness.

After three days behind bars, twenty-two-year-old Cottenham was found guilty in a swift appearance before the county judge and immediately sentenced to a thirty-day term of hard labor. Unable to pay the array of fees assessed on every prisoner-fees to the sheriff, the deputy, the court clerk, the witnesses-Cottenham's sentence was extended to nearly a year of hard labor.

The next day, Cottenham, the youngest of nine children born to former slaves in an adjoining county, was sold. Under a standing arrangement between the county and a vast subsidiary of the industrial titan of the North-U.S. Steel Corporation-the sheriff turned the young man over to the company for the duration of his sentence. In return, the subsidiary, Tennessee Coal, Iron & Railroad Company, gave the county $12 a month to pay off Cottenham's fine and fees. What the company's managers did with Cottenham, and thousands of other black men they purchased from sheriffs across Alabama, was entirely up to them.

A few hours later, the company plunged Cottenham into the darkness of a mine called Slope No. 12-one shaft in a vast subterranean labyrinth on the edge of Birmingham known as the Pratt Mines. There, he was chained inside a long wooden barrack at night and required to spend nearly every waking hour digging and loading coal. His required daily "task" was to remove eight tons of coal from the mine. Cottenham was subject to the whip for failure to dig the requisite amount, at risk of physical torture for disobedience, and vulnerable to the sexual predations of other minors-many of whom already had passed years or decades in their own chthonian confinement. The lightless catacombs of black rock, packed with hundreds of desperate men slick with sweat and coated in pulverized coal, must have exceeded any vision of hell a boy born in the countryside of Alabama-even a child of slaves-could have ever imagined.

Waves of disease ripped through the population. In the month before Cottenham arrived at the prison mine, pneumonia and tuberculosis sickened dozens. Within his first four weeks, six died. Before the year was over, almost sixty men forced into Slope No. 12 were dead of disease, accidents, or homicide. Most of the broken bodies, along with hundreds of others before and after, were dumped into shallow graves scattered among the refuse of the mine. Others were incinerated in nearby ovens used to blast millions of tons of coal brought to the surface into coke-the carbon rich fuel essential to U.S. Steel's production of iron. Forty-five years after President Abraham Lincoln's Emancipation Proclamation freeing American slaves, Green Cottenham and more than a thousand other black men toiled under the lash at Slope 12. Imprisoned in what was then the most advanced city of the South, guarded by whipping bosses employed by the most iconic example of the modern corporation emerging in the gilded North, they were slaves in all but name.

Blackmon (2008, p. 1)

Similar operations, such as Durham Coal and Coke in Georgia, were conducted elsewhere in the South.

Green Cottenham died of illness within a year of entering the mines. Death must have been a relief. Later that same year, white miners and black minors joined together in a strike. Alabama Governor Braxton Comer told union leaders he was, "...outraged at the attempts to establish social equality between black and white miners." He went on to add that he would "not tolerate eight or nine thousand idle niggers in the state of Alabama." He called in the militia to break the strike (Blackmon, 2008, p. 326).

If that doesn't make you think, I don't know what will. Amazing as it seems, the horrors for blacks in post-slavery America were all too often worse than before emancipation. Northern prosperity directly benefited from it. Lynchings as part of the system of white supremacy were common. From 1881 to 1968, 4,742 lynchings occurred in the United States (NAACP, pp. 1). In 1908 in Dallas, Texas, for example, a mob of 2,000 whites tied an 18-year-old black man named Tad Smith, who had been accused of raping a white woman, to a stake in the ground and burned him to death. This type of event was so normal that a front-page headline for the Birmingham Age-Herald, reporting on another murder that same year, read, "Negro Quietly Swung Up by an Armed Mob...All is quiet here tonight" (Blackmon, 2008, p. 326). Beyond the very real threat of violence if a white person was just in a bad mood or didn't like you, the indignities of segregation, of disenfranchisement, of poverty, were like a thousand microaggressions every day. When blacks did prosper against these odds, they were all too often slammed down.

They were especially slammed down by those whites who were most likely to gain by overcoming racism, the working class and the poor (who were often one and the same). During the time of the "Robber Barons," when the gap between the rich and the poor became more dramatic than ever, organized labor was making slow and painful gains while facing some of the same violent opposition from employers and the government that blacks faced daily. The military was used to break the Railway Union in 1894, killing strikers in the streets of Chicago. Instead of reaching out to black workers, organized labor snubbed them. A sign outside the American Federation of Labor (or AFL) headquarters at the turn of the century read "No Colored Need Apply" (Davis, 1990, p. 210).

In 1915, Hollywood got in the act with D. W. Griffith's *Birth of a Nation*, the first feature-length studio production. President Woodrow Wilson screened it at the White House, and afterward reportedly said "My only regret is that it is all so terribly true" (Kendi, 2016, p. 306). By 1916, more than 3 million people had viewed the film in New York alone. Dazzled by this new medium, many likely confused fiction with fact, especially if it fit the biases they already held. Historian Ibram Kendi describes *Birth of a Nation* this way:

> The silent film depicted Reconstruction as an era of corrupt Black suprema-cists terrorizing innocent whites. At the climax, a black male rapist (played by a white actor in blackface) pursues a white woman into the woods until she leaps to her death. "Lynch him! Lynch him!" moviegoers shouted in Houston, and nearly one hundred Blacks were actually lynched in 1915. In the end, the victim's brother in the film organizes Klansman to regain control of southern society. A White Jesus-brown haired, brown eyed, and white robed-appears to bless the triumph of white supremacy as the film concludes. The film revitalized the Ku Klux Klan....
>
> **Kendi (2016, p. 305)**

One has to wonder if it was shown at the movie theater in Greenwood, Oklahoma, a neighborhood also known as Black Wall Street. One hundred years ago (at the time of this writing), Greenwood and the people who built it were destroyed. Picture, in the face of the racism of the times, a prospering community of black people. Despite the most uneven playing field imaginable, the neighborhood of Greenwood, in Tulsa, OK, was thriving in every way. "My grandfather often talked about how you could enjoy a full life in Greenwood, that everything you needed or wanted was in Greenwood. He never had to go anywhere,' said Star Williams, 40, the granddaughter of Otis Grandville Clark, who was 18 during the massacre. 'He talked about seeing Black success and how his sense of identity and pride came from Greenwood" (NY Times, 2021, pp. 15).

Two blacks with vision, Mr. Gurley and Mr. Stradford, among others, purchased the land in the early 1900s literally "on the other side of the railroad tracks" in Tulsa and began building.

> Survivor accounts of the thriving business and social community…recall neighbors getting "gussied up" to gather in Greenwood, with Thursdays being big because of "maids night out." Black domestics, many of them live-in workers who cleaned the homes of white residents across town, were off that day. In Greenwood, residents held more than 200 different types of jobs. About 40% of the community's residents were professionals or skilled craftspeople, like doctors, pharmacists, carpenters and hairdressers, according to a Times analysis of the 1920 census. While a vast majority of the neighborhood rented, many residents own their homes.
>
> **NY Times (2021, pp. 32)**

Ironically, the very segregation designed to hold blacks down, prevented blacks with income from shopping in white shops, and in this rare circumstance helped black businesses thrive. White resentment of the community simmered. Between May 30 and June 2, 1921, the beacon of hope that was Greenwood was wiped out. The trouble began with the all-too-familiar accusation of a young black male assaulting a white woman. Things escalated quickly as "The mob indiscriminately shot black people in the streets. Members of the mob ransacked homes and stole money and jewelry. They set fires, 'house by house, block by block.' The numbers presented a staggering portrait of loss: 35 blocks burned to the ground; as many as 300 dead; hundreds injured; 8000 to 10,000 left homeless; more than 1470 homes burned or looted; and eventually 6000 detained in internment camps…a fire ordinance…prevented black property owners from rebuilding…and insurance companies refused to pay damage claims" (NY Times, 2021, pp. 43).

The only legal prosecution was indictments handed out against six blacks for "inciting a riot." "No compensation has ever been paid under court order or by legislation. To this day, not one person has been prosecuted or punished…" (NY Times, 2021, pp. 61).

Spoiler alert: it's safe to say the playing field wasn't even in 1921. And while one of the worst, the Tulsa Massacre, was by no means the only such incident. Just two years earlier, in what became known as the "Red Summer," violence against black neighborhoods occurred in 25 cities across the US (Kendi, 2016, p. 314). That violence was partially fueled by growing tension as more and more blacks fled the south in the "Great Migration," which had been accelerated by Northern labor shortages during WWI.

Far from being greeted with open and non-racist arms, white reaction was the revival of the Ku Klux Klan in the 1920s, which spread into the north. By 1924, it had 4.5 million members. Two short generations ago, instead of progress, racism in the form of white supremacy was on the rise.

WWII united the country as much as any period in history. Nonetheless, racism continued to come between us, with as many as 242 violent attacks targeting African Americans in 47 US cities occurred in 1943 alone. At the Baltimore Western Electric plant, white women went on strike in protest of having to use the same restroom facilities as black women (Coates et al, 2018, p. 354).

In its time of need, Uncle Sam drafted blacks into the military and many served with distinction. Ambivalence about and the irony of fighting for a country that had and was systemically oppressed blacks did not go unspoken. The following "Draftee's prayer" appeared in one black newspaper (Zinn, 1980, p. 410):

Dear Lord, today
I go to war:
To fight, to die,
Tell me what for?
Dear Lord, I'll fight,
I do not fear,
Germans or Japs;
My fears are here.
America!

A potential draftee told his college professor: "The army jim-crows us. The Navy lets us serve only as messman. The Red Cross refuses our blood. Employers and labor unions shut us out. Lynchings continue. We are disenfranchised, jim-crowed, spat upon. What more could Hitler do than that?" (Zinn, 1980, p. 410).

Segregation didn't legally end until the Civil Rights Act of 1964, and even then, integration had to be enforced at the end of a bayonet.

It's almost endless, the examples of racism that could be documented here. A lot will be covered in the pages ahead, starting with the next section. At risk of skipping important events, it is time to move on.

ATTEMPTS TO MAKE RACISM SCIENTIFIC

Like putting lipstick on a pig, throughout the 1800s and early 1900s, racists tried to cloak racism in a veil of science.

As mentioned in the introduction, German "physical anthropologist" Johaan Blumenbock asserted in 1795 that blond blue-eyed people were the "most handsome and becoming" and had originated in the Caucasus Mountains (Raj Bophal and Usher, 2007, pp. 14). Blumenbock himself concluded that humans were all one species and that superficial physical characteristics were due to climate. Unfortunately, his bias toward which superficial appearance was more attractive and his nonsensical coining of the term "Caucasian" became his primary legacy.

Other prominent scientists kept throwing darts at a science that would explain "white superiority." As the American Psychological Association explains as part of their 2021 apology, in "1869: Francis Galton, who was recognized as an early leader in psychology (among other professions) publishes *Hereditary Genius*, a central early event in the study of individual differences and psychometrics in European and U.S. psychology. In this work, he ranked the 'comparative worth of different races' and concluded that 'the average intellectual standard of the negro race is some two grades below our own'…In 1883, Galton would introduce the word 'eugenics,' described as a science of improving 'racial stock'" (APA, 2021, pp. 22). Galton's Eugenics would be enthusiastically embraced by racists in the US and Europe, including Adolph Hitler, who used eugenics as justification for attempting to rule the world and for the murder of 6 million Jews between 1941 and 1945.

In 1876, Italian prison doctor Caesar Lombroso…"proved" that non-White men loved to kill, "mutilate the corpse, tear its flesh and drink its blood." His *Criminal Man* gave birth to the discipline of criminology in

1876. Criminals were born, not bread, Lombroso said. He believed that born criminals emitted physical signs that could be studied, measured, and quantified, and that the "inability to blush"-and therefore, dark skin- "had always been considered the accompaniment of crime." Black women, in their close "degree of differentiation from the male," he claimed in *The Female Offender* in 1895, were the prototypical female criminals... Lombroso's student, Italian law professor Raphael Garofalo, invented the term "criminology" in 1885. British physician Havelock Ellis popularized Lombroso in the English speaking world, publishing a compendium of his writings in 1890.

Kendi (2016, p. 257)

During this same period, the American Medical Association published among its goals "a scientific process" to decrease the population of the "unfortunate classes" and the "Chicago Ugly Law" of 1911 institutionalized discrimination in a new way, stating that: "Any person who is diseased, maimed, mutilated or in any way deformed so as to be an unsightly or disgusting object, or an improper person to be allowed in or on the streets, highways, thoroughfares or public places in this city shall not therein or thereon expose himself or herself to public view" (Coates et al, 2018, p. 164). The idea of superiority, anointed by science, was reaching new lows.

Beginning with the Immigration Law of 1891, anyone deemed inferior was deported. Immigration officials determined whether immigrants suffered from a "...loathsome or dangerous contagious disease' (which included pregnancy, poverty, and a lack of morals) and applied to any widowed or unmarried women" (Coates et al, 2018, p. 164). To help immigration officials maintain the standards of eugenics, psychologist Henry Goddard developed IQ tests which he claimed showed that about "80% of Jewish, Hungarian, Italian, and Russian immigrants were feeble minded. Deportations for the reason of feeble mindedness increased 350% that year and 570% the next" (Coates et al, 2018, p. 164).

Emboldened by the "science" of eugenics, 33 states enacted laws allowing involuntary sterilization to decrease "undesirable traits." In 1927, the US Supreme Court ruled in favor of the State of Virginia in the case of *Buck v. Bell* that Carrie Buck, a resident at the Virginia Colony for Epileptics and Feebleminded, who had given birth after being raped at age 16, could be involuntarily sterilized. As Justice Oliver Wendell Holmes Jr. explained: "It is better for all the world, if instead of waiting to execute degenerate offspring for crime, or to let them starve for their imbecility, society can prevent those who are manifestly unfit from continuing their kind... Three generations of imbeciles are enough..." (Coates et al, 2018, p. 164). Backed by the courts, by the mid-1930s, more than 60,000 US citizens were forcibly sterilized. Other nations followed the US lead, most notably Nazi Germany. Hitler's "final solution" to purify the Aryan race listed the following categories for extermination: "Jews, homosexuals, Romani gypsies, the disabled, Jehovah's Witnesses, political prisoners, habitual criminals, the asocial, and immigrants" (Coates et al, 2018, p. 165).

The President of the United States from 1923 to 1929, Calvin Coolidge, embraced eugenics. In Coolidge's opinion, "Biological laws tell us that certain divergent people will not mix or blend...The Nordics propagate themselves successfully. With other races, the outcome shows deterioration on both sides" (Kendi, 2016, p. 321).

In 1931, Ernest Hooten authored *Up from the Ape*, which became a staple in physical anthropology courses over the next few decades. "Physical characteristics...which determine race are associated, in the main, with specific intangible and non-measurable but nevertheless real and important, temperamental and mental variations" (Kendi, 2016, p. 333).

In 1932, at the Tuskegee Institute in Macon, Alabama, a "study" involving 600 black men without their consent began (and didn't end until 1972, following exposure by the associated press).

> Syphilis harmed blacks much more than it did whites, argued syphilis expert Thomas Murrell in the *Journal of the American Medical Association* in 1910. But this theory had never been definitively proven. So in 1932, the US Public Health Service began its "Study of Syphilis in the Untreated Negro Male." Government researchers promised free medical care to 600 syphilis infected sharecroppers around Tuskegee, Alabama. They secretly withheld treatment to these men and waited for their deaths, so they could perform autopsies. Researchers wanted to confirm their hypothesis that syphilis damaged the neurological systems of Whites, while bypassing Blacks "underdeveloped" brains and damaging their cardiovascular systems instead.
>
> **Kendi (2016, p. 333)**

If you think, after reading the preceding that taking a different and more balanced look at history isn't important, consider what Lewin wrote about post-WWI Germany:

"We will have to avoid the naive belief that people 'left alone' will choose democracy. We have to avoid building our plans on 'hatred of the enemy,' but we have to also avoid building our plans on wishful thinking and blindness against reality. We should know, for instance, that we have to deal in Germany with a set-up where month after month, day after day, six to seven thousand unwanted women and children are killed in central slaughter houses in occupied territories, and where thousands of people must have grown accustomed to doing such jobs. American newspapers seem to play down such unpleasant truths probably because they wish to prevent a peace based on hatred. Actually, this procedure defies its purpose because in politics as in education a successful action has to be based on a full knowledge of reality"

(Lewin, 1943, 1997, p. 39).

Our discourse about history in the US is far from that standard. To their credit, and as proof of a much more successful reconstruction than what we managed following the civil war in the US, post-WWII Germany has set a much higher bar in terms of teaching accurately about their own past. Unfortunately, attempts to alter what is taught here in the US are sensationalized and met with bitter opposition.

If any or all of what I have written in this chapter seems like a whole new version of US history, and you are having trouble with that, try looking at it this way. Imagine if the people you identify with and love had been conquered and that the conquerors taught your children that they (the conquerors) were superior in every way. Imagine if they tried to teach you that you had been conquered for your own darn good. Do you really think you would put up with it?

Of course, some of the readers don't have to imagine that. They are living it.

We can do better. Blocking attempts to improve what is taught needlessly handcuffs the quality of our educational system and our political discourse. Frankly, it is also disrespectful to the intelligence of upcoming generations. We don't need to cling to past practice. Likewise, we don't need a retelling of history that is one-sided in the opposite direction. We need as balanced a telling of history as possible. Imperfect as it is, that has been my intention here. If you can improve it, or make suggestions, please do so.

In 1942, Ashley Montagu's *Man's Most Dangerous Myth*, in harmony with other new voices, burst on to the international scene and effectively debunked eugenics and all theories that racial superiority was based on any sort of physiology. Racists had to turn to other explanations of racial superiority, such as the inadequacy of the black family, or that there is already "an even playing field" and it is completely up to the individual whether they succeed or fail.

Sadly, the story of why whites are better changed without skipping a beat. When people are more worried about their own situation than about facts, it is easy enough to find "evidence" to support one's beliefs. The same behavior has been used to justify a multitude of sins, by which I mean the dominance of one type of group over another. More often than not, that short-sighted dominance has divided groups that could have a common cause, such as the worthy experiment of working toward social stability and prosperity for all.

Even more sadly, the myth of race, although thoroughly debunked by science, has morphed nonetheless into other bigoted forms including "replacement theory," which as I was finishing this manuscript was part of the diseased thinking that led a young man to go on a rampage in a grocery store in Buffalo. As long as a critical mass of our society clings to the myth of race, and to the related belief that races are in competition with each other, racial violence is bound to occur.

SEXISM AND OTHER FORMS OF PREJUDICE

The division and dominance of one group over another has certainly been true of women and men. As we have seen during the history of England, poor men were for the most part more than willing to be lord and master of women, even if they had nothing else going for them. The same sexism was transplanted to the colonies.

During the battle over civil rights immediately following the civil war, women fought to leverage the moment to extend voting rights to women. In 1866, Susan B. Anthony and Elizabeth Cady Stanton joined with black male suffragists in founding the American Equal Rights Association (AERA). Unfortunately, racism reared its ugly head in this attempted collaboration. At the first annual meeting of the AERA in 1877, Stanton said, "I would not trust a black man with my rights; degraded, oppressed, himself, he would be more despotic...than ever our Saxon rulers are...(while the) elevation of women (would) develop the Saxon race into a higher and nobler life and thus, by law of attraction, to lift all races" (Kendi, 2016, p. 241). It became clear that the white women present, while keen for suffrage for themselves, harbored mixed feelings about suffrage for black men and made no effort to include black women. To make things worse, many of the men present opposed women's suffrage. George Downing, a black activist and businessman, spoke of "women's obedience being God's will" (Kendi, 2016, p. 246). This view was shared widely at the time by white men. When the 15th Amendment only extended suffrage to black men, the white leaders of the women's suffrage movement opposed it. The AERA, a brief moment of potential unity, quickly fell apart.

As Sojourner Truth later noted:

> There is a great stir about colored men getting their rights, but not a word about the colored woman; and if colored men get their rights, and not colored women theirs, you see the colored men will be masters over the women, and it will be just as bad as it was before. So I am for keeping this thing going while things are stirring; because if we wait till it is still, it will take a great while to get it going again…
>
> I am above eighty years old; it is about time for me to be going. I have been fourty years a slave and fourty years free, and would be here fourty years more to have equal rights for all. I suppose I am kept here because something remains for me to do. I suppose I am yet to help break the chain. I have done a great deal of work; as much as a man, but did not get so much pay. I used to work in the field and bind grain, keeping with the cradler; but men doing no more, got twice as much pay…I suppose I am about the only colored woman that goes about to speak for the rights of the colored women. I want to keep the things stirring, now that the ice is cracked….
>
> **Zinn (1980, p. 197)**

Stir she did, and well, but civil rights for women was a long time coming.

When women, with the passage of the 19th Amendment, won the right to vote in 1920 (Zinn, 1980, p. 375), black women in the South, Latinos in the Southwest, and others were still barred from voting by Jim Crow laws and other forms of institutional racism.

A detailed analysis of sexism is beyond the scope of this text but suffice it to say that sexism remains a plague upon the human race. Violence against women, sexual harassment, institutional barriers, wage disparities such as mentioned by Sojourner Truth, and microaggressions such as men talking over women or taking credit for their work and ideas are so commonplace that it boggles the mind. The evidence that education for girls and women-run businesses increase everyone's prosperity is overwhelming, making it even more foolish that men intentionally hold women back. The training methods in Chapter 13 have helped many women find their voice in male-dominated workplaces. The need for action to change institutional sexism remains. The convergence of racism and sexism puts women and girls in the cross-hairs of more abuse than any other humans on the planet.

The same dynamics apply to any group that is discriminated against for any reason. As Historian Ibram Kendi put it, "...to say something is wrong with a group is to say something is inferior about that group" (Kendi, 2016, p. 5). Once you make the choice of saying "those people aren't like us," you are on the same slippery slope that has been taken by anyone who is prejudiced against you for whatever reason. Not going down that path and not staying silent when others are doing so takes courage and discipline, but it is the only path that makes sense. Bigotry toward any group by people who oppose bigotry is hypocrisy that weakens the moral position and damages potential coalitions.

My fellow men, if you value whatever civil rights you enjoy, don't be hypocritical. Support full equality for women.

The LGBTQ community has likewise faced and continues to face discrimination and hatred. The medical profession as recently as the early 1900s deemed their behavior as resulting from eugenic "defects," which justified commitments and incarcerations. "Treatment" consisted of "prefrontal lobotomies, electroshock, castration, and sterilization" (Coates et al, 2018, p. 166). Again, a thorough history of discrimination against LGBTQ is beyond the scope of this book, but standing against further discrimination is part of the gauntlet hurled down in Chapter 7.

The US has not only gone down the path of prejudice we have encouraged and institutionalized it time and again.

Returning to immigration, we find clear examples of the many forms of racism practiced by the US. The Statue of Liberty was completed in 1886, with its famous inscription, "Give me your tired, your poor, your huddled masses yearning to breathe free." The huddled masses came, with 14 million arriving between 1900 and 1920. With "science" explaining that non-whites were "undesirables," anti-immigration sentiment in Washington, D. C., and elsewhere grew. Congress in the 1920s passed a new set of immigration laws setting quotas for who could enter the country: "The quotas favored Anglo-Saxons, kept out black and yellow people, limited severely the coming of Latins, Slavs, and Jews. No African country could send more than 100 people; 100 was the limit for China, for Bulgaria, for Palestine; 34,007 could come from England or Northern Ireland, but only 3,845 from Italy; 51,227 from Germany, but only 124 from Lithuania; 28,567 from the Irish Free State, but the only 2,248 from Russia" (Zinn, 1980, p. 3737).

By that time, at least on immigration policy, the once despised and downtrodden Irish were favored, the Italians were not. Contempt toward Italians and Jews was widespread. Neither were considered "white." As future President Theodore Roosevelt put the sentiment held by many, the lynching of several Italian immigrants in New Orleans was "rather a good thing," and he boasted that he had said as much at a dinner with "…various dago diplomats…all wrought up by the lynching" (Zinn, 1980, p. 293). Such was the discrimination of the immigration system, which severely limited Jewish immigration even once the US had knowledge of the holocaust. Kurt Lewin was allowed to immigrate only because he found a university to sponsor him. Harvard and Stanford turned him down. In the process, imminent psychologist E. G. Boring of Harvard wrote to Stanford professor L. Terman that "In the first place Lewin is a Jew…also the wife is a Jew and their child, who has figured in some of the movies of Lewin's child psychology, is a perfect little yid" (Crosby, 2021a, p. 25). Despite years of effort and money spent, he was unable to get his mother out of Germany. She died in a death camp.

By the 1900s, there were no free spaces left for Native Americans, who had been herded onto the reservations and treated like dogs. The last major military action in the genocide of the indigenous peoples of North America had taken place on December 29, 1890, by members of the 7th Calvary, the same unit that had been defeated in a rare indigenous victory at the Battle of Little Big Horn in 1876. Using the excuse of an "incident" while they were disarming the group that was legally camped at Wounded Knee, South Dakota, on the Pine Ridge Indian Reservation, the 7th Calvary attacked and slaughtered 300 men, women, and children. The "Indian Wars" were over.

Mexicans and Latin Americans weren't treated much better, then or now. Tensions about immigration continue to this day at the Mexican border despite the welcome by American farmers and businesses that depend on the steady stream of low-wage legal and illegal labor from south of the border. In the Mexican-American war of 1846, a blatant war of expansion was justified by the young nation's creed of "manifest destiny,"[5] and the land that Mexico had taken from Native Americans was taken from the Mexicans. In 1848, young senator Abraham Lincoln explained his party's support (at the time, the Whig Party) for the war this way:

> The declaration that we have always opposed the war is true or false, according as one may understand the term "oppose the war." If to say "the war was unnecessarily and unconstitutionally commenced by the president" be opposing the war, then the Whigs have very generally opposed it...The marching an army into the midst of a peaceful Mexican settlement, frightening the inhabitants away, leaving their growing crops and other property to destruction, to you may appear a perfectly amiable, peaceful, unprovoking procedure; but it does not appear so to us...But if when the war had begun, and had become the cause of the country, the giving of our money and our blood, in common with yours, was support of the war, it is not true that we have always opposed the war. With few individual exceptions, you have constantly had our votes here for all the necessary supplies....
>
> **Zinn (1980, p. 151)**

The war, as Lincoln and most historians agree, was obviously provoked by the US. It resulted in a huge acquisition of territory, California and Texas, as well as parts of Colorado, Arizona, New Mexico, Utah, and Nevada.[6] Mexicans already living in the region were granted US citizenship, including the protection of property rights. Instead, by the 19th century, most had been deprived of their land. As was all too familiar in US history, the power of law enforcement was used against Mexican-American landowners, instead of protecting them (Library of Congress, pp. 1).

An idea emerged from opposition to the war with Mexico, an idea important to the battle for equality. To be sure, the idea had been acted on by slaves and by all who opposed oppression, but the articulation was important nonetheless. It was the idea of civil disobedience. As Howard Zinn tells it:

> The war had hardly begun, the summer of 1846, when a writer, Henry David Thoreau, who lived in Concord, Massachusetts, refused to pay his Massachusetts poll tax, denouncing the Mexican war. He was put in jail. His friends, without his consent, paid his tax, and he was released. Two years later he gave a lecture, "*Resistance to Civil Government*," which was then printed as an essay, "*Civil Disobedience*": "It is not desirable to cultivate the respect for the law, so much as for the right...Law never made men a whit more just; and, by means of their respect for it, even the well-disposed

are daily made the agents of injustice.".…His friend and fellow writer, Ralph Waldo Emerson, agreed, but thought it futile to protest. When Emerson visited Thoreau in jail and asked, "What are you doing in there?" it was reported that Thoreau replied, "What are you doing out there?"

Zinn (1980, p. 154)

A beautiful moment in the history of civil disobedience. The question remains one well worth asking today.

In 1963, Martin Luther King Jr. was "in there." In a letter to his jailers, he expressed the importance of civil disobedience this way, "We know through painful experience that freedom is never voluntarily given by the oppressor; it must be demanded by the oppressed…For years now I have heard the word 'Wait!' It rings in the ear of every Negro with piercing familiarity. This 'Wait' has almost always meant 'Never.' We must come to see, with one of our distinguished jurists, that 'justice too long delayed is justice denied'.…One has not only a legal but a moral responsibility to obey just laws. Conversely, one has a moral responsibility to disobey unjust laws. I would agree with St. Augustine that 'an unjust law is no law at all'" (Carson, 1998, p. 191).

Meanwhile, another portion of humanity grouped together arbitrarily by physical appearances, ethnicity, and place of origin, and then viciously discriminated against, were the Chinese. During the California gold rush of 1848–1852, Chinese immigration was welcomed to provide labor on major construction projects and the transcontinental railroad. By 1862, racism against Chinese led to the "Act to Protect Free White Labor against Competition with Chinese Coolie Labor, and to Discourage the Immigration of the Chinese into the State of California" otherwise known as "The Anti-Cooley Act" (Coates et al, 2018, p. 234). Chinese were segregated, resulting in the creation of what came to be known as "Chinatowns," and any significant Chinese immigration was not allowed again until 1943.

Hostility against "Asians," which even now is the official US government racial designation for anyone from India to the Pacific Ocean, is barely below the surface today as the uptick in Asian hate crimes during the pandemic proves and has been on display during three of our major wars.

In 1897, Theodore Roosevelt was itching for a fight: "In strict confidence…I should welcome almost any war, for I think this country needs one" (Zinn, 1980, p. 290). He soon got one that would make him a rising political star, the Spanish-American War. Begun like so many wars on dubious circumstances, wherein the US Battleship Maine blew up in Havana harbor due to causes that have never been explained, Roosevelt and the Rough Riders easily defeated Spain in Cuba. In 1898, along with control of Cuba, the terms of surrender included the annexation of Hawaii, Puerto Rico, Wake Island, Guam, and the Philippines.

Despite the "manifest destiny" of the US, a funny thing happened in the Philippines. Many of the residents didn't appreciate the implementation of President McKinley's vision: "...there was nothing left for us to do but to take them all and educate the Filipinos, and uplift and civilize and Christianize them, and by God's grace do the very best we could by them, as our fellow men for whom Christ also died" (Zinn, 1980, p. 305). This must have been particularly puzzling to any Filipinos who heard it as they had already been a Catholic and fully "Christianized" nation since the Spaniards arrived in 1565.

In 1899, a full-scale revolt against US rule was underway, which lasted three long and bloody years. What conduct on the part of the new US colonial administrators led to an insurrection that took three years to control? Perhaps these words in a letter home from a US soldier once the fighting started are a clue: "Our fighting blood was up, and we all wanted to kill 'niggers'...this shooting human beings beats rabbit hunting all to pieces" (Zinn, 1980, p. 307). Racism and racial violence were running amok in the US at the time. It should be no surprise that it went with us wherever we chose to go. As one correspondent stationed in Manilla described in 1901:

> The present war is no bloodless opera bouffe engagement; our men have been relentless, have killed to exterminate men, women, children, prisoners and captives, active insurgents and suspected people from lads of 10 up, the idea prevailing that the Filipino as such was little better than a dog...Our soldiers have pumped salt water into men to make them talk, and have taken prisoners people who held up their hands and peacefully surrendered. An hour later, without an atom of evidence to show that they were even *insurrectos*, stood them on a bridge and shot them down one by one, to drop into the water below and float down, as examples to those who found their bullet-loaded corpses.
>
> **Zinn (1980, p. 308)**

Racism helps people close their eyes to the inhumanity of their actions. The leadership of the country openly embraced that racism at the time. Senator Albert Beverage said this on the floor of the US Senate: "Mr. President the times call for candor. The Philippines are ours forever...

My own belief is that there are not 100 men among them who compre-
hend what Anglo-Saxon self-government even means, and there are over
5,000,000 people to be governed. It has been charged that our conduct of
the war has been cruel. Senators, it has been the reverse…Senators must
remember that we are not dealing with Americans or Europeans. We are
dealing with Orientals" (Zinn, 1980, p. 306).

The same racism directed toward "Orientals" was openly present during
WWII and again in Vietnam. Throughout the history of war, the "othering"
of the enemy was encouraged to make killing easier. During WWII, one of
the rare wars where the US was actually attacked and where the opponent
was truly the aggressor, the "othering" was turned on US citizens of Japanese
descent; 110,000 men, women, and children were rounded up and placed in
internment camps for years, losing much of their land and possessions in the
process. "White" US citizens of German descent faced no such persecution.

Manifestations of prejudice, both individual and institutional, in US
history are legion. As asserted in the DEI framework, any prejudice begets
more prejudice. We will return to that theme in Chapter 7. Now let us consider the myth of "the even playing field."

NOTES

1. A commitment held by the Samish tribe in Western Washington with whom I've
   had the honor of working.
2. Which I appreciated then and now! It's what I and millions of other boys (and who
   knows how many girls) wanted that year, and it will always be a fond childhood
   memory even though I now see it in a different sociological light.
3. Native Americans faired less well under Grant, who continued the policy of
   "removal" and believed in "assimilation." To his credit, he appointed the first Native
   American to head the Indian Bureau, Ely Samuel Parker, in 1869, and he cracked
   down on corruption and grift in the bureau.
4. The original KKK was crushed, but like Hydra, offshoots of the Klan quickly
   popped up, such as the White League, the Red Shirts, and the Knights of the White
   Camellia. Unlike the Klan, these groups organized in public, and some took public positions that included removing the Republican Party from power (Chernow,
   2017, p. 760).
5. John O'Sullivan, the editor of *The Democratic Review*, had coined the rallying cry
   of American imperialism that stuck into the early 1900s with this passage: "Our
   manifest destiny to overspread the continent allotted by Providence for the free
   development of our yearly multiplying millions" (Zinn, 1980, p. 149).
6. In 1854, the US acquired the remainder of Arizona and New Mexico from the
   Mexican government for $10 million.

6

Accuracy about Privilege & the Playing Field

A blue-collar white man I thought I had established "we feeling" with (mutual respect) looked me in the eye recently and said, "the playing field is even." I almost fell out of my chair, as I had only heard those words from DEI gurus, like DiAngelo, as an example of "microaggression." I challenged the idea, but I didn't have much time and I doubt I changed his thinking.

By now, if you have read the history portion of this book and if you grant it any credence, you must know that blacks have been systematically beaten down in the US during the time thus far covered, which brings us into the 1950s. I was born in 1959. The overt racism of the time was still stunning. The task now is to examine how racism in the US has positioned most blacks compared to whites and whether barriers continue to be placed in the way of racial equity. My hypothesis, which I believe is easily supported by facts, is that if US society was a playing field and blacks were on a football team playing whites, the game would start with a score at least as lopsided as 50–0. Despite that some blacks succeed, but the majority lose.

The uneven playing field, if you are willing to consider it as such, is based on multiple barriers for blacks and privileges for whites. The barriers used to be obvious, announced brazenly by signs proclaiming "whites only" or "negroes need not apply." These days the barriers, partially because of tireless legal defense against overt racism by organizations such as the ACLU and the NAACP, have become more and more stealthy.

Believe it or not, the interstate freeway system, the vast network of concrete that connects the nation, was built with racist intent in most

DOI: 10.4324/9781003335689-8

communities. Starting in 1956, the construction of the highway system is an important example of how racism can be enacted on a massive scale and yet be kept mostly under the radar of public consciousness. A primary source of what became the national approach to the design and construction of the system was New York City's "construction coordinator" Robert Moses. "Our categorical imperative is action to clear the slums," Moses said in a 1959 speech. "We can't let minorities dictate that this century-old chore will be put off another generation or finally abandoned." Moses, who was also the chairman of the New York City Slum Clearance Committee, said that the highway construction must "go right through cities and not around them." Two of the city's main arteries, the Cross-Bronx and Brooklyn-Queens Expressways, did just that, cutting through the heart of the minority populated Bronx and Red Hook neighborhoods (Evans, 2021, pp. 6).

The blueprint was followed nationwide, consistently plowing through predominately black neighborhoods, disrupting minority communities, or being built intentionally as barriers between minorities and whites. Homes were destroyed and those that were left standing suffered from declining property values. Suburban regions connected by or created by the freeway system saw their values go up. In one fell swoop, which had nothing to do with "merit," net worth went up or down depending on what end of the color spectrum you were sitting on. As NFL commentator Chris Berman would say, just based on the racism in the construction of the interstate freeway system, "Come on man!" The score is already Whites 50, Blacks 0, and the game hasn't even started!

In St. Paul, MN, for example, "...the construction of a vast roadway system cut through the Black neighborhood of Rondo in St. Paul, Minnesota, a mixed-class community known for its thriving cultural life, social clubs and integrated schools. Despite neighborhood resistance, an estimated 600 families lost their homes, and 300 businesses were shuttered when I-94 divided the community.

'It wasn't just physical – it ripped a culture, it ripped who we were,' Minnesota governor Tim Walz later commented. 'It was an indiscriminate act that said this community doesn't matter...this convenient place to put a highway so we can cross over this place and go from the city out to the suburbs'" (Evans, 2021, pp. 10).

According to the *LA Times*, more than one million people lost their homes nationwide. "In Nashville, civic officials added a curve to Interstate 40 in

1967 to avoid a white community in favor of knocking down hundreds of homes and businesses in a prominent Black neighborhood. Highway planners in Birmingham, Ala., did the same thing when routing Interstate 59.

After Ku Klux Klan leaders and others destroyed the Greenwood neighborhood of Tulsa, Okla., a century ago in the nation's deadliest race massacre, residents quickly rebuilt the commercial area renowned as 'Black Wall Street.' But the neighborhood <u>was demolished for good</u> when Interstate 244 and U.S. 75 were built through its center in 1971" (Dillon and Poston, 2021, pp. 2). Despicable.

In LA, the California Highway Commission put the freeway right through the affluent black neighborhood of Berkely Square, completely demolishing it. It was a special neighborhood for many reasons, not the least of which for the battle for civil rights that had occurred there just a few years prior. A common practice in the US was racially specific "covenants" written into deeds, assuring "...no Blacks, no Jews..." (Chang et al, 2021, pp. 15). Black homeowners had thrived there after winning a court case in 1945 that struck down the covenants locally and influenced a 1948 Supreme Court ruling (based on the 14th Amendment), in Shelley v Kraemer, which struck them down throughout the US.

NPR describes the once proud neighborhood: "Berkeley Square was part of a larger neighborhood called Sugar Hill, which was named after a wealthy Black section in Harlem. By the 1940s, Sugar Hill was home to some of the most prominent figures of Black Los Angeles – doctors, entrepreneurs, oil barons, even Hollywood stars like 'Gone With the Wind's' Hattie McDaniel. On screen, she may have played a housekeeper or an enslaved person, but here in Sugar Hill, she hosted extravagant soirees in her sprawling mansion where people like Duke Ellington and Ethel Waters would perform" (Chang et al, 2021, pp. 13).

Within a decade of their court victory, so they could own homes, their homes were gone. All that remains is the Santa Monica Freeway.

Between 1956 and 1972, a million minority-owned homes were destroyed in a land where minority homeownership was rare. The playing field, uneven as it already was, tilted like a landslide for one million families 50 short years ago.

Land has been a source of wealth since the dawn of time. Land's modern translation, homeownership, is the most widespread source of increased net worth. It is important then that land has been the arena where the playing field has been and continues to be uneven.

Imagine how you would react if your land was stolen at gunpoint. That was how this nation started. True reparations would include giving back a bunch of it to the indigenous peoples it was stolen from.

Setting that aside (as we are likely to do), let's return to 1865. Sherman granted a small portion of Southern land to the ex-slaves who had produced much of the nation's wealth. As noted, President Andrew Johnson gave it back to the previous white slave-holding owners. The same year Pennsylvania Senator Thaddeus Stevens proposed the redistribution of 400 million acres from the wealthiest 10 percent of Southern landowners. The proposal, which would have gone a long way toward leveling the playing field, was defeated (Kendi, 2016, p. 236).

Instead, black farmers in the South eked out a living, more often than not to be caught in a web of a system rigged to deprive them of their land and drive them further into poverty. Historian Ta-Nehisi Coates relates this all too typical true story: "When Clyde Ross was still a child, Mississippi authorities claimed his father owed $3,000 in back taxes. The elder Ross could not read. He did not have a lawyer. He did not know anyone at the local courthouse. He could not expect the police to be impartial. Effectively, the Ross family had no way to contest the claim and no protection under the law. The authorities seized the land. They seized the buggy. They took the cows, hogs, and mules. And so, for the upkeep of separate but equal, the entire Ross family was reduced to sharecropping.

This was hardly unusual. In 2001, the Associated Press published a three-part investigation into the theft of black-owned land stretching back to the antebellum period. The series documented some 406 victims and 24,000 acres of land valued at tens of millions of dollars. The land was taken through means ranging from legal chicanery to terrorism. 'Some of the land taken from black families has become a country club in Virginia,' the AP reported, as well as 'oil fields in Mississippi' and 'a baseball spring training facility in Florida'" (Coates, 2014, pp. 5).

Ross grew up, fought in WWII, joined the Great Migration's escape from the south, got red-lined by the FHA, and swindled when he turned to unscrupulous lenders. Again, his story was not unusual.

Fast forward to the lending practices of the New Deal, "The Roosevelt administration's new homeowners loan corporation (HOLC) and the Federal Housing Administration (FHA) handed black residents the Old Deal when these agencies drew 'color coded' maps, coloring black neighborhoods in red as undesirable. The maps caused brokers to deny residents new thirty-year year mortgages and prevented black renters from purchasing a home and acquiring wealth" (Kendi, 2016, p. 337). The practice of "red-lining," which greatly inhibited lending to minorities, continued until the mid-60s. White homeownership during the same period boomed. "In 1930, only 30 percent of Americans owned their own homes; by 1960, more than 60 percent were homeowners" (Coates, 2014, pp. 89). *Institutional government supported racism* regarding lending practically tipped the playing field upside down.

Another big reason why white homeownership boomed was the GI Bill, passed by Congress in 1944. Instead of federal oversight, the administration of the funds was placed in the hands of state and local governments. In the segregated South, that was (surprise, surprise) bad news for black veterans. Besides simply being denied benefits by all-white veteran administration officials, black veterans, some of who had only recently braved the German barriers at Normandy, were confronted by a maze of obstacles at home. The segregated school system meant there were not enough black colleges to serve all the veterans who wanted to apply. GI Bill-funded job training could only be qualified for if you had an employer willing to hire you, and because of job discrimination, jobs for blacks were few and far between. Housing loans for veterans, which created a huge post-war housing boom, were administered by banks, and most banks refused to lend to African-Americans (Coates et al, 2018, p. 138). A bill created for all veterans became one more huge advantage for whites. The 50–0 score seems way understated.

Did white veterans deserve those benefits? Of course! Did black veterans deserve them just as much? Absolutely! But that isn't what happened, and now we are talking about forces very recently tilting the playing field further into the uneven direction.

When the government wasn't in the way, bankers and realtors have been happy to pitch in. "As late as 1950, the National Association of Real Estate Boards' code of ethics warned that 'a Realtor should never be instrumental in introducing into a neighborhood...any race or nationality, or any individuals whose presence will clearly be detrimental to property values.' A 1943 brochure specified that such potential undesirables might include madams, bootleggers, gangsters – and 'a colored man of means who was giving his children a college education and thought they were entitled to live among whites'" (Coates, 2014, pp. 90).

Lack of homeownership and lack of access to high-value land restricts wealth: "The income gap between black and white households is roughly the same today as it was in 1970. Patrick Sharkey, a sociologist at New York University, studied children born from 1955 through 1970 and found that 4 percent of whites and 62 percent of blacks across America had been raised in poor neighborhoods. A generation later, the same study showed, virtually nothing had changed...

Black families, regardless of income, are significantly less wealthy than white families. The Pew Research Center estimates that white households are worth roughly 20 times as much as black households, and that whereas only 15 percent of whites have zero or negative wealth, more than a third of blacks do...

And just as black families of all incomes remain handicapped by a lack of wealth, so too do they remain handicapped by their restricted choice of neighborhood. Black people with upper-middle-class incomes do not generally live in upper-middle-class neighborhoods. Sharkey's research shows that black families making $100,000 typically live in the kinds of neighborhoods inhabited by white families making $30,000" (Coates, 2014, pp. 36).

The same article by Coates documents the history of racist behavior in white Chicago neighborhoods, such as a mob of thousands gathering at a black doctor's house soon after he moved in, pelting the house with rocks, and setting the garage on fire. The doctor moved out.

Without homeownership, there is no equity, the biggest source of household net worth. Without homeownership in neighborhoods where equity increases, homeownership has a diminished impact on wealth. "In 2019 the typical Black family had just over one-tenth the net worth of the typical White family, in part because of the value of their homes. The gulf in homeownership also persists: About 74% of White families own a home; among Black families, it's 44%" (Robison and Buhayar, 2021, pp. 26).

Racism in real estate has been so bad that the National Association of Realtors issued an apology in 2020. But discrimination continues. An undercover investigation conducted in 2016 and 2017 documented "steering" of applicants into segregated neighborhoods and other racist practices by realtors: "One Long Island real estate agent told a black man that houses in a predominantly white neighborhood were too expensive for his budget. But the same agent showed houses in the same neighborhood to a white man with the same amount of money to spend.

Another real estate agent warned a white home buyer about gang violence in a mostly minority neighborhood, but she appeared to steer a black buyer with a comparable budget toward homes in that neighborhood.

All told, real estate agents treated people of color unequally 40 percent of the time compared with white people when they searched for homes on Long Island, one of the most racially segregated suburbs in the United States" (Ferre-Sadurni, 2019, pp. 1).

The same investigation caught realtors refusing to show homes unless black buyers were prequalified, yet showing homes to white buyers with similar financial assets and no prequalification.

Speaking of prequalifications, another recent study concludes that "Nationally, loan applicants of color were 40%-80% more likely to be denied than their white counterparts. In certain metro areas the disparity was greater than 250%" (Martinez and Kirchner, 2021, pp. 1). The study goes on to claim that: "…we found that lenders were 40 percent more likely to turn down Latino applicants for loans, 50 percent more likely to deny Asian/Pacific Islander applicants, and 70 percent more likely to deny Native American applicants than similar White applicants. Lenders were 80 percent more likely to reject Black applicants than similar White applicants. These are national rates" (Martinez et al, 2021, pp. 11).

As if all the above isn't enough, there is also evidence of bias during appraisals. A 2020 article in the NY Times puts it this way: "Abena and Alex Horton wanted to take advantage of low home-refinance rates brought on by the coronavirus crisis. So in June, they took the first step in that process, welcoming a home appraiser into their four-bedroom, four-bath ranch-style house in Jacksonville, Fla.

The Hortons live just minutes from the Ortega River, in a predominantly white neighborhood of 1950s homes that tend to sell for $350,000 to $550,000. They had expected their home to appraise for around $450,000, but the appraiser felt differently, assigning a value of $330,000. Ms. Horton, who is Black, immediately suspected discrimination.

The couple's bank agreed that the value was off and ordered a second appraisal. But before the new appraiser could arrive, Ms. Horton, a lawyer, began an experiment: She took all family photos off the mantle. Instead, she hung up a series of oil paintings of Mr. Horton, who is white, and his grandparents that had been in storage. Books by Zora Neale Hurston and Toni Morrison were taken off the shelves, and holiday photo cards sent by friends were edited so that only those showing white families were left on display. On the day of the appraisal, Ms. Horton took the couple's 6-year-old son on a shopping trip to Target, and left Mr. Horton alone at home to answer the door.

The new appraiser gave their home a value of $465,000–a more than 40 percent increase from the first appraisal…

Even in mixed-race and predominantly white neighborhoods, Black homeowners say, their homes are consistently appraised for less than those of their neighbors, stymying their path toward building equity and further perpetuating income inequality in the United States" (Kamin, 2020. pp. 1).

In other words, the playing field when it comes to generational home-ownership is basically a cliff, and the playing field when it comes to securing and getting value from current homeownership is still tilted at a steep angle and covered with ice.

Want more evidence that discrimination is happening now? As mentioned in Chapter 4, one needs to look no further than the COVID-19 relief Payroll Protection Loans of 2020. Covered by the federal government so there was *no risk to the lender,* and hence no reason to be stingy toward anyone, black applicants nonetheless found it much harder to secure the loans than white applicants. Refused by lenders who made the loans on a more personal basis, like small banks, black applicants had to turn to so-called financial technology companies (or fin-techs), where awareness of race was not part of the process (Cowley, 2021, pp. 1). I've seen enough of it first-hand, as indicated in Chapter 4, to find such allegations completely credible.

Imagine being a child at the wrong end of the uneven playing field. Can you overcome it? Of course. Is your environment a variable? You bet your sweet bippy it is. Do you have space and privacy when you need it? How about wi-fi and equipment? Are you surrounded by chaos or relatively calm and supportive adults? Are people helping you advance, or are you on your own? Children living in poverty, which is much more likely in the US if they are black, have significantly more barriers to overcome. They deserve access to the same tools that other kids have. They deserve a society where the adults are doing the right thing. If they fail, it is partially on them, but it is mostly on us.

Instead in many ways, we are going backwards. Affirmative action was an attempt to put a finger in the dike of barriers facing African-Americans, women, and other minorities. Granted, if you don't think the playing field is uneven after everything we have already covered, then nothing else is likely to convince you. But the Kennedy administration, back in 1961, believed that "affirmative steps" had to be taken "to realize more fully the national policy of non-discrimination" (Coates et al, 2018, p. 149). Affirmative action only effects government agencies and private workplaces with large government contracts and only requires action "... where discrimination has been historically documented, and where White women and people of color continue to be excluded in numbers disproportional to their representation in the population" (Coates et al, 2018, p. 149). Affirmative action has been resisted as "reverse racism" from the beginning, and the simplification of quotas to increase representation was struck down by the Supreme Court in the 1972 case of *Regents of the University of California v Bakke*. The claim that "the playing field is already even" is part of the lament. The impact is that the Equal Employment Opportunity Commission (EEOC) has gradually been declawed, and action is rarely taken. In 2016, the EEOC had a growing backlog of 76,000 unresolved cases (Coates et al, 2018, p. 149). Meanwhile, the percentage of black students in California public universities has fallen even though the percentage of black high school graduates has been on the rise (Peele and Willis, 2020, pp. 26).

Here, we have one of the only attempts in the history of this country to level the playing field, being undermined by the myth that it is already level. The cold facts don't support the myth. Furthermore, to give people a chance that haven't had a chance, the mission of equity must matter or those who have already had opportunities will always get the next job because they will have more experience. That might not be "fair" to everyone, but where has that cry been throughout US history? The current system is far from fair, and the degree of unfairness that comes from sticking with the intent of affirmative action is nothing compared to the systemic oppression we are trying to overcome. If you are truly worried about fairness, then you will fight for equity and sleep better at night knowing you are helping move the world toward that even playing field we have heard so much about. Instead, attempts to address unequal access to the best schools are being blocked to this very day, with no alternatives being offered.

We will return to the related topic of hiring and promotions in Chapter 14.

Meanwhile, having overcome every other barrier, picture the young black student, having graduated from college, sending a letter to the faculty in a graduate school program they are considering. In a study checking for bias in responses, the same letters were sent, only the names were changed. The 6500 faculty in the study, *regardless of their own ethnicity or gender*, were much more responsive to white male prospects than to any others, "particularly in higher paying disciplines and private institutions" (Milkman et al, 2012, pp. 1). Wow. Even African-American professors in the study were biased against African-American youth *applying to doctoral programs*. If these young people haven't already proven themselves by earning masters degrees, what in heaven's name do they have to do?

That is a stunning example of how confusing and seductive racism and sexism are for everyone involved.

In a similar study of job applicants, again using the same applications but changing the names, those "with white names needed to send about 10 resumes to get one callback; those with African-American names needed to send around 15 resumes to get one callback" (Francis, 2003 pp. 1). In other words, it took 33% more effort for African-Americans to get considered. Other studies have documented similar and even wider gaps. If their ethnicity is a barrier to even getting interviewed, it's not a big leap to imagine their ethnicity being a barrier to getting hired.

And there are more barriers to an even playing field happening to this very day!

Here's a partial list for the curious:

Environmental racism (including how polluting industries are located near low-income residential areas and are even more likely near black neighborhoods no matter what their socio-economic status) (Ramirez, 2021, pp. 20);

Racism in healthcare (go back to the Tuskegee "experiment" for one example);

Racism in government handouts (since the beginning, when domestic and agricultural workers were excluded from social security, to the present, when the majority of SNAP recipients are white and black farmers have to fight to get crumbs from the billons in farm subsidies handed out annually and during covid) (Gaines, 2020).

The list goes on.

Let us narrow our focus and integrate the concept of "privilege" into the conversation. The concept of "white privilege" can easily invoke defensive responses if not thought through carefully. Many "whites" have worked themselves up from poverty and take pride in keeping themselves from slipping backwards in a system that can be cold and unpredictable. I personally am a preacher's kid. There was no family property or wealth handed down through the generations. My grandfather was an hourly laborer on the railroad near Pittsburgh. My grandmother was a homemaker. They lost their home during the depression. I have worked hard all my life, always bringing a high standard to what I do, and I have still been laid off three times, and still lost my shirt during The Great Recession (and to add insult to injury, as a consultant when it started, I didn't qualify for any unemployment benefits even though my income dropped to zero). I can understand people saying, "What privilege? No one has ever helped me!"

But the individual experience, challenging as it may have been at times, isn't the whole story. Thinking systemically, there is truth to the notion that a rising tide lifts all boats. In the history of this nation, drenched as it is in racism, a rising white tide to a large extent has lifted all white boats. My grandfather, a good, loving, and hardworking man, had a job in an industry where "Negroes Need Not Apply." That was white privilege, not created by him, but he and the family benefited from it nonetheless. The railroads near Pittsburgh thrived in conjunction with the steel industry, which, as we saw in the last chapter, thrived on the brutal re-enslavement of black men in the mines of the South. The prosperity of the Northern working class depended on the same, not to mention on access to land, to FHA loans, etc.

Born in 1959, I spent several childhood years in fully segregated Nashville, Tennessee. My father, a United Methodist Minister, was far from racist, fighting for equity all his life. In 1963, dad confronted the citizens of Wausau, Wisconsin, where we lived prior to Nashville, when they asked him to speak about the "problem" of blacks moving into town and dropping their property values. There were no black homeowners in Wausau at the time. This is what dad said according to the local newspaper: "When freedom is denied to anyone, it is denied to me, and to you. There is no freedom for any citizen unless it is for all." He went on to say that when African-Americans move into a community, property values rise or at least stay the same. Dad continued, "When people talk about property values they're talking about our own society and those who discriminate against the Negro." The paper goes on, "The Rev. Mr. Crosby said that the Negro problem is probably not as great as the White problem. We in Wausau need to have a citizens committee set up to initiate the influx of Negros here," he said, "For if we don't do something to invite them we are really not Christians" (*Wausau Daily Herald*, 1963, p. 11). That was just one example of my father's relentless involvement in civil rights and antiracism. During our Nashville years, he had black friends and their families over for dinner, even though we received hostile phone calls for this behavior. He desegregated the church camps he ran and participated in civil rights action. At 94, he continues his antiracism advocacy to this every day, posting a letter to the editor of his local newspaper just this week as I am writing these words.

Dad and I are in agreement with the assertion that all "whites" in the US have benefited from "white privilege." The school I went to in Nashville was far superior to the schools for black children. The images surrounding me and penetrating my developing brain said all the heroes looked like me. I could easily wear my Daniel Boone coonskin cap with pride because I looked like Daniel Boone. The home we lived in, provided by the church (dad was in charge of camping and T-groups for the National Board of Education of the United Methodist Church at the time), was charming, as was the neighborhood. We were not wealthy, but we were no doubt wealthier than the local black pastors could dream of being. Christmas was abundant, school supplies were a given. I grew up in a society where I could easily get a job. Would I have been hired by my first employer or any of my other employers and customers if I were black? I'll never know, but the odds would surely be lower. I grew up in a society where I could get a car, a home, and other types of loans and credit without much trouble. I live in a world where I can walk into almost any fancy hotel and use the bathroom without anyone questioning why I am there.

As mentioned, the convergence of whiteness and maleness gets me quick service in places where my Jamaican wife and my white female co-workers get ignored.

That's all privilege that I didn't earn nor did I ask for it, but there is no arguing about whether it is there.

And there was something else I took for granted for many years...

But first, a reminder. If you read the history section of this chapter, and you believe enough of it, then you know that the government of the colonies and subsequently the US has been engaged in the legal and violent oppression of blacks since the beginning of the nation[1].

What I took for granted was "officer friendly." What I took for granted was the idea that there were adults who dedicated their lives to protecting all good people everywhere. What I took for granted was that my country was good. I grew up proud that we were winners, that we beat the Nazis, and that we stood for democracy.

I know that there is still truth in some of that. I'm still proud that we beat the Nazis and authoritarianism at that time, but I also know my fellow citizens, especially the white men, but not only the white men, have also been the authoritarians and that far too many continue to want to be.

A white privilege was believing with good reason that if I got lost when I was little, all I had to do was find a police officer, and they would help me. If there was a crime, the obvious thing to do was to call the police. Little did I know that other kids and adults feared the police more than they feared violence within their own community. If something happened in the black side of town, the last thing anyone wanted to do was call the police. Instead, black parents give their kids "the talk." Not the one about the facts of life that all kids need, but the one about what to do if they have to deal with the police. An African-American manager at a manufacturing plant recently told me that he learned early that the only safe place was at home. "Mom taught me not to go outside unless I absolutely had to. If you were outside you might be a suspect." The recent killing of Breeona Taylor, a 26-year-old nurse who was in her bed at home when the police burst in to the wrong apartment with guns blazing, demonstrates that for many blacks even the thread of safety provided by being at home is wishful thinking.

A white privilege has been not living in what for many Americans is a police state where they or their sons are likely suspects because of their complexion. A white privilege has been not living with constant fear. Howard Thurman describes that fear like this:

> Fear is one of the persistent hounds of hell that dog the footsteps of the poor, the dispossessed, the disinherited…The ever-present fear that besets the vast poor, the economically and socially insecure, is a fear of still a different breed. It is a climate closing in; It is like the fog in San Francisco or in London…It has its roots deep in the heart of the relations between the weak and the strong…when the power and the tools of violence are on one side, the fact that there is no available and recognized protection from violence makes the resulting fear deeply terrifying.
>
> **Thurman (1976, p. 36)**

By the time you are reading this, you must know that black people are scared of dying during routine traffic stops because too many of them have been killed. Richard Pryor's comedy routines about police choke-holds were from first-hand experience. He succeeded in talking about what was taboo and making it funny, but it really wasn't. White privilege is getting pulled over less often for the same behaviors and thinking the only thing to worry about is whether or not you are going to get a ticket.

I drove a cab during the Great Recession. A friend of mine, a young man from Cameroon who was also a cab driver at the time, was pulled over in his personal vehicle in the town of Elsmere, Delaware, for "following too close." The cops searched every inch of his vehicle. They even brought in drug-sniffing dogs. My friend was in the trials for the US men's Olympic boxing team. He didn't drink. He didn't smoke. He didn't do drugs. They even reached in and searched his underwear.

Later while he and I were standing by our cabs discussing the incident in another part of Wilmington, Delaware (where we drove our cabs), a little old black lady overheard us and said, "I got pulled over for following too close in Elsmere too!"

Coincidence? Every black driver in this area knows that they are targets in the city of Elsmere.

By now, it's been almost two years since George Floyd was killed. What was unusual about that incident is not that it happened but that it got filmed. Even more unusual was that the officer who perpetrated the killing was sentenced to 22.5 years.

The protests were also unusual in their size and perseverance, especially given the pandemic. The President called for "law and order" and never spoke out against the abuse of power by law enforcement. The media on the right called the mostly peaceful protestors "rioters" over and over again. The same media called the heavily armed white crowd that surrounded the Michigan capital building "protestors." That is what black people have been putting up with since the beginning of the US.

For a long time keeping black people down was part of policing. Times have changed. It would be inaccurate to say all police are racists, just like it is inaccurate to say all whites are racist. But it is accurate to say too many of them are, and that racist actions are supported by too many government leaders and institutions. One grand jury after another has let perpetrators of violence against blacks walk free, making the George Floyd conviction all the more remarkable. Hopefully, that is a sign that the playing field of justice is taking baby steps toward becoming more fair.

Meanwhile please don't harbor any illusions that equality already exists. Here is just a small sample of recent statistics: "Young Black males were 21 times more likely to be killed by police than their White counterparts between 2010 and 2012, according to federal statistics…Black people are five times more likely to be incarcerated than Whites" (Kendi, 2016, p. 1).

Do we care about cops? Then we should make sure they do have social workers and mental health professionals assisting them in handling situations where force can and should be avoided. We should do everything we can to make certain that criminals don't have easy access to guns. We should make sure every officer is wearing a body cam. We should change the system so that municipalities are not pressuring officers to make needless traffic stops just to fund the local government.

Police work is dangerous and necessary work. I would not want to drive on a US freeway without the restraint that law enforcement places on driving behavior. Even with the threat of penalties, people are breaking the rules and driving recklessly. Imagine how drivers would behave without cops? That is just one small example of why I appreciate law enforcement, even if their presence inhibits my own freedom to speed. That curtailment of my freedom has probably saved my life.

We can simultaneously support law enforcement and do much better at holding them to the standard of "to serve and protect" for everyone. When we do, the world will be a better place for the police and for everyone else.

In sum, if the playing field is equal, ask yourself why "White American males constitute only 33% of the population. Yet, they occupy approximately

- 80% of tenured positions in higher education
- 80% of the House of Representatives
- 80-85% of the U. S. Senate
- 92% of Forbes 400 executive CEO-level positions
- 90% of public school superintendents
- 99.9% of athletic team owners
- 97.7% of U. S. presidents" (Sue, 2010, pp. 10).

If you think the answer is that the field has been and is level and white males just happen to be the best candidates for everything 90% of the time, then go stand in the corner of history and rethink your answer.

It's time to do the work required so that "white privilege" is something to study in history books, instead of a virus that continues to be far too alive in the body of our system. Let's level the playing field so that no one has to be embarrassed about advantages, and no one is held back by anything except their own efforts and abilities.

If you fear equity, get over it. Plenty of research shows that when girls get educated, for example, it creates more prosperous communities and even nations. The same applies to everybody. If we create a rising tide that is truly equal, there is no rational reason to believe that tide cannot lift all boats.

NOTE

1. If you don't believe it, please find evidence to the contrary and send it to me! Also feel free to let me know about any historical inaccuracies in my writing. That was a lot of territory to cover!

7

Any Prejudice Begets More Prejudice

If anyone still believes in racial differences, I think he is too backward and narrow. Perhaps he still does not understand man's equality and love.

Bruce Lee

Let's keep this chapter simple. My hypothesis is that we can't eliminate racism while practicing racism or any ism and expect anything but more of the same. We can't say it is ok in this context but not in that. Any such selective thinking will backfire.

Again, this framework operates on Kendi's definition of racist thinking: "My definition of a racist idea is a simple one. It is any concept that regards one racial group as inferior or superior to another racial group in any way (Kendi, 2016, p. 5)," not the more complicated definition offered by DiAngelo and others that "racism – like sexism and other forms of oppression – occurs when a racial group's prejudice is backed by legal authority and institutional control (DiAngelo, 2018, p. 20)."

It also operates on the assumption that race is socially constructed. *We are genetically one race – the human race.* As historian Nell Irvin Painter puts it, "Today most Americans envision whiteness as racially indivisible, though ethnically divided; this is the scheme anthropologists laid out in the mid-twentieth century. By this reckoning, there were only three races ('Mongoloid,' 'Negroid,' and 'Caucasoid') but countless ethnicities. Today however, biologists and geneticists…no longer believe in the physical existence of races-though they recognize the continuing power of racism (the belief that races exist, and that some are better than others)" (Painter, 2010, p. 10).

We are highly divergent even within skin shades, cultures, ethnic groups, and families.

DOI: 10.4324/9781003335689-9

I'm not any more like the next "white" person I will meet than you are like the next person of skin color similar to yours that you will meet. Although we share the same gender, I'm not identical to the man next to me. I'm definitely not the same person as my other family members (just ask them). Whether any one of us agrees with any other person on important subjects like politics, religion, racism, and sexism, is very random, unpredictable, and unlikely, even though we do tend to gravitate toward like-minded people. Lumping people together in groups and believing you know something about them is lazy, and doing the same and believing you know something negative about them is biased.

Holding such bias against a "race" is racist. It also requires holding an opinion that is based on a false hypothesis. Scientifically speaking, race simply doesn't exist. It is beyond doubt a concept that is in the eye of the beholder. Like Whoopie Goldberg seemed to do (at least until her recent snafu), do you think of Jewish people as white? Many people in the contemporary US do, but not the very people who are most attached to the concept of race, the white supremacists. From the perspective of contemporary white supremacy, Jewish people are both racially inferior and part of a vast conspiracy, hence the recent bombing of the synagogue in Pittsburgh. If you are attached to the idea of race, you and anyone who believes in white supremacy have something in common.

Painter adds, "Although science today denies race any standing as objective truth, and the U.S. census faces taxonomic meltdown, many Americans cling to race as the unschooled cling to superstition. So long as racial discrimination remains a fact of life and statistics can be arranged to support racial difference, the American belief in races will endure" (Painter, 2010, p. 11).

The current US census classifications are White, Black or African-American, American Indian or Alaska Native, Asian, and Native Hawaiian or Other Pacific Islander, or Some Other Race. Where do you fit in that categorization? Where does a person from India? How about anyone from the Middle East? How about Jesus of Nazareth? How about his fellow Jewish people?

My wife is clear that even though she gained her US citizenship, she is first and foremost "Jamaican," not "Black" (although she identifies that way at times), and certainly not "African-American." Do you think relatively light-skinned Russian, German, Italian, Polish, French, Spanish, and English people are all the same "race"? How about Brazilians? How about everyone lumped under Asian?

That last designation is a mindboggling simplification of the majority of the human population if ever there was one! Try telling a Japanese person and a Chinese person and a Filipino person that they are all the same race. Try convincing two ethnic groups in China that they are the same race.

Adding to this confusion, the concepts of ethnicity and "race" easily blur, and understandably so. Ethnicity is based on shared attributes, mostly cultural but also geographical and physical. "Race" is based mostly on physical attributes, but ignores huge differences evident to the local populations but easily overlooked by people on the outside looking in. As more than one of my Jamaican friends have said, "all white people look alike." "Asians" don't consider themselves the same as all other "Asians" (a word which in ancient Greek apparently meant "from where the sun rises") any more then far left democrats consider themselves the same as far right republicans here in the US.

What the heck is an Australian according to the US census? A Pacific Islander? The most scientifically accurate response would be if every citizen of the US checked "Some Other Race."

It is time to face facts: *race is socially constructed* (in other words "made up"). *There are no actual races.* The "white race" was made up by the Virginia upper classes to divide and control the lower classes (see Chapter 5), and racist ideas are "…any concept that regards one racial group as inferior or superior to another racial group in any way" (Kendi, 2016, p. 5).

In that light, claiming that Samuel L Jackson's advice in *Die Hard 3* to two black kids, "Never trust whitey," isn't racist is confusing and threatens to deteriorate the conversation into fighting about how to talk instead of fighting against racism itself. Such thinking by Jackson's character is biased, bigoted, and racist no matter who says it, what group they are talking about, what the power structure is, etc.

It's easy and tempting to identify with such thinking when it bucks up against a power structure, but that doesn't make it any less prejudiced. Another example is the line from the Mary Poppin's song, *Sister Suffragette*, that goes, "Though we adore men individually, we must admit that as a group they're rather stupid." That is a completely sexist line but whimsical and endearing in the context of women resisting sexism.

If racism only happens in the context of power, is there racism in my beloved Jamaica where the people in charge are predominately black? If so, is any individual or institutional action only racist if darker-skinned people are the ones committing the act? They have the power. Does racist behavior by whites count as racist there? Or does the local power structure get outweighed by the global power structure? Social science needs to apply in any society to be valid and reliable. A socially constructed concept that tries to only link racism to power doesn't hold up much better than the construct of race itself.

Has the construct of race been wielded to hold power? Absolutely. Does that excuse racism by groups that don't hold power? Not in this book. Does that mean the Palestinians can't be racist against the Israelis? Or that the Israelis can't be racist because of the historical and current racism against Judaism? Any such "Get out of jail free" card would be absurd.

Bottling people in about what is and is not racism is fighting the wrong fight. It further divides us, which is what the original creators of race were trying to do in the first place. Resist!

By the definition here, the *Die Hard* quote above is an example of racism. It is an understandable sentiment by a black American, to some extent wise, and in the context of the movie, even humorous. Thank heavens comedy can help to explore and lighten sensitive subject matter. Is it still racist even in the context of the power structure? Absolutely. Trying to say that racism isn't racism depending on the circumstances defies common sense even though it is accepted in many sociological circles. Such a claim complicates the needed conversation more than it helps.

If one can be racist because the power structure is against them, what is to keep one from staying racist and perpetuating racism even if the power structure is eliminated? Who is going to help people tell the difference between "acceptable" racism and "unacceptable" racism?

We can do better than that. We can fight racism and prejudice without resorting to it in any way, shape, or form.

8

Social Justice Is Spiritual

Human beings are members of a whole,
In creation of one essence and soul.
If one member is afflicted with pain,
Other members uneasy will remain.
If you've no sympathy for human pain,
The name of human you cannot retain!

The Persian poet Saadi (circa 1257 AD)

Not all the important voices working to end racism are from spiritual sources, but there is no denying that some of the most influential, such as Gandhi, Howard Thurman, Martin Luther King, Jr., Desmond Tutu, and many others, drew voices from a deep spiritual well. This well reflects the original meaning of the word "religion." While there are different interpretations of the origin of that word, mythologist Joseph Campbell favored the derivation from *ligare:* "to bind, connect," probably from a prefix *re-ligare*, i.e., *re* (again) + *ligare* or "to reconnect." Interpretations that fit well with the definition of spirituality are being stated here:

Spirituality is the aspect of humanity that refers to the way individuals seek and express meaning and purpose and the way they experience their connectedness to the moment, to self, to others, to nature, and to the significant or sacred.

**Christina Puchalski, MD, Director of the George Washington
Institute for Spirituality and Health**

Or as Joseph Campbell put it, *"Tat Tvam Asi,* 'Thou art that'" (Osbon, 1991, p. 7).

DOI: 10.4324/9781003335689-10

We are one. That does not mean that racism hasn't and doesn't exist. It means that we are reclaiming ourselves by coming together and ending the foolishness that divides us. That coming together is an act of love, an act that is necessary to heal the deep wounds of humanity, an act that is balm for the spirit. That is the essence of antiracism work, and it has drawn people of faith since the beginning, as well as people of good will regardless of their attachment or lack of attachment to any particular faith.

Religion has also been used in the service of racism. We must no longer tolerate any such foolishness nor the use of religion to justify any prejudice. No faith requires it, even if proponents of faith preach it. Like Howard Thurman's grandmother, whoever you are, you are as much a child of God[1] as anyone.

That said, spirituality is deeply personal, and I am not here to preach to you. Instead, here are some quotes that seem relevant, antiracist, and inspiring:

> As the body without the spirit is dead, so faith without deeds is dead.

James (James 2:26)

> Love your neighbor as yourself.

Jesus (Mathew 22:37–22:39 and Mark 12:30–12:31)

> We have been given the duty to live in balance and harmony with each other and all living things.

Excerpt from the Mohawk version of the Haudenosaunee Thanksgiving Address which was published in 1993 and provided courtesy of the Six Nations Indian Museum and the Tracking Project.

> In a common Tibetan meditation on compassion you view all sentient beings as if they were your mother, bearing in mind that in some past life they all must have actually been your mother. This is done to arouse a sense of affection and gratitude by focusing on the person who has shown you the greatest love and compassion.

B. Alan Wallace in dialogue with the Dalai Lama (Goleman, 2003, p. 143)

> ...if you hold anything against anyone, forgive them...

Jesus (Mark 11:25)

Forgiveness liberates the soul, it removes fear. That's why it's such a powerful weapon.

Nelson Mandela

If you can find it in yourself to forgive, then you are no longer chained to the perpetrator.

Archbishop Desmond Tutu

Non-violence and forgiveness is not just an idea, but it is a way of living for me…We were taught not to hate, not to become bitter, but to believe in the philosophy and discipline of non-violence, in the way of peace, in the way of love, the way of forgiveness and reconciliation.

Congressman John Lewis (1940–2020)

In February 2009, Lewis recalled an encounter with the son of a man who had attacked him at a bus station on May 9, 1961 in Atlanta. This young man had been encouraging his father to seek out the people that he had wronged during the height of the movement, and it led them to Lewis' office. Lewis remembered, 'The father was a few years older than I am. In 1961, I was 21 years old and he was probably 24, maybe a little older. But they beat me and my seatmate and left us lying in a pool of blood at the Greyhound bus station.' Lewis recalled that the father, accompanied by his son, came to his office after so many years and asked 'Mr. Lewis will you forgive me? Do you accept my apology?' He said, 'Yes I forgive you, I accept your apology.' At this point, Lewis continued, 'the man's son started crying, he started crying and they hugged me and I hugged them both back and I started crying too, they started calling me brother and I called them brother.'

Manojlocik (2014, p. 1)

So in everything, do unto others what you would have them do unto you.

Jesus (Mathew 7:12)

The root of violence is the illusion of separation – from God, from being one with oneself and everything else, and from Being Itself. When we don't know how to consciously live out of union (which is called love), we resort to violence, fighting anything that is not like us and that we cannot control. Contemplative practice teaches us to honor differences and also realize that we are all much more than our nationality, skin color, gender, or other labels which are all aspects of the passing and thus false self. Contemplation brings us back to our True Self, who we are in God.

Richard Rohr, Franciscan Friar

An eye for eye only ends up making the whole world blind.

Mahatma Gandhi

My study of Gandhi convinced me that true pacifism is not nonresistance to evil, but nonviolent resistance to evil. Between the two positions, there is a world of difference. Gandhi resisted evil with as much vigor and power as the violent resister, but he resisted with love instead of hate. True pacifism is not unrealistic submission to evil power, as Niebuhr contends. It is rather a courageous confrontation of evil by the power of love, in the faith that it is better to be the recipient of violence than the inflictor of it, since the latter only multiplies the existence of violence and bitterness in the universe, while the former may develop a sense of shame in the opponent, and thereby bring about a transformation and change of heart.

Martin Luther King Jr. (Carson, 1998, p. 26)

Anger is a righteous emotion. It is almost necessary to your being.

Martin Luther King, Jr.

Don't get me wrong, righteous indignation is, well, righteous. More than that, it fuels good and necessary work. But if we allow that anger to make us bitter, cynical, or hateful, we are forgetting the reason we want justice so badly, the reason we are angry in the first place: our love of justice for all people. We are angry because of our love.

Martin Luther King, Jr. (Letter from a Birmingham jail)

I have learned to use my anger for good…Without it, we would not be motivated to rise to a challenge. It is an energy that compels us to define what is just and unjust.

Mahatma Gandhi

NOTE

1. Or Yahweh, or the Tao, or the Universe, or the Great Spirit, or the Goddess, or whatever word you use.

Section III

It's Not Always about Racism

9

All Are Affected, All Must Be Invited

Why do you look at the speck of sawdust in your brother's eye and pay no attention to the plank in your own eye? How can you say to your brother, 'Brother, let me take the speck out of your eye,' when you yourself fail to see the plank in your own eye? You hypocrite, first take the plank out of your eye, and then you will see clearly to remove the speck from your brother's eye.

Jesus (Luke 6:41–6:42)

When you make it about race when it's not about race, this doesn't mean it's about race. That means it's about you.

Sometimes people do stuff that isn't based on prejudice but still gets in the way. Ironically, making everything about race is a behavior that gets in the way. As stated at the beginning of the book, we must be able to examine situations and behaviors through the lens of racism and other isms, but we must also be able to examine them without that lens. Put simply, not everything is about racism. That should be obvious, but the leaders of the DEI workshop I have mentioned, when they did reveal their thinking, framed every bit of interpersonal tension as racism or defensiveness about racism. They proposed no other way of looking at things and labeled any suggestion that there were other dynamics as "denial." In her writing, Robin Di Angelo holds the same bias. One of the elephants in the room is the very fact that these leaders aren't willing to look at interpersonal tension through any other lens. *The Interpersonal Gap* provides one such lens.

Another dynamic that complicates DEI progress is the belief that if members of the group that has been in power work on equity, they are possibly acting off and reinforcing the myth that they are superior to the people that have been and are being oppressed. This type of thinking leads

DOI: 10.4324/9781003335689-12

toward resentment at attempts to help, defensiveness about how the "help" is received, and further separation of both parties. It's a good example of how inequality can create confusion and hypersensitivity (or fragility). Think about it. Are we really going to fight racism by dividing by "race?" That's a self-inflicted wound.

If you are "white" and are reading this, please get it that any such reaction is based on centuries of minorities being lorded over by whites, who haven't exactly done a great job of running things. See Chapters 4 through 6 if you need a reminder. Any behavior that seems like more of the "great white hope" behavior where the self-absorbed white person (especially the men) are there to fix everything for the poor, helpless, less gifted rest of the world, can easily be misunderstood. Even in the unlikely eventuality that you are the smartest person in the room, like Einstein almost always was, you would be even wiser if you noted the humor and humility with which he carried himself. If you believe you are smarter than everyone, that's probably just your ego speaking. If you believe you are smarter than everyone and you show it, then you deserve the reaction you are bound to get. Furthermore, nobody is smarter about being themselves and more knowledgeable about what they face than each and every human being. There are technical smarts (there are people who are genuinely better than me at doing brain surgery or flying airplanes, for example), and then there is wisdom and knowledge from our own lives. Each person is a source of that intelligence and deserves respect. No one needs Tarzan, the great white man, to swing in and save the day.

That backdrop aside, the framework proposed here keeps the quagmire of who is in and who is out simple. We are all in this together and we need all the help we can get. Let's greet anyone with open arms who is willing to join the cause. If Scrooge wakes up tomorrow morning from his classism and his greed[1] and decides to help, let's welcome him! If Tarzan swings in, give him a seat at the table. Give everyone a seat at the table, regardless of race, gender, etc.

The fight against prejudice isn't easy! It is even harder because so many think they can make exceptions! I've been in numerous churches where the service is going wonderful, and then the pastor throws in something prejudiced about gays or about "the place" of women. Yes, the bible has passages that can be interpreted that way, just as the white slave owners used to cherry-pick the passages that seem to support slavery. Is that the focus one wants to keep when most of the bible, certainly the New Testament, teaches love?

If the human race is the Titanic, prejudice in the form of racism and all other isms is the iceberg. Greed and lust for power are perhaps even bigger icebergs lurking below the surface, but if we don't steer clear of the iceberg of prejudice, we are going down. We need "all hands on deck" to change the course of history, and we can't accomplish that by selectively insulting our crewmates and violating the very values we are fighting for. "I am against discrimination...except for you, you and you" isn't going to cut it. If you have a bias that is hard to let go of, recognize it, forgive yourself, and get to work not letting it control your behavior.

Let us turn back now for guidance from Kurt Lewin. Based on his Jewish experience, and his faith in reason, Lewin was able to deeply feel the plight of the minority without resorting to simply scapegoating the majority. As he put it: "Inter-group relations is a two-way affair. This means that to improve relations between groups both of the interacting groups have to be studied.

In recent years we have started to realize that so-called minority problems are in fact majority problems, that the Negro problem is the problem of the white, that the Jewish problem is the problem of the non-Jew, and so on" (Lewin, 1946, 1997, p. 151).

In other words, racism is everyone's problem, and we need all the help we can get from every corner of society. Black people don't need to fix this themselves nor do white people. We need each other. As we shall see in the next chapter, we need people with power, and we need people who, relatively speaking, have no power. We need to heed Lewin's group dynamics wisdom and include everyone we can in dialogue about the challenges we face so they can come up with their own solutions. That is messy but effective.

However, we are not throwing the baby out with the bath water. Some imposed solutions are important for systemic change, such as eliminating discriminatory laws, increasing oversight when people are behaving badly, and enforcing standards that are for the good of the community and consequently for the good of the individual. Seatbelts are a good example. So are voting rights. We must act collectively at times and nationally. Nonetheless, the vast majority of change that sticks is generated "locally" by the people who must make the change.

In a nutshell, lasting change cannot over-rely on the "expert model," where solutions and behaviors are imposed and have to be policed. We must not exclude the people we are trying to change from the problem-solving process! It doesn't matter if they aren't like you! It doesn't matter if you think they are your enemy! If anything, over-rely on inviting *everyone* into the dialogue and the generation of solutions. Use that as your guiding light. And use this book. We will elaborate more on practical steps for leading change in Chapter 14.

You don't have to be perfect at it. Lewin's methods were meant for anyone to use. Don't spend years studying the problem! The time for action is now!

You want change? You want less gun violence, for example? You need the gun owners and gun dealers and gang members and the police and everyone from the high crime communities and everyone else that can influence or cares in the room and at the table. An Australian customer of mine watching this approach once said, "I get what you are doing. My dad used to say, 'It's better to have everyone inside the tent pissing out, than to have anyone outside the tent pissing in." Get whoever you can inside the tent. Treat each with respect. Create a process where each can participate without any dominating the others. To repeat the immortal words of Mahatma Gandhi, "Be the change you want to see in the world."

NOTE

1. Everybody was white in that story as far as I recall, so I am not aware of what he thought about race.

10

Family Systems Theory, Self-Differentiation, & EQ[1]

(Jesus) recognized with authentic realism that anyone who permits another to determine the quality of his inner life gives into the hands of the other the keys to his destiny. If a man knows precisely what he can do to you or what epithet he can hurl against you in order to make you lose your temper, your equilibrium, than he can always keep you under subjugation. It is a man's reaction to things that determines their ability to exercise power over him.

Thurman (1976, p. 28)

Dr. Murray Bowen's family systems therapy concept of "self-differentiation" offers a way to be the way you want to be in difficult situations, to be different than others despite pressure, and to calm one's own emotional reactions to people and situations. Self-differentiation is vital to influencing change and to establishing emotional health in any confusing and dysfunctional system. It is a model that fits nicely with Emotional Intelligence (EQ), *The Interpersonal Gap*, and Kurt Lewin's social science (Figure 10.1).

EQ, by the way, while woven into this text, is only touched on lightly. That doesn't mean it is not important. Simply put, EQ is your ability to actively and accurately experience your own emotions and those of others, to connect emotionally, and to *influence* your own emotions and those of others. To influence your own emotions, you must understand the cause and effect of your emotional reactions. For accuracy about how your emotional states get triggered, reread *The Interpersonal Gap* in Chapter 3.

DOI: 10.4324/9781003335689-13

It may seem at first glance that self-differentiation is a concept that excludes the collective. That would be a misunderstanding of the concept. It does help one differentiate (or separate) from aspects of society that one does not want to be part of, such as racism. It would be a mistake, however, to think of self-differentiation as some sort of Western versus Eastern thought polarity (a contrast often included in DEI conversations and which we will examine further in Chapter 13). Rather, it is a concept about how to be yourself within the collective, a dynamic that is managed differently in different cultures but is nonetheless a universal human experience. It is a path toward creating a community that isn't just based on people pretending to fit in. Self-differentiation is essential for real dialogue and intentional influence.

Self-differentiation is the ability to separate and clearly see each element of what Bowen called the "inner guidance system." It is an EQ skill because, in moments of high emotional intensity, it is easy to have these elements "fuse" and cause confusion. Let us explore the three elements of the "guidance system."

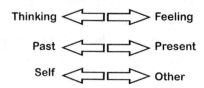

FIGURE 10.1
Bowen's inner guidance system.

ABILITY TO SEPARATE SELF AND OTHER

Object theory in psychology tells us we are born fused and only gradually learn to differentiate between ourselves, our primary caretakers, and the world around us. Small wonder that in moments of emotional intensity we return to fusion. We begin life so attached that we literally think we are one.

Without early attachment, humans, and our closest relatives in the natural world, mammals, wither and die. Early experiments with perfectly sterile infant care wards demonstrated that food and shelter are not enough. Without human interaction and contact, most of the unlucky infants in the experiment perished (Lewis et al., 2000, p. 68). We are primed for relationships and wired into each other long before we have the capacity to use words. Emotions ripple through relationships, groups, and nations and even spread on a global level. When a person in proximity to you becomes tense, it's hard not to become tense yourself and vice versa. While most communication moves as slow as mud, rumors spread like wildfire, riding on a wave of fear. Likewise, when the mood of a group suddenly lightens up, everyone is likely to feel lighter. We are more wired together than our social construction of reality has led us to believe.

Bowen refers to this as "the emotional field." Individuals with high EQ recognize their role in cocreating the field and their vulnerability to it. That person who drives you crazy at home or at work is partially the way they are toward you because *you* are probably tense if you even anticipate running into them, let alone are actually in their presence. In other words, your own tension fuels their reactions (tension, fear, etc.) and vice versa. Calming yourself by recognizing your own tension and using the "mindfulness" technique of taking slow, deep breaths through your nose and deep into your belly is one of the surest pathways to creating calmer relationships. This is equally vital when the initial tension is coming from others.

Imagining others feel the way *you* feel and/or think the way you think is another form of fusion of self and others. It may or may not be accurate, but it is especially easy to believe in moments of high intensity. Imagining others feel or think things that you *differ with* and believing what you are imagining to be "the truth" is another form of fusion. That's also called projection and is an easy mistake to make in the field of ambiguity and tension that comes within a system of inequality.

If you can't differentiate yourself from others – if you can't get clear about what is really you and what is really them – you will be prone to creating needless drama. It's one thing to wonder if someone is holding something against you. It's another thing to be in the habit of concluding that others are holding something against you and, in turn, hold that conclusion as if it were a fact. That is the mistake one can easily make when applying concepts such as microaggressions. Figuring out what is really just your own stuff and what is really in others is vital to having sane DEI conversations. When it is actually about others, building the capacities to let go, confront, and/or improve relationships that you want to improve is also vital.

Like *The Interpersonal Gap*, self-differentiation requires a blend of trusting yourself and questioning yourself. Try starting with the assumption that there is a misunderstanding when someone seems to be "against you." You may indeed have an irresolvable conflict, as any Jewish person did with Hitler, but most people jump to that conclusion way too fast in less extreme circumstances out of fear of getting burned. Psychologist Carl Rogers said start with "unconditional positive regard." Jesus said, "Love your enemies" (Mathew, 5:44).

If you can't differentiate your own emotional experience from others, you're like a puppet on a string. They get mad, you get mad. They get anxious, you get anxious. Starting any emotionally intense moment by blaming others, even silently in your head, is a form of fusion. If that is your pattern, break it. Don't indulge in blaming them for "being tense" or "defensive." Be the source of calm for yourself and for others. There are many simple pathways to managing intensity, such as deep breathing or mindfully focusing on behavioral skills (four of which are described in more detail in Appendix B). Take responsibility and calm yourself when the intensity goes up, and you will be a calming influence not only for yourself but for others. That will go a long way toward fostering collaboration and better outcomes for everyone involved.

Ability to Separate the Past from the Present (Here & Now)

The emotional field also involves fusion of the past with the present. Neuroscience shows that we are wired for this. The hippocampus, embedded deep in the brain in close proximity to the reptilian brain, begins storing emotional memory before we can even think. We project our emotional experience of our early caretakers onto others, especially important others such as authority figures and spouses, throughout the rest of our lives.

Emotional intensity is a clue that the brain is being reminded of past experiences. These experiences could have been five minutes ago, when you felt offended, ten years ago, when you thought a person intentionally humiliated you (whether or not they did intend it), or in the first moments of your life. One of the highest EQ skills is to assume that intensity in the present isn't just about the person or persons you are dealing with now but also what you are carrying from the past.

The same applies when you are an actual authority figure. Everyone dependent on you is wrestling with the same fusion of their past and present when they are dealing with you. It would be wise to recall the Mayan advise from Chapter 3: "Don't take anything personally" (Ruiz, 1997, p. 47). In his modern representation of ancient Mayan Toltec thought, Ruiz goes on to explain, "Nothing other people do is because of you. It is because of themselves.

All people live in their own dream, in their own mind; they are in a completely different world from the one we live in" (Ruiz, 1997, p. 47). In this way of thinking, everything coming from you and coming at you is a projection or more about our inner world than the outer world. With this in mind, it is wise to not spew your own past intensity onto people in the present. Differentiate between what you are carrying, such as anger at some past authority figure, and what really is about what is happening now. It is easier said than done because we are talking about highly irrational processes here, but a worthy goal nonetheless, with high returns when we need it the most.

Separating the past from the present requires the ability and willingness to be fully present in the here and now. That brings us back to the spiritual nature of DEI work. Breathing, calming yourself, taking in the moment, and being truly present is at the heart of spiritual practice from many sources.

Really being present requires setting aside your concerns about knowing what to do next. Really being with another requires setting feelings from the past and worries about the future aside. Really being alive requires the same. There is a time for planning; there is a time for reflecting. Separate the past from the present, whether the distant past or what happened just a few moments ago. Make sure you are giving yourself and others the gift of being truly present in the here and now. Buddhist monk Thich Nat Hanh put it this way, "…happiness is possible only in the present moment. Of, course, planning for the future is part of life. But even planning can only take place in the present moment" (Hanh, 1991, p. 6). The same is true of taking action. As Zen philosopher Eckhart Tolle puts it, "If not now, when?" (Tolle, 1999, p. 43).

Ability to Separate Thinking and Feeling

Bowen describes differentiation as dependent on the degree to which a person is "…able to distinguish between the feeling process and the intellectual process. Associated with the capacity to distinguish between feelings and thoughts is the ability to *choose* between having one's functioning guided by feelings or by thoughts" (Bowen and Kerr, 1988, p. 97). Without this inner differentiation between feelings and thoughts, one will operate more on emotion, including the emotional cues from one's primary social groups (this includes family, work, and larger entities, such as nations). In other words, one will be more prone to "fit in" by only behaving in a manner that is accepted by others or behaving in the opposite extreme – establishing their sense of identity by habitually rebelling. Either extremes are a form of fusion in family systems theory...the opposite of differentiation. Even though the fused person will be convinced they are acting independently, they are primarily forming their identity in reaction to others. To be a person who can connect to others while still respecting their own *inner guidance system* of thoughts and feelings, it is essential to separate these aspects of our inner experience.

As Eckhart Tolle puts it, "Be present as the watcher of your mind – of your thoughts and emotions as well as your reactions in various situations" (Tolle, 1999, p. 45).

Self-differentiation, then, is about being yourself in relationship to others. Easier said than done in emotionally intense situations. Self-differentiation is also about being a calming influence in whatever emotional field you are in, from interpersonal, to family, to group, to nation, and to the world. Fields overlap, and we both influence and are influenced by them. Edwin Friedman, Bowen's protégé, used the metaphor of being a "step-up or step-down transformer" in the emotional system. If you are acting like a step-up transformer, at precisely the time the system needs clear, calm leadership (whether formal or informal), the leader's own anxiety spikes and increases the emotional intensity in the system. To be a self-differentiated leader, you must function the majority of the time as a "step-down transformer," helping the emotional system stay cool, calm, and focused during difficult moments, *even if you yourself are anxious and uncertain of the outcome.*

At any given moment, you are either a calming influence on the emotional field or a source of increased tension. It is possible to be both, at times, calm and aware and yet occasionally flooded with tension. Even the best of us get reactive at times. A high EQ aspiration is to decrease the amount of reactivity and to de-escalate faster when reactivity happens. This is vital to the DEI needs of managing difficult topics and fostering collaboration.

Living completely nonreactive is unlikely. Friedman describes self-differentiation this way:

The following ten statements complete the sentence that starts with "self-differentiation is":

- Being clear about one's own personal values and goals
- Taking maximum responsibility for one's own emotional being and destiny rather than blaming others or the context

- Charting one's own way by means of one's own internal guidance system, rather than perpetually eyeing the "scope" to see where others are at
- Knowing where one ends and another begins
- The capacity to take a stand in an intense emotional system
- Saying "I" when others are demanding "we"
- Being able to cease being one of the system's emotional dominoes
- Maintaining a nonanxious presence in the face of others
- Containing one's reactivity to the reactivity of others
- A lifetime project, with no one ever getting more than 70% of the way to the goal (from "Bowen Theory and Therapy" by Edwin Friedman in the *Handbook of Family Therapy, Volume II*, edited by Gurman and Kniskern, 1991)

Let's elaborate on two of these. By "maintaining a non-anxious presence in the face of anxious others," Friedman doesn't mean you will never feel anxious. Anxiety, in the right dose, is an important self-motivating emotion. What he does mean is that you will be a calming presence when the going gets tough and emotional intensity is running high in others. You will be the step-down transformer in the emotional system. "A lifetime project, with no one ever getting more than 70 percent of the way to the goal," means that moments of self-differentiation come and go and that even the best of us will only be self-differentiated 70% of the time. You will be 100% differentiated at times and fused (and confused) at others. Give yourself a break when it happens, learn what you can from the experience, and figure out what to do next.

It is important to remember that the theme of this section is that not every interpersonal, group, and societal tension is about racism or other isms. A lack of self-differentiation can cause tension in any system. Systems can then get too organized around "making everyone happy." When that happens, the most reactive people hold emotional sway, and the system is likely to stay stuck. When dealing with DEI education and action, an important variable is the degree of self-differentiation versus reactive fusion in the people involved. This is especially important for leadership in the fight for equity. The leader's degree of self-differentiation sets the tone. Racism and other inequalities are dramatic enough. The question for leaders and for each person is this: is the way we relate to others increasing the drama or decreasing it?

There is much more that can be explored regarding self-differentiation. The content is an important part of the DEI learning approach covered in Chapter 13. For now, let us turn our attention to understanding and managing conflict, another vital dynamic in DEI work.

NOTE

1. This chapter draws heavily on excerpts used with permission from Chapter 3 of Crosby (2021b). *Spirituality and Emotional Intelligence: Wisdom from the World's Spiritual Sources Applied to EQ for Leadership and Professional Development*. New York, NY. Routledge.

11

Conflict Beliefs and Behaviors[1]

Lewin showed us that we can create needless conflict while trying to drive change. His research on group dynamics clearly showed that if people come together to solve problems through effectively facilitated dialogue, there is a much higher reliability that they will get results. Let us review Lewin's wisdom regarding how the approach one takes to change either increases or decreases tension:

TWO BASIC METHODS OF CHANGING LEVEL OF CONDUCT

For any type of social management, it is of great practical importance that levels of quasi-stationary equilibria can be changed in either of two ways: by adding forces in the desired direction or by diminishing opposing forces. If a change…is brought about by increasing the forces toward…the secondary effects should be different from the case where the same change of level is brought about by diminishing the opposing forces…

In the first case, the process…would be accomplished by a state of relatively high tension, in the second case, by a state of relatively low tension. Since increase of tension above a certain degree is likely to be paralleled by higher aggressiveness, higher emotionality, and lower constructiveness, it is clear that, as a rule, the second method will be preferable to the high pressure method (Lewin, 1999, p. 280).

In other words, it doesn't work to impose one's "thou shalt" on others, and it makes no sense to then blame them for their defensiveness. It's needless in most cases, it's tiresome, and it's ineffective. Instead, we

DOI: 10.4324/9781003335689-14

need to bring people together and build a broad coalition against racism. To do so, we need skills for managing conflict. Anyone leading DEI work especially needs these skills. They need to establish how conflict will be managed, and they need to walk the talk, especially when they are part of the conflict.

These skills, of course, apply whether the conflict is related to inequality or to any of the plethora of human differences that can result in conflict.

Conflict, according to subject matter expert, Dr. Jay Hall, "is a natural part of human interaction...the way we, as individuals, think about and choose to handle conflict is more important in determining its outcome than the nature of the conflict itself[2]." In other words, having differences, whether large or small, is inevitable. How we interpret each other during moments of difference and our beliefs about conflict complicate or simplify the resolution of differences.

If you tend to blame the other for causing the conflict, or if you believe that all conflicts are bad and signs that you are failing in a relationship, then the intensity will go up. The ability to reconcile the actual difference (the toothpaste cap, for example) will go down.

On the other hand, if you can own your part in the cocreated dance, remember to breathe, be behaviorally specific when giving feedback, work harder on understanding than on being understood, you can manage and even build respect through your moments of difference. You can build stronger and richer relationships tapping into the diversity of thoughts, feelings, and aspirations that is present in each and every human being.

To do so requires self-awareness:

What words come to mind when you think of the word "conflict"?
How do you handle conflict?
How do you think you arrived at your current beliefs about conflict?
How was conflict handled in your family during childhood?
What contrasts, similarities, and connections do you see between then and now?
What do you *want* to believe about conflict?
How do you want to handle it?

Dr. Hall suggested that there are five basic behavioral tendencies during conflict. These are habitual responses that you may slip into before realizing what is happening. They may last for a few seconds or go on for years.

My summaries of Dr. Hall's tendencies are listed below. Check the tendency that you think is truest of you:

Avoid/Withdraw: Your first impulse is to keep your mouth shut and go inward into your thoughts, or even better, actually physically remove yourself from the conflict. You may feel overwhelmed when conflict arises and hold beliefs that "nothing good ever comes of it." The upside of this behavior is not engaging when you are reactive and not engaging in issues that may seem important at the moment, but less so or not at all with time. The downside is letting things fester and avoiding when you would be better off engaging.

Preserve/Yield: Your first impulse is to make sure that relationships are ok, even at the expense of your own goals and preferences. You tend to give in to what others want, focus on their needs, invite their thoughts, do a lot of active listening, and possibly slip into placating (pretending you're happy when you are not). When there is conflict, you may feel impatient with whoever seems to be the source but will likely keep that to yourself, thinking things like "Why can't they just relax" and "Don't they see how they're affecting people?" The upside of this behavior is an ability to tune in to others and to keep things light. The downside is a tendency to neglect your own needs, wants, and opinions. Eventually, any such imbalance may increase the very tension one is trying to avoid.

Compromise: Your first impulse is to look for a middle ground. You believe "you have to be realistic" when it comes to conflict. Everyone can't get what they want, and if you can come away without badly damaging the relationship, that's success. You want to keep things controlled and come up with a solution which is good enough. You value being fair. The upside of this behavior is the ability to negotiate an acceptable outcome for all that balances both goals and relationships. The downside is a willingness to settle for less (both the goals and the relationships may be "compromised") and possible impatience with those who want to work the conflict at a deeper level.

Win/Win: Your first impulse is to engage, going for your goals while simultaneously respecting the wants and perspectives of others. You believe that when it's important enough to you, with time and effort, you can achieve both. Even though you have your reactive moments, you are relieved when conflict emerges because you'd rather have differences in the open than have them hidden away where you believe they will tend to fester. You take the risk of raising conflicts, go directly to others when you have issues, and encourage them to come directly to you. The upside is the tendency to be true to yourself while simultaneously respecting others. The downside is a tendency to be impatient to "work things now," when time and space might ease the conversation (or even resolve the need for one), and to "work things to death" in the eyes of others.

Win/Lose: Your first impulse is to meet your needs and goals. You figure others can and must take care of themselves. You may think and say things like, "This is nothing personal" and "Let's not get emotional," especially at work. You see competition as a natural part of human affairs, go after your goals with vigor, and probably get rewarded for it. You may believe people who tend to avoid/withdraw are spineless, those who tend to preserve/yield are too worried about how people feel, and that people tending toward the win/win style are unrealistic dreamers. You may occasionally value help from those who can compromise. The upside of this behavior is that you are not afraid of conflict, stand up for yourself, and tend to get things done. The downside is you may "walk all over people," erode relationships, and eventually wear out both your welcome and your ability to accomplish anything that depends on the support of others.

In Dr. Hall's theory, you are likely to have a primary style (although two or more of these behaviors could essentially be tied as a tendency), and you are likely to shift into other styles, depending on the situation and other variables. You would have to push yourself to do whatever styles are least habitual for you.

Which style do you think you tend to slip into the most in your personal life?

Which style at work?

Are they the same?

After you start with one style, what do you think you will do next?

What behaviors do you want to engage in?

What behaviors do you think you are least likely to do?

As mentioned, each of these five behaviors has an upside and a downside. The challenge is to accurately identify your own conflict habits/patterns and to not be stuck in them. Carefully read the upside of whichever style you think you are least likely to engage in. In terms of these styles, that is your blind spot, and there is almost certainly value in stretching in that direction.

These behaviors are not limited to times of conflict. You can experiment in any relationship by doing more of the Jay Hall behaviors that are less habitual to you. If you do most of the talking, try talking less (which corresponds to avoid/withdraw) or actively listening with your Wallen skills (which corresponds to preserve/yield). If you rarely take clear stands about what you want, experiment by taking one (win/lose). Combine taking clear stands and being open about what you want, think, and feel with active listening (tuning in to what they want, think, and feel), and you are on the path of win/win, which is also the skill set needed for collaboration. Balance the wants of self and others and make a deal that is good enough for both of you, and you have compromised.

When conflict does arise, remember to breathe. Conflict is neither good nor bad; it is what we do with it that matters. Ground yourself by being intentional about your conflict behavior. Be as self-differentiated as possible, and don't give into your own reactivity. Choose what you do.

The following are two models of understanding and managing conflict. The first was developed by Sherwood, Glidewell, and my colleague and mentor, John Scherer. Another colleague, Mark Horswood, here puts their theory into his own words.

THE PINCH THEORY: A MODEL FOR CONFLICT MANAGEMENT

Kurt Lewin, the renowned social psychologist, once said, "There is nothing so practical as a good theory." That is my experience with the Pinch Theory – it is practical.

For many, conflict is a reoccurring drama where the supporting actors and plots may change, but the action remains the same. On reflection, we may find patterns in our emotional reactions to conflict. Our approach to conflict may drive familiar thoughts, words, and reactions in ourselves and others. It is wise to ask, is our approach "working?" If not, awareness of our tendencies in conflict is the first step toward creating what we want.

The Pinch Theory suggests that relationships develop in predictable phases and that, in the course of any relationship, just as predictably, conflict will show up. The theory also describes some common responses to conflict and the likely effects of these responses.

Allow me to define, for our purposes, the terms relationship and conflict. Relationships exist in any instance where you have some expectation of and/or are impacted by another. This includes the obvious examples of relationships such as spouse, family, friend, and coworker. In addition, you have a relationship with the person that delivers your paper, your waitress, your clients, and so on.

There may be differences in expectations, values, opinions, goals, or desiring the same goal when there is not enough to go around. Conflict can be activated by differences between any two parties who are connected to one another. The conflict may remain internal or be expressed outwardly.

Sharing Information and Negotiating Expectations

In the beginning phase of a relationship, the parties share information about themselves and expectations of how they will "be" in the relationship. This is an attempt to create a common understanding. The process is often an accumulation of inferences and unspoken expectations.

Role Clarity and Commitment

At a point where a sufficient amount of information has been shared (formally and/or informally), the parties settle into their roles. I know what is expected of me and what I can expect of the other. Verbalizing and committing to expectations helps to clarify the roles. However, especially in new relationships, some or most aspects of "role clarity" are likely to be based on unspoken expectations, which may not surface until there is a pinch or a crunch.

Stability and Productivity

Stability develops once expectations and commitments are met with an acceptable degree of reliability. At this phase, the parties experience a level of satisfaction in the relationship. The stability and resulting satisfaction creates a productive environment for the relationship.

Disruption of Shared Expectations

Inevitably, something happens that disrupts the status quo. *Quite possibly, only one of the parties sees it as a violation* of their previous "commitment." This is called a "pinch." Pinches are inevitable for many reasons. First, many of the expectations are implied and/or assumed. Who could possibly share all that information explicitly? Another is the fact that humans are complicated, open organisms – subject to change. Another is what my wife calls "EDB" – Early Dating Behavior. That is when two people, in the beginning of a relationship, have a strong tendency to be at their very best behavior, show their best side, and only see the best of the others. In this case, there is much information missing (Figure 11.1).

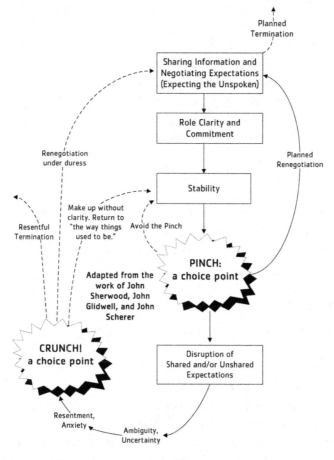

FIGURE 11.1
The PINCH Theory.

Pinch Stage – Choice Point: "Pay Now or Pay Later"

The following is a list of choices in the Pinch stage:

- Planned renegotiation/reconciliation of roles, expectations, & commitments
- Planned termination after negotiation
- Ignore the pinch – "I'm not going to let it bother me" – return to stability (with history of pinch[es] building up)

Crunch Stage – Choice Point: "Something's Gotta Give"

Choices in the Crunch stage – when dissatisfaction worsens:

- Renegotiate under duress
- Ignore or "make-up" superficially – attempt to return to "the way things used to be" with the likelihood of lingering resentment and emotional resignation (quit and stay)
- Resentful termination of the relationship (with likelihood of carrying this pattern to a new relationship)

Most people, when presented with the pinch theory, agree that the most functional approach is to attempt to renegotiate the relationship at the pinch, when tensions are real but small, rather than waiting for the crunch, which is complicated by the baggage of past (ignored) pinches and emotional intensity. The part that most people have trouble with is resolving a pinch.

Addressing a Pinch

Follow this practical five-step road map to negotiate your way through a Pinch:

Step 1 – Frame It: In most situations, I am reasonably confident that once we get talking about a conflict, we can work it out. The hitch for me is where to begin. This first step (framing the issue) helps break the ice by conveying to the other party my inner experience as I bring up the issue. It lets them know what's going on for you and gives them an opportunity to get on the same page. Scan your awareness as you go to speak with the other. Get as clear with yourself about thoughts, feelings, and wants as possible. The "frame" may be something like "Hey, I'd like to talk to you a moment about something that's been bugging me for a couple days." Or "I don't want to make a big deal out of this, but there is something I'd like to clear up with you." Or "I have something to talk to you about and I'm worried that it may affect our relationship if I ignore it."

Step 2 – Describe the Behavior: The key here is to identify the behavior(s) that triggered your reactions. As you can probably imagine, confronting others with your interpretation of them, such as "You're rude" or "I think you are a jerk" will have dubious results. Describing the behavior keeps the focus on the situation rather than the person. Maybe you thought they were rude or a jerk when they left a meeting you were in (or left the cap off the toothpaste, etc.). State the behavior: "When you walked out of the meeting…"

Step 3 – Describe the Impact on You: Relate the emotional impact the event had on you - how you felt about it. The impact and emotion are yours – own them as yours. This keeps the focus from being "blaming" the other person. They may be more open to hearing the issue and less defensive. "When you walked out of the meeting, I felt _____ (mad/glad/sad/afraid, etc.)."

Step 4 – Describe what You Want: This is a hard one for many people, not just verbalizing their wants but being aware of a want in the first place. It seems to go against some internal code that says, "Don't be selfish." Basically, you are visualizing a preferred future if the situation comes up again. "If you must leave, I want to know why."

Step 5 – Check for Impact on the Other: Life would be simple if situations got resolved before you get to this step. But it takes two to tango. In this step, make certain you "check in with them." Give the other some space to state their thoughts, feelings, and wants. Listen! Do this as early in the talk as possible! The relationship is most likely to prosper if you forge mutual agreement on how you both intend to respond should pinches and/or the specific situation arise again.

What pinches are you ignoring? What unspoken expectations do you hold of others that aren't getting met? What do you want to do about it?

The next model was created by my father, Robert P. Crosby. I edited this version about 30 years ago. It can be a helpful reminder of the dynamics of conflict and what to pay attention to when trying to work things out.

THE VOMP MODEL

VOMP is not intended as a rigid or linear process for dealing with conflict, but rather a description of what takes place, in some form, when interpersonal conflict is truly resolved. Furthermore, VOMP, as is the case with most behavioral tools, is most effective when applied to understanding your own behavior (i.e., "This isn't going the way I want it to – am I owning my piece of this conflict? Do I really understand what the other is conveying to me?") and least effective when applied as a technique to change or manipulate the other ("If I own, maybe then they will see/own that it's really their fault…").

V *Ventilation.* If emotions have built up, there needs to be some way to let the "steam" out. Be patient with others when they vent and use skills such as deep breathing, active listening, and behavior description to patiently shift from venting toward something more productive.

Traps

1. Being so afraid of venting "getting out of hand" that you avoid addressing pinches. Staying stuck in avoidance or placating patterns of behavior.
2. Not accepting or understanding the other person's style of ventilation. Conversely, not being aware that you are venting. We all do it differently, some with high intensity, others with little or no emotional expression (for example, "logical debating" can be a form of venting, as can slamming a door: the possible variations are endless).
3. Ventilating in such a way that progress cannot be made to the next stage. Accusations, sarcasm, angry questions, and judgments are likely to trigger reactivity.
4. Ventilating to someone other than the person with whom you are upset and avoiding the person or group you are actually in

conflict with. This is called triangulation in family systems theory and is otherwise known as gossip.

5. Getting upset that the other person is upset. Both parties may spend time being angry that the other is angry, thus ignoring and avoiding the original disagreement altogether.

6. Thinking that this theory gives you some sort of "Get out of Jail Free" card for venting. Put yourself in the other's shoes and treat them the way you would like to be treated.

O *Own/Open.* If I can't see my own contributions to what isn't working between us, I have no power to make changes. Ownership is essential to creating a climate of learning as opposed to a climate of blame. Ownership, when genuine, can be a beginning to bridging the gap.

Openness is being straight with the other, throughout the course of the dialogue, about what I want, think, and feel.

Traps with Owning

1. Remaining defensive. Believing the other will take advantage of you if you admit your part in the problem.
2. Owning too quickly. Trying to bring peace before its time.
3. "Owning" with judgments ("I never do things right") instead of behavior specifics.
4. Believing "it's all my fault."
5. Using "owning" as a technique to get the other to own.

Traps with Openness

1. Being "open" in a derogatory fashion.
2. Waiting for the other to be open before you're willing to risk.
3. Being "open" with judgments ("You're a micro-manager") instead of with behavior specifics ("I think I could be making my own decision on that").
4. Blaming: "You're the problem."

M *Moccasins.* In step with, or even proceeding, taking ownership, both parties begin to acknowledge that they can understand the experience of the other.

Traps

1. Saying "I understand" and then moving on without actually verbally verifying your understanding. Paraphrase, paraphrase, paraphrase! The likelihood early on in a conflict is that you don't "understand," but even if you do, the other may not know it, and so half the value of "understanding" gets lost.
2. Being empathic too early. Like number two under owning, trying to make peace before you have been heard.
3. Attending to the other person's experience and ignoring your own. You may forge a temporary peace, but you'll pay for it over time.

P *Plan.* If the other stages have been worked through, the plan usually comes naturally. The best plan is one that is about process ("When that happens again, let's agree to talk about it") and prevention ("Let's get together periodically and talk about how it is going").

Traps

1. Promising that neither of you will ever do it (whatever it was) again.
2. Promising things that you cannot deliver, like "I will never feel upset again."
3. Expecting the impossible of the other ("I want you to always listen to and understand me").

In summary, your ability to resolve conflict successfully is directly related to your ability to do the following:

1. Calm yourself. Breathe! Ground yourself in other ways!
2. Be in touch with and able to communicate your "here and now" experience, i.e., what you want, think, and feel.
3. Listen actively to the other person's experience. Paraphrase! Tuning in effectively and nondefensively to them will help ground both of you! Make sure you understand what they want, think, and feel!
4. Keep focused on doing your part. You cannot control whether the other party does theirs.

These behaviors are especially important if you are leading. Be transparent about how you intend to be when there is conflict and what you are looking for in others. Create a space for dialogue about difficult topics that isn't just full of judgments and blame. Above all else, start with yourself and be the change you want to see in the world.

NOTES

1. Significant portions of this chapter are adapted with permission from: Crosby (2008). *Fight, Flight, Freeze: Emotional Intelligence, Behavioral Science, Systems Theory & Leadership*. Seattle, WA. Crosby OD Publishing.
2. This quote is from Dr. Hall's highly valid and reliable self-assessment instrument, the "Conflict Management Survey" (CMS), which can be ordered at Teleometrics. com for a reasonable price (I gain nothing from this!). My colleagues and I have used the CMS in our workshops for decades.

12

Power, Authority, and Leadership[1]

Power properly understood is nothing but the ability to achieve purpose. Is the strength required to bring about social, political, and economic change...And one of the great problems of history is that the concepts of love and power have usually been contrasted as opposites-polar opposites-so that love is identified with the resignation of power, and power with the denial of love. Now we've got to get this thing right. What (we need to realize is) that power without love is reckless and abusive and love without power is sentimental and anemic...It is precisely this collision of immoral power with powerless morality which constitutes the major crisis of our time.

Martin Luther King, Jr.

Power and one's personal beliefs about power are important to this conversation. As described in detail in Chapter 5, the social construction of race was written into the legal code by people desperately trying to hold on to power in the colony of Virginia. In my eyes, it was power wielded without morality. Some politicians, too many, still try to increase their political power to this very day by using diversity to divide us.

It is easy to hold strong opinions and reactions to power and authority. As we have discussed, our beliefs and reactions form in our earliest experiences. Many had such negative experiences of power when they were growing up that they want a world where no one has any power over another. As Kurt Lewin put it, "Few aspects are as much befogged in the minds of many as the problems of leadership and of power...power itself is an essential aspect of any and every group..." His social science asserts human social relation without any power structure is a fantasy.

Everyone wants to influence the groups they are in, including their families, and there is nothing wrong with that. Use your influence, your

DOI: 10.4324/9781003335689-15

personal power, to make the world a better place. Don't let "thou shalt" get in your way. Authority is necessary for any functioning group and for a functioning democracy. Just as being power hungry is destructive, so aversion to power is counterproductive. Power exists, and so it must be recognized openly, used wisely, and checked and monitored to prevent abuse. The struggle for equity requires assertion of power.

That runs counter to the instincts of many of the people who are drawn to the struggle. Looking at almost any group, even the groups that most dislike each other, it is evident that there is a strong antiauthority streak running through the United States. The field of organization development (OD), a field that owes much to Lewin's influence, and the DEI movement are no exceptions.

The leaders of the DEI workshop I attended certainly seemed ambivalent toward authority, including their own. They insisted they had no agenda, no intended outcome, and no interest in influencing. The person I considered the lead facilitator sent me this note: "Thank you for your inquiry of: 'Are you getting the conversation you hoped for?' It is rather difficult for me to address the first inquiry because there was/is no anticipated 'hoped for' concerning these sessions. I will not speak for (the other facilitator), however I came to this with a curiosity and not a prefixed destination." Further inquiry was met with increasing impatience. It's a safe bet there was a big gap between my intent and the impact on them. My intent was to genuinely understand and learn about their beliefs and goals. Thinking in terms of the PINCH Theory from the last chapter, we clearly had different unspoken expectations. About halfway through, I created the rough draft of the framework presented in this book. I wrote this note to the two facilitators and sent them the framework: "While I wish there was more structure, I do find myself being inspired by this group experience. This came to life from within me last night and this morning as a framework for how to facilitate DEI dialogue." They never responded to it.

It became increasingly clear that one thing they *did want to influence* was to get me to stop asking! I reluctantly took the hint. Avoidance led to a tenuous decrease in overt tension, but it certainly didn't foster real dialogue.

Such conflict is predictable if people care deeply about how power happens but are so strongly antiauthority that they do not recognize their own craving for influence. Referring back to the JOHARI Window from Chapter 3, a blind spot like that tends to lead toward conflict-adverse behavior. Tensions are then expressed in indirect ways, are likely to simmer unresolved, and manifest in what could reasonably be described as "passive-aggressive" behavior. That was certainly my experience of the aforementioned DEI workshop, and that is why it is important for the leaders of such processes to be as transparent as possible about their own authority beliefs and biases. We will say more about that in Chapter 13.

The same applies to organization development, and leadership in general. OD people with authority issues have been trying to get businesses to flatten, to operate through leaderless teams, and to otherwise eliminate authority relationships for decades. The message is often delivered as dogma and as if it were new. Authority relationships are "scientifically" regarded as outdated relics of the past and the root cause of many problems. The dogma is often delivered with an escape clause from responsibility. If chaos erupts when authority is eliminated in a system, the explanation is that the system failed because the people who were told to implement it weren't committed. The results are usually a disaster, but somehow people keep getting paid to tell manufacturing plants that they will run better if they just get rid of the front-line supervision (or at least change their names to something friendly like "facilitators"). Then they call someone like me in to help figure out how to recover (hint: part of the process is to help people figure out how to support each other in whatever role they are in). Roles, including authority roles, are not inherently good nor bad. They help create structure. That's why we have a president, a congress, etc.

We need leadership in the struggle against racism. That leadership can come from people in positions of formal authority. It can also come from anyone, as Rosa Parks famously demonstrated[2].

On to Lewin. I wrote the following article because I sincerely believe Lewin's leadership model applies to all situations, and because it is based on combining power with deep love and respect.

LEWIN'S DEMOCRATIC STYLE OF SITUATIONAL LEADERSHIP – A FRESH LOOK AT A POWERFUL OD MODEL[3]

Kurt Lewin had a clear-eyed vision of authority as an essential function in human systems. As Lewin put it: "... power itself is an essential aspect of any and every group ..." (Marrow, 1969, p. 172). Authority in Lewin's theory is neither good nor bad; it is simply an ever-present aspect of group dynamics and leadership.

Lewin concluded this about leadership: "Autocracy, democracy, and laissez-faire should be perceived as a triangle. In many respects, autocracy and democracy are similar: They both mean leadership as against the lack of leadership of laissez-faire; they both mean discipline and organization as against chaos. Along other lines of comparison, democracy and laissez-faire are similar. They both give freedom to the group members in so far as they create a situation where the members are acting on their own motivation rather than being moved by forces induced by an authority in which they have no part" (Lewin, 1999, p. 286). Lewin's democratic principles of leadership hold the only corner of the triangle that combines leadership (or structure) *and* freedom, as illustrated in Figure 12.1.

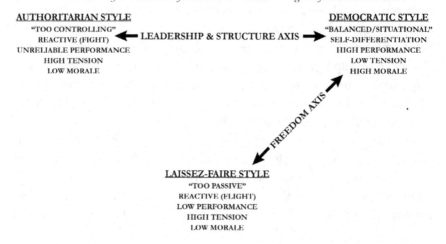

FIGURE 12.1
Lewin leadership style triangle.

Lewin's model first emerged from research in which leadership styles were rotated so that groups of children experienced each. Initially, two styles were identified – "democratic" and "authoritarian." The authoritarian leader told the kids what to do, who to work with, what materials to use, and solicited no questions. The democratic leader also told the kids what the task was, and then encouraged dialogue and influence.

In one of Lewin's classic "Ah ha" moments, a leader attempting the democratic style hardly led at all. Lewin then identified and included passive leadership as a third style, which he called laissez-faire. He established clearer standards of behavior. *Even the adult leaders had to learn Lewin's model of active democratic leadership.* As Lewin put it, "Autocracy is imposed on the individual. Democracy he has to learn" (Lewin, 1997, p. 66).

The kids knew how to comply with an authoritarian leader, even though they didn't like it. They floundered under the laissez-faire style. They flourished under the democratic style.

In Lewin's research, the leaders periodically left the rooms. In their absence, the kids in the authoritarian *and* the laissez-faire groups would stop working and start fighting with each other. When the leader left the democratic group, the kids cheerfully kept working. *That is true engagement.*

The autocratic leader got results, but only while they were present. The laissez-faire style produced neither results nor harmony. My own experience indicates that while having an autocratic boss is feared by many, *overly passive bosses are far more prevalent and create far more chaos.* It has been easier over the years to help leaders who are "too controlling" move toward the democratic style than to help "too passive" leaders become more active. In both cases, what Lewin called "group decision" – based on dialogue, feedback, and commitment to action – is the most reliable path toward change.

Lewin's placing of the democratic style into the triangle creates an effective situational frame. New employees need leaders who will slide to the left along the "leadership & structure" axis and then gradually slide back as employees become more experienced. Highly experienced workers need leaders who will slide down the freedom axis while being careful not to spill over into laissez-faire. Every employee and every group should be involved in an ongoing dialogue regarding the right blend of structure and freedom.

Because of my father's OD career, which dates back to his first T-group in 1953, I found myself, at the tender age of 24, facilitating just such a dialogue in every workgroup in two tomato processing plants. The CEO said, "Thou shalt do this process." Each work team generated survey data, engaged in dialogue, came up with their own solutions, and implemented them. Each group adjusted their own degrees of structure and freedom. This design, even in the hands of a novice facilitator, resulted in productivity and morale increases throughout the system! Lewin's principles have yielded similar results throughout our careers, including a 72% productivity increase reported by *Business Week Magazine* (1992) after supervisors were *restored* in a system that had attempted the laissez-faire approach of self-managed teams.

Lewin's research indicates that his democratic principles can even decrease prejudices such as racism, sexism, and the role-based biases held in organizations, such as mistrust between management and labor. When people begin to blameless, interact more, support each other's roles (whether they be bosses or subordinates, operators or engineers, etc.), and begin to see everyone as peers in their fundamental humanness, ongoing objective dialogue about how much freedom and how much structure is optimal can take place.

OD must work with the power structure, not against it. Effective leadership requires the capacity to empower the people below and support the people above. Based on the research and practice to date, it is my thesis that Lewin's democratic principles deserve a renaissance in the profession of OD.

That's where the article ends. It is a strength of Lewin's social science that his methods apply in all arenas. For political democracy to function, we need leaders who will lead and who will do so with the interests of democracy in mind. Organizational leadership, to achieve high morale and high performance, must lead, and must do so with the "democratic principle" of balancing freedom and structure. DEI learning and action require the same.

Lewin was idealistic, but not naively so. He believed that a democratic leader had to assert authority. He made the following observations toward the end of WWII: "The democratic leader is no less a leader and, in a way, has not less power than the autocratic leader. There are soft and tough democracies as well as soft and tough autocracies; and a tough democracy is likely to be more rather than less democratic. The difference between autocracy and democracy is an honest, deep difference, and an autocracy with a democratic front is still an autocracy...

It is particularly interesting to consider what might be called an efficient 'tough democracy.'

The gospel of inefficiency of democracies has been preached and believed not only in Nazi Germany. We ourselves are somewhat surprised to see the democratic countries execute this war rather efficiently. When Lippitt's first study (1940)[4] showed the beneficial effects which the democratic atmosphere has on the overt character of the member, how it changes his behavior from hostility to friendliness, from egocentrism to we-feeling, and to an objective matter-of-fact attitude, the argument was frequently presented that these results may hold in the friendly settings of a boys' club, but that the advantages of the democratic atmosphere would not stand up in a tough situation such as an industry requiring high efficiency" (Lewin, 1944, 1999, p. 287).

Lewin believed that democracy had to be learned by each generation, and that for democracy to work, freedom has to have limits. As we struggle to maintain our own democracy today, these words from Chapter 2 bear repeating. Having watched firsthand the rise of the Nazis in Germany, Lewin concluded the following: "A democratic world order does not require or even favor cultural uniformity all over the world. The parallel to democratic freedom for the individual is cultural pluralism for groups. But any democratic society has to safeguard against misuse of individual freedom by the gangster or – politically speaking – the 'intolerant.' Without establishing to some degree the principle of tolerance, of equality of rights, in every culture the 'intolerant' culture will always be endangering a democratic world organization. Intolerance against intolerant cultures is therefore a prerequisite to any organization of permanent peace" (Lewin, 1943, 1997, p. 36.)

Edwin Friedman, reflecting on the same dynamics, warns that empathy for the "rights" of the intolerant will only be used against the empathetic: "The form of human colonization that functions most similarly to a virus or a malignant cell is the totalitarian nation. No human entity is more invasive. The totalitarian nation is equally invasive of the lives of its citizens and the space of its neighbors...The two are linked...by the absence of self-regulation; they make no attempt to regulate their drive in either direction. They infect what they touch and they seek to replicate their own being by taking over any host they 'occupy.' They certainly do not know when to quit. It is this same lack of self-regulation and the inner integrity required for self-definition that makes totalitarian states as notoriously untrustworthy of agreements and treaties as a crime syndicate...and this brings us back...to the irrelevance of empathy in the face of a relentless force" (Friedman, 1999, p. 148).

Lewin would certainly have agreed. In several papers, he used the history of post-WWI Germany as a case study for the way in which authoritarian-minded people can use democracy to undermine it:

> It has been one of the tragedies of the German Republic that the democratically minded people who were in power immediately after the war confused democracy with "being unpolitical"...It was a tragedy that they did not know that "intolerance against the intolerant" is...essential for maintaining and particularly for establishing a democracy...above all it was a tragedy that they did not know that strong leadership and an efficient positive use of the political power by the majority is an essential aspect of democracy. Instead, Germany congratulated herself on having 'the freest Constitution in the world' because technically even a small minority gets its proportional representation in the parliament. Actually, this set-up led to dozens of political parties and to the permanent domination of the majority by a minority group...

> **Lewin (1943, 1997, p. 37)**

Democracy will likely always face this challenge. The use of racism as a political weapon has perpetuated inequality and increased the power of a minority over the majority. Such maneuvering is inherently antidemocratic. To really achieve equity, we must resist any attempts to divide us into hostile subgroups and work instead together on truly creating as even an economic and political playing field as possible. We must lead, and not be afraid to lead. We must follow, and not be afraid to follow. We must not tolerate the intolerant.

NOTES

1. Significant portions of this chapter are adapted with permission from Chapter 7 of: Crosby, G. (2021a). *Planned Change: Why Kurt Lewin's Social Science is Still Best Practice for Business Results, Change Management, and Human Progress*. Boca Raton, FL. Taylor & Francis Group.
2. If you don't know who Rosa Parks is, Google her.
3. Reprinted from and in accordance with the guidelines of *The Journal of Applied Behavioral Science*, 1–4, ©Gilmore Crosby, 2020, DOI: 10.1177/0021886320979810
4. Ron Lippitt, along with Ralph White, led the aforementioned leadership study of groups of children, under Lewin's supervision.

Section IV

Leading DEI Education and Action

13

Leading DEI Education

Let us reason together. As Lewin put it: "To believe in reason is to believe in democracy, because it grants to the reasoning partners a status of equality. It is therefore not an accident that not until the rise of democracy at the time of the American and French Revolutions was the 'goddess' of reason enthroned in modern society. And again, it is not an accident that the very first act of modern Fascism in every country has been officially and vigorously to dethrone this goddess and instead to make emotions and obedience the all-ruling principles in education and life from kindergarten to death" (Lewin, 1939, 1997, p. 67).

The goal of this type of DEI education is to reason together and, while doing so, maximize learning, decrease division, and encourage action toward equity (Figure 13.1). Transparency about goals, intentions, and beliefs is an important part of the process. We will start with the framework (or something similar...this is not intended as the only possible way), so that all the participants know what to expect and where the process is headed. We attempt to spread the responsibility for learning rather than holding it all in the hands of an expert.

Let us revisit the framework.

DOI: 10.4324/9781003335689-17

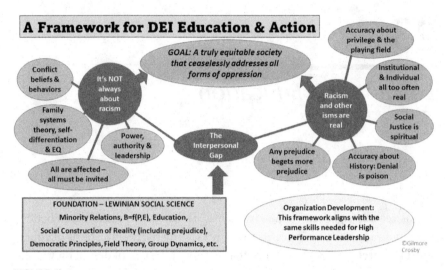

A Framework for DEI Education & Action

GOAL: A truly equitable society that ceaselessly addresses all forms of oppression

It's NOT always about racism

Conflict beliefs & behaviors

Family systems theory, self-differentiation & EQ

Power, authority & leadership

All are affected – all must be invited

The Interpersonal Gap

Accuracy about privilege & the playing field

Institutional & Individual all too often real

Racism and other isms are real

Social Justice is spiritual

Any prejudice begets more prejudice

Accuracy about History: Denial is poison

FOUNDATION – LEWINIAN SOCIAL SCIENCE
Minority Relations, B=f(P,E), Education, Social Construction of Reality (including prejudice), Democratic Principles, Field Theory, Group Dynamics, etc.

Organization Development: This framework aligns with the same skills needed for High Performance Leadership

©Gilmore Crosby

FIGURE 13.1
A framework for DEI education and action.

Education of this kind, whether in a workshop or in a classroom, can begin with a review of the framework and then proceed by exploring each element throughout the course. The agenda can look something like this:

1. A framework for DEI education and action
2. Lewinian social science
3. The interpersonal gap, microaggressions, and defensiveness
4. Racism and other "isms" are real
    4.1. Institutional and individual are all too often real
    4.2. Accuracy about history: Denial is poison
    4.3. Accuracy about the playing field
    4.4. Any prejudice begets more prejudice
    4.5. Social justice is spiritual
5. Seeing without the filter of isms
    5.1. All are effected, all must be invited
    5.2. Family system theory, self-differentiation, and EQ
    5.3. Conflict beliefs and behaviors
    5.4. Power is part of equation then and now
6. Application

This book and/or other materials can be used to speed up the learning process through preworkshop reading and homework assignments so as to minimize lectures and maximize dialogue during class time.

IMAGE 13.1
At the Connecticut workshop (from left to right): Frank Wright (possibly Dr. Frank Simpson[1]), Leah Gold Fine, Kurt Lewin, Leland Bradford, and Ken Benne.

Ideally, such workshops will be built on Lewin's T-group methodology. The T-group was first conducted in 1947, 75 years ago at the time of this writing. It was first experienced by my father in 1953 and conducted by mentors, peers, and myself continuously ever since. The T-group was invented in 1946 during a workshop that was designed to improve race relations in the State of Connecticut. The following picture was taken during the workshop.

My first experience as a participant in a group learning process was as a kid in the segregated south at an interracial church camp led by my father. Groups of black and white children got to know each other in a unique way. What precise impact that had on little me and the others is a mystery, but I appreciate the intent. It certainly brought us together when society was trying to keep us apart.

Coming together is essential if we are to overcome racism, but fostering dialogue among adults is easier said than done. T-group learning takes time and skilled facilitation. In a nutshell, T-group workshop participants learn in a lecture-style presentation, albeit with lots of interaction and activities designed to enhance engagement and learning, and then they spend time in T-group, where they learn by attempting to apply the theories they have heard and by talking about their actual interactions as they unfold. It's radically different than most educational experiences and takes getting used to.

The process proceeds like this: theory, T-group, theory, T-group, and so on. The ideal amount of time is a week, and the ideal faculty-to-student ratio is no more than 12 participants to every 1 experienced faculty. Most insist on having 2 faculty to every 12 students.

Because of these requirements (the facilitators must be experienced, the process takes time, and the group size must be kept relatively small), it is a serious commitment. It also works, hence the demand on my colleagues and me for the past 70 years. The T-group allows for unique dialogue, including with the instructors. The dialogue leads to learning at both the level of beliefs and behavior, learning that sticks. You can do less with less, but I don't recommend it.

Appendix C provides more information on T-group-based learning.

Whether or not you use T-group methodology, you are invited to use the DEI Framework in this book or your own version of it. Hopefully you value transparency and have similar goals. Whatever the case, we don't have to design effective learning from scratch. With so many pieces of the puzzle now in place, let us revisit some of the same territory as in Chapter 2.

As you may recall, Lewin used his social science to study how people learn, especially how to change deep-seated beliefs like racism. To do so we must understand and apply his "democratic principles." An assumption is that even though we play different roles, including roles of formal authority, we all are equals in our basic humanity and want to be treated as such. With this in mind, in any intervention, social science must be applied not just to the participants but also to the conduct of the leader. In OD circles, this is called "the use of self." An important aspect of this "use of self" (although not the only aspect) is how the social scientist and/or leader relates to people. *In Lewin's model, they must not only guide the process but also engage as human peers.* Staying aloof and separate as "the expert" can actually become a restraining force when conducting planned change. To influence a group, the social scientist must actually, even if only temporarily, become a part of the group.

Establishing that "we feeling," as Lewin put it, has to happen early and has to be extended to everyone involved. If the leaders only identify with subgroups, then they are perpetuating division. A skilled facilitator can invite everyone into the shared values necessary for learning, despite their gender or the color of their skin. I've experienced this both as a participant and as a facilitator, and (as a participant) I've experienced the opposite.

There is an art and a science to helping adults unlearn beliefs and behaviors and learn new ones. This is why Lewin's social science is such a critical foundation for DEI work. It cannot be emphasized too much that not only must the leader establish peer rapport with the participants, but the participants must be allowed and encouraged to think for themselves. Once again, here is a passage that is so important that it bears repeating:

> When re-education involves the relinquishment of standards which are contrary to the standards of society at large (as in the case of delinquency, minority prejudices, alcoholism), the feeling of group belongingness seems to be greatly heightened if the members feel free to express openly the very sentiments which are to be dislodged through re-education. This might be viewed as another example of the seeming contradictions inherent in the process of re-education: Expression of prejudices against minorities or the breaking of rules of parliamentary procedures may in themselves be contrary to the desired goal. Yet a feeling of complete freedom and a heightened group identification are frequently more important at a particular stage of reeducation than learning not to break specific rules.
>
> **Lewin (1945, 1997, p. 55)**

In other words, if people are cowed into thinking, they can't say what they really think, and if they are controlled by a process that prevents them from speaking, they are less likely to internalize the intended lessons and more likely to reject them. The odds of a lasting change in beliefs come instead from the aforementioned "we feeling," and then from ample opportunities for conversations between peers. This can occur both in small group discussion, such as the T-group, and in pairs where people are allowed to talk privately with one another and sort things out without the constant presence of the workshop leader. It is through wise use of group dynamics that people are more likely to ponder their beliefs and consider other possibilities.

As Lewin put it: "…it is easier to change ideology or cultural habits by dealing with groups than with individuals" (Lewin, 1944, 1999, p. 289). He goes on to say: "Perhaps one might expect single individuals to be more pliable than groups of like-minded individuals. However, experience in leadership training, in changing of food habits, work production, criminality, alcoholism, prejudices – all seem to indicate that it is usually easier to change individuals formed into a group than to change any one of them separately. As long as group values are unchanged the individual will resist changes more strongly the further he is to depart from group standards. If the group standard itself is changed, the resistance which is due to the relation between individual and group standard is eliminated" (Lewin, 1947, 1997 p. 329). The group and the individuals in it must be allowed to do their own exploration of the facts before them. "It can be surmised that the extent to which social research is translated into social action depends on the degree to which those who carry out this action are made a part of the fact-finding on which the action is to be based" (Lewin, 1945, 1997 p. 55).

The brilliance of Lewin's approach is that the entire group is engaged in teaching, learning, and influencing. "Lecturing is a procedure by which the audience is chiefly passive. The discussion, if conducted correctly, is likely to lead to a much higher degree of involvement" (Lewin, 1948, 1999, p. 271). The restraining force of the lecturer being activate and the students or participants being passive is removed, and the homeostasis is broken and shifted toward a more democratic, truly inclusive norm. The group dynamics of functional democracy and effective learning are one and the same: "Learning democracy means, first, that the person has to do something himself instead of being passively moved by forces imposed on him. Second, learning democracy means to establish certain likes and dislikes, that is, certain valences, values, and ideologies. Third, learning democracy means to get acquainted with certain techniques, such as those of group decision" (Lewin, 1942, 1997, p. 223).

> In democracy, as in any culture, the individual acquires the cultural pattern by some type of "learning." Normally such learning occurs by way of growing up in that culture…experiments indicate that autocracy can be "imposed upon a person." That means the individual might "learn" autocracy by adapting himself to a situation forced upon him from outside. Democracy cannot be imposed upon a person; it has to be learned by a process of voluntary and responsible participation.
>
> **Lewin (1943, 1997, p. 38)**

The learning method and the social goals of democracy, equity, and inclusion, using Lewinian methods, are one and the same. In this manner, we are not doing one diametrically opposed thing in pursuit of another. We are walking the talk toward a sustainably equitable society.

It is a blessing that DEI education and the world we want to create are best implemented using the same principles. For such learning to stick, we must really reach the level of beliefs that requires engaging more than just the thinking brain. "The re-educative process affects the individual in three ways. It changes his *cognitive structure*, the way he sees the physical and social world, including all his facts, concepts, beliefs, and expectations. It modifies his *valances and values,* and these embrace both his attractions and aversions to groups and group standards, his feelings in regard to status differences, and his reactions to sources of approval or disapproval. And it affects *motoric action,* involving the degree of the individual's control over his physical and social movements" (Lewin, 1945, 1997, p. 50).

Lewin crafted learning that engaged one's entire experience, cognitive, emotional, and "motoric" (practice/actually doing). It's an experiential approach, a concept misunderstood by many. As noted in Chapter 2, random learning through experiences is an important part of life, but that is not what is meant by experiential learning. Nor does it simply mean having conversations, participating in "simulations" or games, doing role plays, etc. At its core, experiential learning requires having *a structured approach to assess experiences* so as to maximize learning. Lewin called that "fact-finding about the results of the action" (Lewin, 1946, 1997, p. 146). Experiential learning and Lewin's "action research" are one and the same. One must plan, do, and assess in a continuous cycle that leads to the next action, the next assessment, and so on. T-group learning, as conducted by Lewin, is an experiential design (see Appendix C for a contemporary version) well suited for DEI learning because it gets quick results. DEI education must work relatively fast. It must also reach deep within the individual. To do so and to have it last requires a process in which the individual willingly and actively reassesses their own behaviors and beliefs.

If behavior is only enforced from outside, DEI learning will fail to impact enough people, and for many, it will have the opposite effect. As Lewin put it: "Re-education is frequently in danger of only reaching the official system of values, the level of verbal expression and not of conduct; it may result in merely heightening the discrepancy between the super-ego (the way I ought to feel) and the ego (the way I really feel), and thus give the individual a bad conscience. Such a discrepancy leads to a state of high

emotional tension, but seldom to correct conduct. It may postpone transgressions, but it is likely to make the transgressions more violent when
they occur. A factor of great importance in bringing about a change in
sentiment is the degree to which the individual becomes actively involved
in the problem. Lacking this involvement, no objective fact is likely to
reach the status of a fact for the individual concerned and therefore influence his social conduct" (Lewin, 1945, 1997, p. 52).

If people are simply lectured at – moralized at by a critical authority
figure – then all they are likely to learn is to watch what they say. Such
approaches increase polarization instead of decreasing it. Conflict goes
underground, where it simmers. To foster real and lasting change, the
individual, in concert with the group, must be facilitated in doing genuine
action research on themselves. They must test beliefs, old and new, and
test new behaviors through dialogue and interaction. They will only do so
if they are genuinely respected in the process. That respect includes being
transparent about what the process is and by walking the talk by applying
the same standards to the leaders of the process.

Lewin's methods establish a reliable field of forces for DEI learning
and for organizing toward equity action, and when done effectively,
achieve dramatic results. We don't have to reinvent this wheel. We know
what to do.

Let us further consider what not to do. It's clear that a Lewinian
approach doesn't rely on lecturing people and claiming that you know the
truth about them and further claiming that if they disagree, they are in
denial. That is the dogma referred to in the title and already documented
throughout these pages (see the Introduction and Chapter 3 in particular).
My own research has stumbled upon other practices common to dogmatic
DEI that are counterproductive.

The DEI workshop I keep mentioning had us start by taking a test, known
as the Implicit Association Test, or IAT. A valid and reliable instrument
for testing bias could be an asset in the learning process. Unfortunately,
the IAT is neither.

I approached it with curiosity and was open to using it in my own work.
I was a little nervous that it might point to biases I am unaware of, but to
the best of my knowledge, I had an open mind.

The question by the way, is not whether we have biases. Of course we do.
The question is whether any of our biases include prejudice toward others
based on race, gender, etc.

As mentioned, the workshop started with a short film that set the stage for exploring bias. The film offered several clues as to something that had happened. I watched it and overlooked what seemed obvious later. I had focused instead on what I expected was the right stuff to focus on. This is called confirmation bias. More often than not, we only see what we expect to see. This is an outcome of only focusing on what we think is important. Without the capacity to narrow one's focus, one would go crazy. There's too much to possibly take in at any given time: the entire past, everything within range in the present, such as the texture of everything your body is touching at this moment, the lighting, the temperature, everything within sight (if you are sighted), everything you can hear, taste, smell, and everything that you can imagine and anticipate about the future. Our ability to tune out and focus is a wonderful capacity of human perception. Mindfulness depends on it. That very same capacity means we miss things. The movie we watched illustrated that well.

Was it supposed to imply something else? Such as, we have biases we are unaware of, including racial biases? Unfortunately, one could only speculate because that was not something the facilitators were willing to explain. As mentioned, the facilitators adamantly claimed that they had no agenda or intentions in terms of what they were teaching. Rather an odd claim when designing a curriculum, but my hunch is that their intention was to let the participants think for themselves, an intention I support even while differing with the means.

To make a long story short, perceptual bias is real, but that doesn't mean it always manifests in one way. Using myself as an example, one of my biases is that I am more afraid of men than women, especially if I am alone at night in a rough part of any city.

"Rough" to me doesn't automatically mean black. I clarify that because Robin Di Angelo contends all white people speak in a code, and the code for a "bad area" equals black. As she puts it, "In fact, the classification of which neighborhoods are good and which are bad is always based on race" (DiAngelo, 2018, p. 65). That triggers a thought I often had while reading her book, "Speak for yourself please." I'm more nervous in areas that have obvious poverty, especially if I am alone, on foot, at night. Those areas in my world might be populated by any ethnic groups, including whites. If young males, alone or in a group, approach me or are in my path, I am on alert. If I encounter a female, it generally has the opposite effect. I am mindful to try and be as unthreatening as possible because I assume my maleness may put *them* on alert. In other words, I see race. I also see gender, size, age, and attire. As we have attempted to establish, not everything is about race.

So that is one of my biases, and it runs counter to the stereotype that white people are afraid of black men. Under the circumstances just mentioned, I am wary of men, period. Furthermore, I am going to continue to hold that cautionary bias. I won't hold it against you if you don't, but I still will respect my own alarm bells and I won't be shamed or intimidated out of them.

Another bias of mine is a tendency to identify with people who have been oppressed. I think I do a good job of not holding that against people who, like me, are male and have light skin, but I am unabashedly drawn to the underdog. I am also biased toward people who favor democracy, diversity, inclusion, and equity. What that means in specific instances varies and is worthy of dialogue, but if you are consciously opposed to any of those values, we differ. If you are unconsciously doing things that reinforce inequality, such as insisting that we have already achieved an "even playing field" and that all hiring and promotion should be based purely on "merit," then I hope Chapters 4 through 6 have you reconsidering. Chapter 14 will further address how to create equity in hiring and other decisions.

In sum, those are my biases, at least some of the ones I'm aware of, and I'm sticking to them. Including my bias that bias, when it takes the form of prejudice, is a false hypothesis and is detrimental to the individual and society. Perceptual bias in general is part of the human condition and is neither good nor bad. Demonizing it is not helpful and is, ironically, a type of bias. Please be thoughtful about how to lead regarding concepts like this because the problems we are tackling are complicated enough already.

Back to the IAT implicit bias test. I took it again a third time just prior to writing this and got my third result. Once you have taken it, you can access the part of the website that says: "Disclaimer: These IAT results are provided for educational purposes only. The results may fluctuate and should not be used to make important decisions. The results are influenced by variables related to the test (e.g., the words or images used to represent categories) and the person (e.g., being tired, what you were thinking about before the IAT). How does the IAT work? The IAT measures associations between concepts (e.g., Light Skinned People and Dark Skinned People) and evaluations (e.g., Good, Bad). People are quicker to respond when items that are more closely related in their mind share the same button. For example, an implicit preference for Light Skinned People relative to Dark Skinned People means that you are faster to sort words when 'Light Skinned People' and 'Good' share a button relative to when 'Dark Skinned People' and 'Good' share a button (Project Implicit)."

The key assumption is, "People are quicker to respond when items that are more closely related in their mind share the same button." The first time I took it, I realized about two-thirds of the way through that the process was repetitious and that I understood how to take it, so I decided to speed up and worry less about making mistakes. I had two segments out of seven left and they happened to be segments where you were required to associate bad with dark-skinned people and good with light-skinned people. I sped through those two segments and thus my results indicated a strong preference for light-skinned people because I had moved slowly through the first five segments (which included dark-skinned good, light-skinned bad)!

As noted, but unknown to me at the time, the test assumed that speed during that portion meant it was easier for me to associate light-skinned with *good*, and dark skinned with *bad*. As the disclaimer admits, the speed at which I answered the first five segments and the speed at which I answered the last two segments influenced the outcome. I decided to take it again, this time answering everything as quickly as I could (i.e., replicating the same speed with which I had completed the last two segments of the first test). This time, the results said I moderately favored dark-skinned people over light-skinned. My third try indicated I moderately favored light-skinned people again. This time, the ending associated dark-skinned people with *good*, and I had no trouble matching the correct keyboard response for good to the faces of dark-skinned people or bad to the faces of light-skinned people. However, I noticed I made more mistakes, such as pushing the wrong button for word associations, such as "bad" for the word "fabulous." That must be how the most recent version of my alleged bias was "detected."

Prior to the workshop, skeptical about both results, I began searching the Internet for articles about the validity of the IAT. It wasn't hard to find a plethora of research, none of which indicated that the test was valid or reliable. In other words, there is no scientific evidence that it measures what it claims to be measuring. One of the articles combines research from many sources on IAT and concludes this: "An unbiased assessment of the evidence shows no compelling evidence that the race IAT is a valid measure of implicit racial bias; and without a valid measure of implicit racial bias it is impossible to make scientific statements about implicit racial bias" (Schimmack, 2019, pp. 45).

Does it matter? Of course it does! Many people are going to believe what the test tells them! California is even considering using the IAT in police hiring decisions! If you can't believe the results, why use the test? It is certainly below my standards. It's frankly unethical unless you add your own disclaimer along the lines of, "this test gives random results, so disregard them." The disclaimer on the website hints at that, but there really should be information pointing people to the abundance of data that discredits the IAT. The website also reveals this: "In addition to the publicly available IAT project implicit provides consulting services, lectures, in workshops on implicit bias, diversity and inclusion, leadership, applying science to practice, and innovation business (Project Implicit)." In other words, what they disclose about the problems with the IAT should be taken with a grain of salt, given that they are conducting a thriving business based on the IAT.

On a related note, new research indicates that extensive "implicit bias" work done by a company called Fair and Impartial Policing, LLC, with 36,000 NYPD officers, had no measurable impact on actual behavior. Similar training has been conducted with police departments across the country. The study "…hypothesized that the training would lead to reductions in racial/ethnic disparities in enforcement actions, including stops, frisks, searches, arrests, summonses, and uses of force. We examined enforcement disparities at multiple levels of analysis – at the aggregate level of commands and the level of individual enforcement events. To isolate the effect of the training from other factors, the NYPD adhered to a protocol for a randomized controlled trial that provided for grouping commands into clusters scheduled for training by random assignment. This experimental control was supplemented by statistical controls in the analytical models. Overall, we found insufficient evidence to conclude that racial and ethnic disparities in police enforcement actions were reduced as a result of the training" (Worden et al, 2020, p. vi).

Meanwhile, more than 3 million people had taken the IAT by December 2015, with 68% of the results indicating a slight to strong bias of light-skinned people over dark-skinned people and another 18% showing no bias either way. The results are not just random. If so, the totals would come out even. Since the individual result is not reliable, it is only fair to wonder if the entire test is biased in favor of telling people they are biased against dark-skinned people. Only 18% received results indicated the opposite bias. No doubt millions more have taken it since. Not that the totals indicating many are biased against dark-skinned people are shocking. An accurate instrument might tell us the same about the overall results. But unfortunately, the IAT isn't that.

Let us return to the workshop. A white female participant was disturbed by her IAT results, which had indicated bias against dark-skinned people. We were split into two groups by that time, one white and the other black. This was, we were told, to prepare us for the interracial conversation to come. This splitting of the groups along racial lines was another experiment I was curious about and then disappointed by. The white male facilitator was with the white group. Rather than say anything about the validity of the instrument, he encouraged her "to explore her bias." Having been told to be open and honest, I asked if the facilitator was concerned about the IAT's validity and mentioned the research I found. The facilitator said it didn't matter, and when I expressed surprise and concern over that, a white male participant, obviously upset with me, said, "why can't you just learn from it?" The facilitator didn't do anything to discourage this or to explore the question I was raising, so I dropped the subject. The pattern of one or both of them fighting with much of what I said continued through the remaining five sessions, never with any kind of overt ownership, and always with the implication that I was the problem. They revealed over time that they had known each other prior to the workshop, were friends, and shared many of the same beliefs about DEI. These dynamics made it very hard to continue. Other participants defended me, which was nice of them, but the whole thing was highly dysfunctional.

Interestingly, instead of bringing the two groups together by the third session as they had planned, the facilitators chose to keep us apart for one more week, with the vague explanation that "we weren't ready." What they meant by "not ready" they either weren't able or willing to elaborate on. We continued on in segregated groups until the fourth session, when apparently we were deemed "ready."

A strength of the workshop was that there were many opportunities to talk in pairs, a structure my colleagues and I also rely on. In my pairings at least, and as reported by others, there was an easy synergy between the participants, male and female, black and white, when we were allowed to talk privately. As far as I know, the conflicts in the group, which weren't just about me, thank heavens, were mostly between participants and the facilitators, not between blacks and whites. As noted, not everything is about race.

I was hoping that when we got to the combined group, the African-American woman who seemed to be the lead facilitator (although that was never acknowledged) would lead in a way that would help people work and explore differences. I know groups in conflict can move toward constructive dialogue with help because that is what I do. Unfortunately, that simply wasn't in their model, at least not overtly. Instead of facilitating in such a way that gaps were closed, both facilitators continued to be step-up transformers in the emotional system (as discussed in Chapter 10). The lead facilitator implied near the end that I was rebelling against her leadership because she was a black woman. Every conflict was viewed in terms of racism and sexism, and it was a long and tiring experience.

At the end, the facilitators said they welcomed feedback. I kept it to myself that I had offered feedback throughout the entire process and had been fought with every time I opened my mouth.

One of the only intentions the facilitators did reveal at the very beginning was that the workshop was not going to be a conversation based on "shame and blame." I mention this because I share that value 100%. Unfortunately, this standard was quickly dashed as I ended up being served a whole heap of blame for having a different point of view, with a chaser of shame in hopes I would swallow the blame. I would have preferred a spoonful of sugar. I still share the goal 100%.

The facilitators said they wanted everyone to be open and honest, and then they fought with me tooth and nail. They said that they had no preconceived ideas, and then they disagreed with almost everything I said. I don't think that is any way to build common ground, which I sincerely believe they wanted to do. I would love to someday have a different conversation with them.

We have the same goals of equity and social justice, and the facilitators obviously poured their hearts into the workshop. There were many lovely moments, and I was mindful to reinforce the other participants and the facilitators when I thought it was warranted. Unfortunately, if there was a framework, it wasn't shared, nor was it evident. It was much needed. What's worse, there are a bunch of people running DEI workshops all over the US, and it's safe to say many are making up their own approach or following the guidance of a dysfunctional approach. The same thing happened to T-groups in the 60s and 70s. They became hugely popular, and then people began running them without any training or clarity. Before anyone realized what was happening, there were so many painful experiences in T-groups that the "T-group movement" basically imploded and disappeared, with a few exceptions. I don't want the same thing to happen to DEI learning. The goal is too important. Backlash could and is happening. We have to do better to ensure we don't lose momentum and increase the odds of staying stuck in the homeostasis of inequality.

There was unfortunately one more thing in the workshop for us to learn from in terms of "what not to do." To be fair, this has been in the DEI conversation for years. I'm referring to the attempt to contrast eastern and western thought and the assertion that western thought has too long dominated. That last complaint is reasonable, but this conversation too often idealizes eastern thought as if in compensation and demonizes a stereotyped version of western thought. As usual, such "all good" versus "all bad" thinking doesn't hold water and doesn't contribute as much as it polarizes. What we need instead is accuracy, so we can move forward to a social construction that incorporates east and west, instead of rejecting either.

None of the voices I have heard on this seem to have studied the history of this claim of cultural polarity, or at least they don't include that in their presentations. The original contrast of eastern and western thought was the Greek world and the Persian Empire. In this contrast, the "west" was democratic and the "east" autocratic. In other words, the west was based on a collective social order, the east on an autocratic hierarchy. Paradoxically, Greek democracy was also built on the rights of the individual citizen (*free men,* that is). In that sense, individualism was honored in a new way in the "west." The stereotype often highlighted about east and west is collectivism versus individualism. There is truth to this, and yet it is a huge oversimplification, as is the division of humanity by east and west.

If this is geographical, where are we talking about? Israel? Where a colleague of mine (who endorsed this book) laments the western dominance in the field of OD? When I point out that the OD I practice was invented by a Jewish man and talk about the techniques, such as solutions being generated by the people facing the problems, he says, "I don't mean your OD." Then he goes back to lamenting the domination of the west (by which he really means certain popular practices of OD from the US, which I also believe are flawed)[2].

The stereotype of collectivism versus individualism is also questionable. Is democracy less collective than the hierarchical cultures of many "eastern" nations and cultures? If so, how? And are we really fighting racism by stereotyping "western" culture?

Bottom line: if we are going to make cultural contrasts, we shouldn't just make things up. We should try to be accurate. Yes, I am suggesting a passion for high levels of accuracy to be a standard that equates to a "thou shalt." Not all "thou shalts" are bad. Thou shalt resist racism!

The aforementioned DEI workshop took the east-west concept and transformed it into "Indigenous and Western." Table 13.1 is a model that I cobbled together off of the Internet. It is very similar to what they presented, although with some important differences, such as changing the words "Health and wellness focus" and "Illness/disease focus" to the words "Natural and spiritual healing" and "Science-based healing," in an attempt, not necessarily perfect, to decrease bias and increase accuracy:

TABLE 13.1

Indigenous and Western strawmen.

INDIGENOUS	WESTERN
Collectivism	Individualism
Egalitarian	Hierarchical
Oral	Written
One with nature	Dominion over nature
Natural and spiritual healing	Science based healing
Time – qualitative	Time – sequential
Identity informed by ancestors	Identity defined by self and accomplishments
Intuitive	Empirical – must be verifiable to hold validity
One with Creator	Separate from Creator

I call this a strawman (my word, not theirs) because a strawman in academic circles is a weak version of something one wants to debate against. It's a technique for making sure you win the debate. It's not a method that values accuracy. There was no discussion following this presentation, and I had by then begun protecting myself by keeping my mouth shut. An obvious question is who is indigenous? Are African cultures considered indigenous in this division? Are they considered western? Or are they simply ignored? Specifically, what about Egypt? East, west, or indigenous? The African Imhotep is the first known physician (writing on the subject 2200 years before Hippocrates), architect (designed the first pyramids), astronomer, as well as a mathematician and a poet. He is rightly a source of African pride and deserves to be widely known. He is also from a rigidly hierarchical culture that maintained slavery for thousands of years. How does *that* fit into this chart?

I like the idea of comparing and learning from cultures, if that is the intent, but this chart on its own leaves many questions unanswered. With a bias for accuracy, let's examine it row by row.

Rows 1 and 2 immediately run into the same stereotype mentioned earlier that indigenous culture is "collective" and "egalitarian" and western culture is "individual" and "hierarchical." Sounds nice, but try explaining the egalitarian lack of hierarchy to the average Aztec and their subjugated neighbors. Each culture then and now is different, and each has its own balance of the individual and the collective. Many indigenous cultures *are and were* more egalitarian compared to the US (but not necessarily compared to other "western" nations, such as Norway). For example, matrilineal property and descent were not uncommon in the Americas, Africa, and the Pacific, greatly elevating women's status relative to men. I find that type of egalitarianism admirable, especially in light of the goal of equity. Lumping all indigenous cultures together as egalitarian, however, requires omitting many uncomfortable facts. Defining western culture as "hierarchical" requires ignoring democracy in the west and ignoring hierarchy in indigenous cultures. That is closer to fantasy than fact.

Ignoring individuality in indigenous thinking also requires omitting facts. The Mayan wisdom of don Miguel Ruiz infused into Chapter 3 is a guide for individual consciousness, as is Buddhism and many other spiritual practices regardless of where you find them on earth. As historian Nell Irvin Painter points out, while critiquing simplistic attempts to define East and West (or as she puts it, "...an obsession with purity-racial and cultural..."): "Furthermore any attempt to trace biological ancestry quickly turns into legend, for human beings have multiplied so rapidly: by 1000 or more times in some 200 years, and by more than 32,000 times in 300 years. Evolutionary biologists now reckon that the six to 7 billion people now living shared the same small number of ancestors living two or three thousand years ago. These circumstances make nonsense of anybody's pretensions to find a pure racial ancestry. Nor are notions of western cultural purity any less spurious. Without a doubt, the sophisticated Egyptian, Phoenician, Minoan, and Persian societies deeply influenced the classical culture of ancient Greece..." (Painter, 2010, p. 14). Not only does the social construction of race hold no water – we are one race, the human race – but attempts to separate us by Eastern and/or Indigenous culture as differentiated from Western culture are flimsy at best.

Can we learn from cultural differences? Absolutely. Let's be as accurate as possible while doing so. Let us also be as accurate as possible about history. We aren't going to advance by distorting history. There has been far too much of that already. Carelessness about the facts undermines credibility and gives fuel to the forces currently fighting against more accurate teaching of history in US schools. We don't have to be perfect, that would be a tough claim for any historian, but we can and must do our best.

There is no arguing with this chart that western religion has often been hierarchical (not that the chart specifies that), but my own religious experience rooted in western tradition (and eastern and indigenous influence) is not. The reformation was resistance to the established hierarchy. The Christian mystics, from the beginning, have sought their own experience of God. In my own religious experience, I am one with the creator and with nature – they are one – and I need look no further than "western" pastor Howard Thurman for reinforcement of the same.

In sum, there is truth in this chart but there is also distortion, confusion, and ambiguity.

Racism and inequality are already infused with distortion, confusion, and ambiguity. We need not add more. To overcome the past, we must move beyond old ways of thinking, such as stereotyping cultures as "all good" and "all bad." To create a better world, we must (with high standards of accuracy) learn from and draw on the best of all cultures. We must truly be the change we want to see in the world.

Thankfully, I've also attended DEI sessions where there was a high regard for accuracy, respect for differences, and where I felt very much welcomed. I am far from alone in those values and in this quest. I have also personally led DEI conversations where the participants were able to let down their guard and explore together in new and profound ways. I can't speak for everyone that attended, but the majority were openly appreciative. We can do this in such a way that we build an ever-stronger community. We must.

NOTES

1. Whoever wrote the caption in Alfred Marrow's autobiography of Kurt Lewin mistakenly mixed up Benne and Bradford (corrected above). Dr. Frank Simpson was the commission member who solicited Lewin's services and I suspect a second mistake was misnaming him "Wright."
2. But that is a windmill to charge on another day.

14

Leading DEI Action

...we see the need for nonviolent gadflies...

Martin Luther King, Jr.

INSTITUTIONAL CHANGE

Building a world of peace which will be worth at least the name 'better than before' includes many problems: political, economic, and cultural. Each of them is loaded with difficulties. Yet all of them have to be considered together and attacked together as interdependent aspects of one dynamic field if any successful step forward is to be achieved.

Lewin (1943, 1997, p. 35)

It doesn't matter so much what people think. What matters more is what they do. If you bring people together and change things, *that* is the most direct path to changing what people think! We don't need therapy (not that therapy would hurt), we need action! The action will be the best therapy! Have a bias for action! Instead of spending your energy soul-searching for evidence in your thoughts and behaviors that you have unconscious biases, put your energy into doing something about institutional racism! Or do both, but favor action over insight!

Instead of holding a diversity training, have a cross-section (including the CEO) of your organization do a Lewinian force-field analysis of any inequities in your system and take action to address them!

Here is what Martin Luther King Jr. wrote to his jailers about "direct action" as he sat in his jail cell in Birmingham, Alabama: "You may well

DOI: 10.4324/9781003335689-18

ask: 'Why direct action? Why sit ins, marches and so forth? Isn't negotiation a better path?' You are quite right in calling for negotiation. Indeed, this is the very purpose of direct action. Nonviolent direct action seeks to create such a crisis and foster such a tension that a community which has constantly refused to negotiate is forced to confront the issue. It seeks to so dramatize the issue that it can no longer be ignored. My citing the creation of tension as part of the work of the nonviolent resister may sound rather shocking. But I must confess that I am not afraid of the word 'tension.' I have earnestly opposed violent tension, but there is a type of constructive, nonviolent tension which is necessary for growth. Just as Socrates felt that it was necessary to create a tension in the mind so that individuals could rise from the bondage of myths and half truths to the unfettered realm of creative analysis and objective appraisal, so must we see the need for nonviolent gadflies to create the kind of tension in society that will help men rise from the dark depths of prejudice and racism to the majestic heights of understanding and brotherhood. The purpose of our direct action program is to create a situation so crisis packed that it will inevitably open the door to negotiation. I therefore concur with you in your call for negotiation. Too long has our beloved Southland been bogged down in a tragic effort to live in monologue rather than dialogue" (Carson, 1998, p. 190).

Here are some issues you can take direct action on:

Hiring and promotion in your organization and in public organizations such as the police department. Reread chapter 6 if you must, but the assumption here is that *the playing field isn't even.* Until it is, a simple opportunity to walk the talk on equity is to give extra opportunity to those who have been denied opportunity in the past. If you act as if there is an even playing field and you only hire based on proven qualifications and experience, you will only hire those who have had the opportunity to gain that experience. In many fields, that will favor white males. No individual is at fault here, and each should be carefully considered, but when all things are relatively equal, giving opportunities to minority and female candidates with potential but with less experience is the right thing to do. The same goal of leveling the playing field should be applied to promotions.

Carefully consider whether you are really reaching out to minority candidates. Don't assume it is already happening. Reaching out will likely take extra effort. If you choose not to do so, you are choosing to perpetuate the homeostasis of inequality.

As Archbishop Desmond Tutu put it, "If you are neutral in situations of injustice, you have chosen the side of the oppressor."

Recent legal challenges, as discussed in Chapter 6, have gutted the equal opportunity act. Just because the country is going backwards legally is no excuse for you and your organization to do the same.

Police hiring illustrates how uneven the playing remains to this very day. Here is an excerpt from a recent article by the associated press:

"Racism trips up Black police candidates at the very start of the application process and later as they seek promotion, complicating efforts to make law enforcement agencies more diverse, experts, officers and Black police associations say.

Black applicants to law enforcement agencies are often filtered out early through racially biased civil service exams, accusations spelled out in multiple lawsuits over the years. And applicants are rejected thanks to criminal background checks that turn up drug and traffic offenses attributable (in part) to discriminatory policing, and poor financial histories that can stem from racial profiling, records and interviews show.

'Black and brown candidates-they'll gig them on credit issues, they'll gig them on minor brushes previously with law enforcement, they'll gig them on what they perceive as attitude issues,' said Charles Wilson, national chairman of the National Association of Black Law Enforcement Officers...

Black and Hispanic men have disproportionately high rates of contact with law enforcement at an early age, leading to records that often disqualify them from becoming police officers, said Ronnie Dunn, a Cleveland State University urban affairs professor.

In Pittsburgh, a 2012 federal lawsuit alleged the city police department systematically rejected Black applicants at the outset of the process after background checks turned up traffic tickets or drug offenses. But the city didn't disqualify 'Caucasian applicants for entry level police officer positions who have committed offenses similar to or even more serious,' the lawsuit said...

Last year, the US Justice Department sued Maryland's Baltimore County, alleging its written exams for hiring police officers have discriminated against Black applicants for years" (Welsh-Huggins, 2020, pp. 1–8).

In a similar article, a Black applicant in Philadelphia was rejected because of being in a car crash in which she was not even the driver.

Bias can find ways to maintain the status quo. Data can reveal that bias. It is up to us to examine the data of our own organizations and to insist on seeing the data of organizations we support as citizens, taxpayers, and customers.

Chapter 6 covered racial bias in lending. Ask your bank what their data shows.

Take action for equity with your vote! Vote for people who don't race bait or try to divide us! Vote for antiracism! That does not limit your vote to one party over the other. Vote Republican all you want, but if you care about social equity, vote for what used to be called moderate republicanism, as exemplified by former Representative Mike Castle of Delaware, former Senator Dan Evans of Washington State, and many others. Vote for people who support inclusion in democracy through voting rights. Protecting against fraud does not require restricted access to voting!

Don't let anyone divide us based on race, gender, and sexuality! Fool us once, shame on them. Fool us for centuries? Shame on us! We can realize the potential for this nation to truly stand for equality and democracy, but we must fight to get it done!

COMMUNITY ACTION

Like my father, let Kurt Lewin's methods be a guide for community action. Dad has worn many hats, including that of a community organizer. In that role, he brought people together who had no formal authority over each other to collaborate on contentious community issues. We must do the same.

Gun violence is a burning platform for such action. We have by far the highest rates of gun violence of any "first world" country, violence which disproportionately impacts African Americans while terrorizing us all. If Lewin were alive today, he would invite everyone into the tent. Gun owners, gun dealers, gun manufacturers, police, anyone living in high violence areas, gang members and anyone involved in gun violence, and anyone else who cares about the issue. Everyone would look at the available information, at the known solutions (warts and all), and then reason together until they came up with their own version of what to do. United by the goal, what the gun dealers chose to implement, what the police chose to do, and what the grandparents living in the high crime areas try will be unique to each group and sometimes to individuals who have their own vision for action. The organizer's job is not to come up with the solutions but rather to help each party carry on their effort, including bringing everyone back together to assess progress, make adjustments to strategy, and celebrate success.

Experts don't need to lead each community action, and each community action doesn't need to be organized the same way, but something close to what was just described can move us forward in ways that most of the past and present efforts have not. Keep in mind that a Lewinian approach would invite those currently working on the issue into the tent, so as to align with, learn from, and support rather than compete. Use the Lewinian Knowledge Retrieval Implication Derivation (KRID) method in Appendix E to get the best possible results from the utilization of experts.

Anything would be better than the current homeostasis on this issue! Let us come together and create a safer nation for all! Let us unite and address all the community problems we face! What have we got to lose?

CONFRONTING BIGOTS

There is another type of community action each of us can do. As mentioned in Chapter 2, one of Lewin's action research projects examined how to respond to bigoted statements in public places. Out of 513 participants, 80% "strongly preferred any answer at all to silence." It was agreed that silence could be mistaken as consent. In the study, two distinctly different types of responses were used: "One, calm and quiet; the other, excited and militant...65% preferred the calm answer...four out of five bystanders did not want to see the bigot go unchallenged. This meant that the individual who spoke up in public against stereotyped slurs on minorities could be assured that a typical group of bystanders would be on his side" (Marrow, 1969, p. 218).

The same calm, quiet, challenge to any and all bigoted behavior, be it subtle microaggressions or flat-out overt racism, sexism, or any prejudice, is needed today. That is all the more reason why the development of behavioral skills for handling conflict is vital to DEI.

CONCLUSION

We created racism and every other ism, and we can rid ourselves of them if we are determined, organized, and persistent. Just as the social construction of race is a lie, so is the belief that we are in a racial competition. Just as improving the lot of girls and women has proven to increase the prosperity of men, so can the rising tide of equity lift all boats. The best part of the founding of this nation was the faith in democracy and reason. That heritage can lead us forward. It's time to admit, learn from, and overcome the sins of the past and the present. We must do that without shame or blame, yet with intolerance of current and continuing attempts at oppression. Let us truly strive to be one nation, undivided, with religious freedom, and liberty and justice for all. These are the right values. The right time is now.

Appendix A

Action Research and Minority Relations[1]

In the last year and a half I have had occasion to have contact with a great variety of organizations, institutions, and individuals who came for help in the field of group relations. They included representatives of communities, school systems, single schools, minority organizations of a variety of backgrounds and objectives; they included labor and management representatives, departments of the national and state governments, and so on.

Two basic facts emerged from these contacts: there exists a great amount of good-will, of readiness to face the problem squarely and really to do something about it. If this amount of serious good-will could be transformed into organized, efficient action, there would be no danger for inter-group relations in the United States. But exactly here lies the difficulty. These eager people feel themselves to be in the fog. They feel in the fog on three counts: 1. What is the present situation? 2. What are the dangers? 3. And most important of all, what shall we do?

We have been conducting an interview survey among workers in inter-group relations in the State of Connecticut. We wanted to know their line of thinking, their line of action, and the major barriers which they encounter. Not a few of those whose very job is the improvement of inter-group relations state that perhaps the greatest obstacle to their work is their own lack of clarity of what ought to be done. How is economic and social discrimination to be attacked if we think not in terms of generalities but in terms of the inhabitants of that particular main street and those side and end streets which make up that small or large town in which the individual group worker is supposed to do his job?

One of the consequences of this unclearness is the lack of standards by which to measure progress. When the inter-group worker, coming home from the good-will meeting which he helped to instigate, thinks of the dignitaries he was able to line up, the stirring appeals he heard, the impressive setting of the stage, and the good quality of the food, he cannot help feeling elated by the general atmosphere and the words of praise from his friends all around. Still, a few days later, when the next case of discrimination becomes known he often wonders whether all this was more than a white-wash and whether he is right in accepting the acknowledgment of his friends as a measuring stick for the progress of his work.

This lack of objective standards of achievement has two severe effects:

1. It deprives the workers in inter-group relations of their legitimate desire for satisfaction on a realistic basis. Under these circumstances, satisfaction or dissatisfaction with his own achievement becomes mainly a question of temperament.
2. In a field that lacks objective standards of achievement, no learning can take place. If we cannot judge whether an action has led forward or backward, if we have no criteria for evaluating the relation between effort and achievement, there is nothing to prevent us from making the wrong conclusions and to encourage the wrong work habits. Realistic fact-finding and evaluation is a prerequisite for any learning. Social research should be one of the top priorities for the practical job of improving inter-group relations.

CHARACTER AND FUNCTION OF RESEARCH FOR THE PRACTICE OF INTER-GROUP RELATIONS

The research needed for social practice can best be characterized as research for social management or social engineering. It is a type of action-research, a comparative research on the conditions and effects of various forms of social action, and research leading to social action. Research that produces nothing but books will not suffice.

This by no means implies that the research needed is in any respect less scientific or "lower" than what would be required for pure science in the field of social events. I am inclined to hold the opposite to be true. Institutions interested in engineering, such as the Massachusetts Institute of Technology, have turned more and more to what is called basic research. In regard to social engineering, too, progress will depend largely on the rate with which basic research in social sciences can develop deeper insight into the laws which govern social life. This "basic social research" will have to include mathematical and conceptual problems of theoretical analysis. It will have to include the whole range of descriptive fact-finding in regard to small and large social bodies. Above all, it will have to include laboratory and field experiments in social change.

INTEGRATING SOCIAL SCIENCES

An attempt to improve inter-group relations has to face a wide variety of tasks. It deals with problems of attitude and stereotypes in regard to other groups and to one's own group, with problems of development of attitudes and conduct during childhood and adolescence, with problems of housing, and the change of the legal structure of the community; it deals with problems of status and caste, with problems of economic discrimination, with political leadership, and with leadership in many aspects of community life. It deals with the small social body of a family, a club or a friendship group, with the larger social body of a school or a school system, with neighborhoods and with social bodies of the size of a community, of the state, a nation and with international problems.

We are beginning to see that it is hopeless to attack any one of these aspects of inter-group relations without considering the others. This holds equally for the practical and the scientific sides of the question. Psychology, sociology, and cultural anthropology each have begun to realize that without the help of the other neither will be able to proceed very far. During the last five years first timidly, now very clearly, a desire for an integrated approach has become articulated. What this integration would mean specifically is still open. It may mean an amalgamation of the social sciences into one social science. It may mean, on the other hand, merely the co-operation of various sciences for the practical objective of improving social management. However, the next decade will doubtless witness serious attempts of an integrated approach to social research. I am of the opinion that economics will have to be included in this symphony if we are to understand and to handle inter-group relations more effectively.

TWO TYPES OF RESEARCH OBJECTIVES

It is important to understand clearly that social research concerns itself with two rather different types of questions, namely the study of general laws of group life and the diagnosis of a specific situation.

Problems of general laws deal with the relation between possible conditions and possible results. They are expressed in "if so" propositions. The knowledge of laws can serve as guidance for the achievement of certain objectives under certain conditions. To act correctly, it does not suffice, however, if the engineer or the surgeon knows the general laws of physics or physiology. He has to know too the specific character of the situation at hand. This character is determined by a scientific fact-finding called diagnosis. For any field of action both types of scientific research are needed.

Until recently, fact-finding on inter-group relations has been largely dominated by surveys. We have become somewhat critical of these surveys of inter-group relations. Although they are potentially important, they have, as a rule, used rather superficial methods of poll taking and not the deeper searching of the interview type used by Likert which gives us some insight into the motivations behind the sentiments expressed.

The second cause of dissatisfaction is the growing realization that mere diagnosis – and surveys are a type of diagnosis – does not suffice. In inter-group relations as in other fields of social management the diagnosis has to be complemented by experimental comparative studies of the effectiveness of various techniques of change.

THE FUNCTION AND POSITION OF RESEARCH WITHIN SOCIAL PLANNING AND ACTION

At least of equal importance to the content of the research on inter-group relations is its proper placement within social life. When, where, and by whom should social research be done?

Since we are here interested in social management let us examine somewhat more closely the process of planning.

Planning starts usually with something like a general idea. For one reason or another it seems desirable to reach a certain objective. Exactly how to circumscribe this objective, and how to reach it, is frequently not too clear. The first step then is to examine the idea carefully in the light of the means available. Frequently more fact-finding about the situation is required. If this first period of planning is successful, two items emerge: namely, an "overall plan" of how to reach the objective and secondly, a decision in regard to the first step of action. Usually this planning has also somewhat modified the original idea.

The next period is devoted to executing the first step of the overall plan.

In highly developed fields of social management, such as modern factory management or the execution of a war, this second step is followed by certain fact-findings. For example, in the bombing of Germany a certain factory may have been chosen as the first target after careful consideration of various priorities and of the best means and ways of dealing with this target. The attack is pressed home and immediately a reconnaissance plane follows with the one objective of determining as accurately and objectively as possible the new situation.

This reconnaissance or fact-finding has four functions. First it should evaluate the action. It shows whether what has been achieved is above or below expectation. Secondly, it gives the planners a chance to learn, that is, to gather new general insight, for instance, regarding the strength and weakness of certain weapons or techniques of action. Thirdly, this fact-finding should serve as a basis for correctly planning the next step. Finally, it serves as a basis for modifying the "over-all plan."

The next step again is composed of a circle of planning, executing, and reconnaissance or fact-finding for the purpose of evaluating the results of the second step, for preparing the rational basis for planning the third step, and for perhaps modifying again the overall plan.

Rational social management, therefore, proceeds in a spiral of steps each of which is composed of a circle of planning, action, and fact-finding about the result of the action.

With this in mind, let us examine for a moment the way inter-group relations are handled. I cannot help feeling that the person returning from a successful completion of a good-will meeting is like the captain of a boat who somehow has felt that his ship steers too much to the right and therefore has turned the steering wheel sharply to the left. Certain signals assure him that the rudder has followed the move of the steering wheel. Happily he goes to dinner. In the meantime, of course, the boat moves in circles. In the field of inter-group relations all too frequently action is based on observations made "within the boat" and too seldom based on objective criteria in regard to the relations of the movement of the boat to the objective to be reached.

We need reconnaissance to show us whether we move in the right direction and with what speed we move. Socially, it does not suffice that university organizations produce new scientific insight. It will be necessary to install fact-finding procedures, social eyes and ears, right into social action bodies.

The idea of research or fact-finding branches of agencies devoted to improving inter-group relations is not new. However, some of them did little more than collect newspaper clippings. The last few years have seen a number of very significant developments. About two years ago the American Jewish Congress established the Commission on Community Interrelations. This is an action-research organization designed primarily to function as a service organization to Jewish and non-Jewish bodies in the field of group interrelations. It is mainly interested in the group approach as compared to the individual approach on the one hand and the mass approach by way of radio and newspaper on the other. These latter two important lines are the focus of attention of the research unit of the American Jewish Committee.

Various programs try to make use of our educational system for betterment of inter-group relations, such as that of the American Council on Education, the College Study in Inter-group Relations at teachers colleges, the Citizenship Education Study in Detroit, and, in a more overall way, the Bureau for Intercultural Education. They all show an increased sensitivity for a more realistic, that is, more scientific, procedure of evaluation and self-evaluation. The same holds in various degrees for undertakings specifically devoted to Negro-White relations, such as the American Council on Race Relations in Chicago, the Urban League, and others. It is significant that the State Commission Against Discrimination in the State of New York has a subcommittee for co-operation with research projects and that the Inter-Racial Commission of the State of Connecticut is actively engaged in research. The recent creation of major research institutions at universities has also helped to broaden the vistas of many of the existing action organizations, making them more confident of the possibilities of using scientific techniques for their purposes.

I cannot possibly attempt even in the form of a survey to discuss the many projects and findings which are emerging from these research undertakings. They include surveys of the methods which have been used until now, such as reported in *Action for Unity*;[2] studies of the development of attitudes in children; studies of the relation between inter-group attitudes and such factors as political belief, position in one's own group; experiments about how best to react in case of a verbal attack along prejudice lines; change experiments with criminal gangs and with communities; the development of many new diagnostic tests; and last but not least, the development of more precise theories of social change. Not too many of the results of these projects have yet found their way into print. However, I am confident that the next few years will witness rapidly increased output of significant and practical studies.

EXAMPLE OF A CHANGE EXPERIMENT ON MINORITY PROBLEMS

One example may illustrate the potentialities of co-operation between practitioners and social scientists. In the beginning of this year the Chairman of the Advisory Committee on Race Relations for the State of Connecticut, who is at the same time a leading member of the Interracial Commission of the State of Connecticut, approached us with a request to conduct a workshop for fifty community workers in the field of intergroup relations from all over the state of Connecticut.

A project emerged in which three agencies co-operated, the Advisory Committee on Intergroup Relations of the State of Connecticut, The Commission on Community Interrelations of the American Jewish Congress, and the Research Center for Group Dynamics at the Massachusetts Institute of Technology. The State Advisory Committee is composed of members of the Interracial Commission of the State of Connecticut, a member of the State Department of Education of the State of Connecticut, and the person in charge of the Connecticut Valley Region of the Conference of Christians and Jews. The state of Connecticut seems to be unique in having an interracial commission as a part of its regular government. It was apparent that any improvement of techniques which could be linked with this strategic central body would have a much better chance of a wide-spread and lasting effect. After a thorough discussion of various possibilities the following change-experiment was designed co-operatively.

Recent research findings have indicated that the ideologies and stereo-types which govern inter-group relations should not be viewed as individual character traits but that they are anchored in cultural standards, that their stability and their change depend largely on happenings in groups as groups. Experience with leadership training had convinced us that the workshop setting is among the most powerful tools for bringing about improvement of skill in handling inter-group relations.

Even a good and successful workshop, however, seems seldom to have the chance to lead to long-range improvements in the field of inter-group relations. The individual who comes home from the workshop full of enthusiasm and new insights will again have to face the community, one against perhaps 100,000. Obviously, the chances are high that his success will not be up to his new level of aspiration, and that soon disappointments will set him back again. We are facing here a question which is of prime importance for any social change, namely the problem of its permanence.

To test certain hypotheses in regard to the effect of individual as against group settings, the following variations were introduced into the experimental workshop. Part of the delegates came as usual, one individual from a town. For a number of communities, however, it was decided the attempt would be made to secure a number of delegates and if possible to develop in the workshop teams who would keep up their team relationship after the workshop. This should give a greater chance for permanency of the enthusiasm and group productivity and should also multiply the power of the participants to bring about the desired change. A third group of delegates to the workshop would receive a certain amount of expert help even after they returned to the community.

The first step in carrying out such a design calls for broad fact-finding about the different types of inter-group problems which the various communities have to face. Communities and teams of group workers in the communities would have to be selected so that the results of the three variations would be possible to compare. In other words, this project had to face the same problems which we mention as typical for the planning process in general.

The experiences of the members of the State Advisory Board of the Interracial Commission of the State of Connecticut were able quickly to provide sufficient data to determine the towns which should be studied more accurately. To evaluate the effect of the workshop a diagnosis before the workshop would have to be carried out to determine, among other things, the line of thinking of the community workers, their main line of action and the main barriers they have to face. A similar re-diagnosis would have to be carried out some months after the workshop.

To understand why the workshop produced whatever change or lack of change would be found, it is obviously necessary to record scientifically the essential happenings during the workshop. Here, I feel, research faces its most difficult task. To record the content of the lecture or the program would by no means suffice. Description of the form of leadership has to take into account the amount of initiative shown by individuals and subgroups, the division of the trainees into subgroups, the frictions within and between these subgroups, the crises and their outcome, and, above all, the total management pattern as it changes from day to day. These large-scale aspects, more than anything else, seem to determine what a workshop will accomplish. The task which social scientists have to face in objectively recording these data is not too different from that of the historian. We will have to learn to handle these relatively large units of periods and social bodies without lowering the standards of validity and reliability to which we are accustomed in the psychological recording of the more microscopic units of action and periods of minutes or seconds of activity.

The methods of recording the essential events of the workshop included an evaluation session at the end of every day. Observers who had attended the various subgroup sessions reported (into a recording machine) the leadership pattern they had observed, the progress or lack of progress in the development of the groups from a conglomeration of individuals to an integrated "we" and so on. The group leaders gave their view of the same sessions and a number of trainees added their comments.

I have been deeply impressed with the tremendous pedagogical effect which these evaluation meetings, designed for the purpose of scientific recording, had on the training process. The atmosphere of objectivity, the readiness by the faculty to discuss openly their mistakes, far from endangering their position, seemed to lead to an enhancement of appreciation and to bring about that mood of relaxed objectivity which is nowhere more difficult to achieve than in the field of inter-group relations which is loaded with emotionality and attitude rigidity even among the so-called liberals and those whose job it is to promote inter-group relations.

This and similar experiences have convinced me that we should consider action, research, and training as a triangle that should be kept together for the sake of any of its corners. It is seldom possible to improve the action pattern without training personnel. In fact today the lack of competent training personnel is one of the greatest hindrances to progress in setting up more experimentation. The training of large numbers of social scientists who can handle scientific problems but are also equipped for the delicate task of building productive, hard-hitting teams with practitioners is a prerequisite for progress in social science as well as in social management for intergroup relations.

As I watched, during the workshop, the delegates from different towns all over Connecticut transform from a multitude of unrelated individuals, frequently opposed in their outlook and their interests, into co-operative teams not on the basis of sweetness but on the basis of readiness to face difficulties realistically, to apply honest fact-finding, and to work together to overcome them; when I saw the pattern of role-playing emerge, saw the major responsibilities move slowly according to plan from the faculty to the trainees; when I saw, in the final session, the State Advisory Committee receive the backing of the delegates for a plan of linking the teachers colleges throughout the state with certain aspects of group relations within the communities; when I heard the delegates and teams of delegates from various towns present their plans for city workshops and a number of other projects to go into realization immediately, I could not help feeling that the close integration of action, training, and research holds tremendous possibilities for the field of inter-group relations. I would like to pass on this feeling to you.

Inter-group relations are doubtless one of the most crucial aspects on the national and international scene. We know today better than ever before that they are potentially dynamite. The strategy of social research must take into account the dangers involved.

We might distinguish outside adversities and barriers to social science and the inner dangers of research procedures. Among the first we find a group of people who seem to subscribe to the idea that we do not need more social science. Among these admirers of common sense we find practitioners of all types, politicians and college presidents. Unfortunately there are a good number of physical scientists among those who are against a vigorous promotion of the social sciences. They seem to feel that the social sciences have not produced something of real value for the practice of social management and therefore will never do so. I guess there is no other way to convince these people than by producing better social science.

A second threat to social science comes from "groups in power." These people can be found in management on any level, among labor leaders, among politicians, some branches of the government, and among members of Congress. Somehow or other they all seem to be possessed by the fear that they could not do what they want to do if they, and others, really knew the facts. I think social scientists should be careful to distinguish between the legitimate and not legitimate elements behind this fear. For instance, it would be most unhealthy if the findings of the Gallup Poll were automatically to determine policy for what should and should not become law in the United States. We will have to recognize the difference between fact-finding and policy setting and to study carefully the procedures by which fact-finding should be fed into the social machinery of legislation to produce a democratic effect.

Doubtless, however, a good deal of unwillingness to face reality lies behind the enmity to social research of some of the people in power positions.

A third type of very real anxiety on the part of practitioners can be illustrated by the following example. Members of community councils to whom I have had the occasion to report results of research on group interrelations reacted with the feeling that the social scientists at the university or in the research arm of some national organization would sooner or later be in the position to tell the local community workers all over the states exactly what to do and what not to do.

They obviously envisaged a social science "technocracy." This fear seems to be a very common misunderstanding based on the term "law." The community workers failed to realize that lawfulness in social as in physical science means an "if so" relation, a linkage between hypothetical conditions and hypothetical effects. These laws do not tell what conditions exist locally, at a given place at a given time. In other words, the laws don't do the job of diagnosis which has to be done locally. Neither do laws prescribe the strategy for change. In social management, as in medicine, the practitioner will usually have the choice between various methods of treatment and he will require as much skill and ingenuity as the physician in regard to both diagnosis and treatment.

It seems to be crucial for the progress of social science that the practitioner understand that through social sciences and only through them he can hope to gain the power necessary to do a good job. Unfortunately there is nothing in social laws and social research which will force the practitioner toward the good. Science gives more freedom and power to both the doctor and the murderer, to democracy and Fascism. The social scientist should recognize his responsibility also in respect to this.

RESEARCH ON MAJORITIES AND MINORITIES

It has not been the intention of this paper to discuss detailed findings of social research in inter-group relations. I feel, however, that I should mention two points which illustrate, I think, basic aspects.

Inter-group relations is a two-way affair. This means that to improve relations between groups both of the interacting groups have to be studied.

In recent years we have started to realize that so-called minority problems are in fact majority problems, that the Negro problem is the problem of the white, that the Jewish problem is the problem of the non-Jew, and so on. It is also true of course that inter-group relations cannot be solved without altering certain aspects of conduct and sentiment of the minority group. One of the most severe obstacles in the way of improvement seems to be the notorious lack of confidence and self-esteem of most minority groups. Minority groups tend to accept the implicit judgment of those who have status even where the judgment is directed against themselves. There are many forces which tend to develop in the children, adolescents, and adults of minorities deep-seated antagonism to their own group. An over-degree of submissiveness, guilt, emotionality, and other causes and forms of ineffective behavior follows. Neither an individual nor a group that is at odds with itself can live normally or live happily with other groups.

It should be clear to the social scientist that it is hopeless to cope with this problem by providing sufficient self-esteem for members of minority groups as individuals. The discrimination which these individuals experience is not directed against them as individuals but as group members and only by raising their self-esteem as group members to the normal level can a remedy be produced.

Many whites in the South seem to realize that one prerequisite for progress is the enhancement of self-esteem of the southern Negro. On the other hand, the idea of a positive program of increasing group loyalties seems to be paradoxical to many liberals. We seem to have become accustomed to linking the question of group loyalty and group self-esteem with jingoism.

The solution, I think, can be found only through a development which would bring the general level of group esteem and group loyalty which in themselves are perfectly natural and necessary phenomena to the same level for all groups of society. That means every effort should be made to lower the inflated self-esteem of the 100 percenters. They should learn the prayer from the musical-play, Oklahoma. "Dear God, make me see that I am not better than my fellow men." However it is essential to learn the second half of this prayer that goes something like "but that I am every darn bit as good as he." From the experiences thus far I would judge that raising the self-esteem of the minority groups is one of the most strategic means for the improvement of inter-group relations.

The last point I would like to mention concerns the relation between the local, the national, and the international scenes. No one working in the field of inter-group relations can be blind to the fact that we live today in one world. Whether it will become politically one world or two worlds, there is no doubt that so far as interdependence of events is concerned we are living in one world. Whether we think of the Catholics, or the Jews, the Greeks, or the Negroes every group within the United States is deeply affected by happenings in other places on the globe. Inter-group relations in this country will be formed to a large degree by the events on the international scene and particularly by the fate of the colonial peoples. It will be crucial whether or not the policy of this country will follow what Raymond Kennedy has called the international Jim Crow policy of the colonial empires. Are we ready to give up the policy followed in the Philippines and to regress when dealing with the United States' dependencies to that policy of exploitation which has made colonial imperialism the most hated institution the world over? Or will we follow the philosophy which John Collier has developed in regard to the American Indians and which the Institute of Ethnic Affairs is proposing for the American dependencies? This is a pattern which leads gradually to independence, equality, and co-operation. Whatever the effect of a policy of permanent exploitation would be on the international scene, it could not help having a deep effect on the situation within the United States. Jim Crowism on the international scene will hamper tremendously progress of inter-group relations within the United States and is likely to endanger every aspect of democracy.

The development of inter-group relations is doubtless full of danger and the development of social science in this field faces many obstacles.

The picture, however, which I have been able to paint, of the progress of research and particularly of the progress that the organization of social research has made during the last few years, makes me feel that we have learned much. A large scale effort of social research on inter-group relations doubtless would be able to have a lasting effect on the history of this country.

It is equally clear, however, that this job demands from the social scientists an utmost amount of courage. It needs courage as Plato defines it: "Wisdom concerning dangers." It needs the best of what the best among us can give, and the help of everybody.

NOTES

1. Reprinted with permission from: Lewin, Kurt. (1997). *Resolving Social Conflicts and Field Theory in Social Science* (pp. 143-156). American Psychological Association.
2. Goodwin Watson, *Action for Unity*, New York, Harper and Brothers, (1946).

Appendix B

Four Key Skills[1]

Wallen identified four skills which are helpful in closing or minimizing interpersonal gaps. They are:

- **Behavior description**
- **Feeling Description**
- **Perception Check**
- **Paraphrase**

See Appendix C for a DEI version of the Behavior Description Quiz.

FEELING DESCRIPTION – EXERCISE F-1

Introduction

Any spoken statement can convey feelings. Even the factual report, "It's three o'clock" can be said so that it expresses anger or disappointment. However, it is not the words that convey the feelings. Whether the statement is perceived as a factual report or as a message of anger or disappointment is determined by the speaker's tone, emphasis, gestures, posture and facial expression.

This exercise does not deal with the non-verbal ways that we express feelings. It focuses on the kind of verbal statements we use to communicate feelings.

We convey feeling by:

- Commands – "Get out!" "Shut up!"
- Questions – "Is it safe to drive this fast?"

- Accusations – "You only think about yourself!"
- Judgements – "You're a wonderful person." "You're too bossy."

Notice that, although each of the examples conveys strong feeling, the statement does not say what the feeling is. In fact, none of the sentences even refers to the speaker or what he or she is feeling.

By contrast, the emotional state of the speaker is the content of some sentences. Such sentences will be called "description of feeling." They convey feeling by naming or identifying what the speaker feels. "I am disappointed." "I am furiously angry!" "I'm afraid going this fast!" "I feel discouraged."

The goal of this exercise is to help you recognize when you are describing your feelings and when you are conveying feelings without describing them. Trying to describe what you are feeling is a helpful way to become more aware of what it is you do feel.

A description of feelings conveys maximum information about what you feel in a way that will probably be less hurtful than commands, questions, accusations and judgments. Thus, when you want to communicate your feelings more accurately you will be able to do so.

Procedure

This is not a test. Complete only one item at a time, as the steps show.

1. Mark your answers for item 1 only; do NOT do item 2, 3, etc., yet.
2. Compare your responses to item 1 with your learning partner(s) (if working alone, skip this step). Discuss the reasons for any differences.
3. Turn to the back pages titled <u>Discussion of Responses to Exercise F-1</u>. Read and discuss item 1 only.
4. Repeat steps for item 2. Then continue this process for each item in turn until you have completed all ten items.

The sets of sentences below convey feelings. Each sentence in a set, however, may be communicating the same feelings using different methods.

Put a "D" before each sentence that conveys the feeling by describing the speakers feeling.

Put a "NO" before each sentence that conveys the feeling but does not describe the speaker's feeling.

1. (___) a. Shut up! Not another word out of you!
   (___) b. I'm really annoyed by what you just said.
2. (___) a. Can't you see I'm busy? Don't you have eyes?
   (___) b. I'm beginning to resent your frequent interruptions.
   (___) c. You have no consideration for anybody else's feelings. You're completely selfish.
3. (___) a. I feel discouraged because of some things that happened today.
   (___) b. This has been an awful day.
4. (___) a. You're a wonderful person.
   (___) b. I really respect your opinion. You're so well-read.
5. (___) a. I feel comfortable and free to be myself when I'm around you.
   (___) b. We all feel you're a wonderful person.
   (___) c. Everybody likes you.
6. (___) a. If things don't improve around here, I'll look for a new job.
   (___) b. Did you ever hear of such a lousy place to work?
   (___) c. I'm afraid to admit that I need help with my work.
7. (___) a. This is a very poor exercise.
   (___) b. I feel this is a very poor exercise.
8. (___) a. I feel inadequate to contribute anything to this group.
   (___) b. I am inadequate to contribute anything to this group.
9. (___) a. I am a failure; I'll never amount to anything.
   (___) b. That teacher is awful, he didn't teach me anything.
   (___) c. I'm depressed because I did so poorly on that test.
10. (___) a. I feel lonely and isolated in my group.
    (___) b. For all the attention anybody pays to what I say, I might as well not be in my group.
    (___) c. I feel that nobody in my group cares whether I'm there or not.

Discussion of Responses to Exercise F-1

1. a. **No.** Commands such as these convey strong emotion but do not name what feeling prompted the speaker.

   b. **D.** Speaker says he feels annoyed.

2. a. **No.** Questions that express strong feeling without naming it.

   b. **D.** Speaker says he feels resentment.

   c. **No.** Accusations that convey strong negative feelings. Because the feelings are not named, we do not know whether the accusations stemmed from anger, disappointment, hurt or something else.

3. a. **D.** Speaker says he feels discouraged.

   b. **No.** The statement appears to describe what kind of day it was. In fact, it expresses the speaker's negative feelings without saying whether   he feels depressed, annoyed, lonely, humiliated, rejected or what.

4. a. **No.** This value judgement reveals positive feelings about the other but does not describe what they are. Does the speaker like the other, respect, enjoy, admire or love him/her?

   b. **D.** The speaker describes his positive feeling as respect.

5. a. **D.** A clear description of how the speaker feels when with the other.

   b. **No.** First, the speaker does not speak for himself but hides behind the phrase, "we feel." Second, "you're a wonderful person" is a value judgment and not a feeling.

   c. **No.** The statement does name a feeling (likes) but the speaker attributes it to everybody and does not make clear that the feeling is within the speaker. A description of feeling must contain, "I," "me," "my" or "mine" to make clear that the feelings are the speaker's own or are within him/her. Does it seem more affectionate for a person to tell you, "I like you" or "everybody likes you."

6. a. **No.** Conveys negative feelings by talking about the condition of things in this organization. Does not say what the speaker's inner state is.

   b. **No.** A question that expresses a negative value judgement about the organization. It does not describe what the speaker is feeling.

   c. **D.** A clear description of how the speaker feels in relation to his job. He feels afraid.

   Expressions a and b are criticisms of the organization that could come from the kind of fear described in c.

Negative criticisms and value judgements often sound like expressions of anger. In fact, negative value judgements and accusations often are the result of the speaker's fear, hurt feelings, disappointment or loneliness.

7. a. **No.** A negative value judgment that conveys negative feelings but does not say what kind they are.

b. **No.** Although the speaker begins by saying, "I feel…" he/she does not name the feeling. Instead, he passes a negative value judgment on the exercise. Merely tacking the words "I feel" on the front of a statement does not make it a description of feeling. People often say "I feel" when they mean "I think" or "I believe," for example, "I feel the Yankees will win" or "I feel you don't like me."

Many persons who say they are unaware of what they feel – or who say they don't have any feelings about something – habitually state value judgements without recognizing that this is the way their positive or negative feelings get expressed.

The speaker could have said she/he felt confused or frustrated or annoyed, etc. She/he then would have been describing her/his feelings without evaluating the exercise itself.

Many arguments could be avoided if we were careful to <u>describe</u> our feelings instead of expressing them through value judgements. For example, if Joe says the exercise is poor, and Fred says it is good, they may argue about which it "really" is. However, if Joe says he was frustrated by the exercise and Fred says he was interested and stimulated by it, no argument should follow. Each person's feelings are what they are. Of course, discussing what it means that each feels as he does may provide helpful information about each person and about the exercise itself.

8. a. **D.** Speaker says he feels inadequate.

b. **No.** Careful! This sounds much the same as the previous statement. However, it states that the speaker actually <u>IS</u> inadequate – not that she/he just currently feels this way. The speaker has evaluated her/himself – has passed a negative judgment on her/himself – and has labeled her/himself as inadequate.

This subtle difference was introduced because many people confuse feeling and being. A person may <u>feel</u> inadequate to contribute to a group and yet make helpful contributions. Likewise she/he may

<u>feel</u> adequate and yet perform very inadequately. A person may feel hopeless about a situation that turns out not to <u>be</u> hopeless.

One sign of emotional maturity may be that a person does not confuse what she/he feels with the nature of the situation around him/her. Such as person knows he/she can perform adequately even though she/he <u>feels</u> inadequate to the task. She/he does not let her/his feelings keep her/him from doing her/his best because she/he knows the difference between feelings and performance and that the two do not always match.

9. a. **No.** The speaker has evaluated her/himself – passed a negative judgment – and labeled her/himself a failure.

b. **No.** Instead of labeling her/himself a failure, the speaker blames the teacher. This is another value judgement and not a description of feelings.

c. **D.** The speaker says she/he feels depressed.

Statements a and c illustrate the important difference between passing judgements on one self and describing one's feelings. Feelings can and do change. To say that I am now depressed does not imply that I will or must always feel the same. However, if I label myself as a failure – if I truly think of myself as a failure – I increase the probability that I will act like a failure.

One woman stated this important insight for herself this way, "I have always thought I was a shy person. Many new things I really would have liked to do I avoided – I'd tell myself I was too shy. Now I have discovered that I am not shy, although at times I feel shy."

Many of us avoid trying new things and thus learning, by labeling ourselves. "I'm not artistic." "I'm not creative." "I'm not articulate." "I can't speak in groups." If we could recognize what our feeling is beneath such statements, maybe we would be more willing to risk doing things we are somewhat fearful of.

10. a. **D.** The speaker says he feels lonely and isolated.

b. **No.** Conveys negative feelings but does not say whether he/she feels lonely, angry, disappointed, hurt or what.

c. **No.** Instead of "I feel," the speaker should have said, "I believe." The last part of the statement really tells what the speaker believes the <u>others feel</u> about him/her not what she/he feels.

Expressions c and a relate to each other as follows: "Because I believe that nobody in my group cares whether I am there or not, I feel lonely and isolated."

PARAPHRASE

A Basic Communication Skill for Improving Interpersonal Relationships

by John Wallen

The problem: Tell somebody your phone number and he will usually repeat it to make sure he heard it correctly. However, if you make a complicated statement most people will express agreement or disagreement without trying to insure that they are responding to what you intended. Most people seem to assume that what they understand from a statement is what the other intended.

How do you check to make sure that you understood another person's ideas or suggestions as he intended them? How do you know that his remark means the same to you as it does to him?

Of course, you can get the other person to clarify his remark by asking, "what do you mean?" or "tell me more" or by saying, "I don't understand." However, after he has elaborated you still face the same question: "Am I understanding his idea as he intended it to be understood?" Your feeling of certainty is no evidence that you do in fact understand.

The Skill: If you state in your own way what his remark conveys to you, the other can be begin to determine whether his message is coming through as he intended. Then if he thinks you misunderstand, he can speak directly to the misunderstanding that you have revealed. I will use the term "paraphrase" *for any means of showing the other person what his idea or suggestion means to you.*

Paraphrasing, then, is a way of revealing your understanding of the other person's comment in order to test your understanding.

An additional benefit of paraphrasing is that it lets the other know that you are interested in them. It is evidence that you do want to understand what they mean.

If you can satisfy the other that you really do understand their point, they will probably be willing to attempt to understand your view.

Thus, paraphrasing is crucial in attempting to bridge the interpersonal gap:

1. It increases the accuracy of communication and, thus, the degree of mutual shared understanding.

2. The act of paraphrasing itself conveys feeling – your interest in the other, your concern to see how they view things.

Learning to paraphrase: People sometimes think of paraphrasing as merely putting the other persons' words in another way, then try to say the same thing with different words. Such word-swapping may merely result in the illusion of mutual understanding as in the following example:

Sarah: Jim should never have become a teacher.
Fred: You mean teaching isn't the right job for him?
Sarah: Exactly! Teaching is not the right job for him.

Instead of trying to re-word Sarah's statement, Fred might have asked himself, "What does Sarah's statement mean to me?" In that case, the interchange might have sounded like this:

Sarah: Jim should never have become a teacher.
Fred: You mean he is too harsh on the children? Maybe even cruel?
Sarah: Oh no. I meant that he has such expensive tastes that he can't ever earn enough as a teacher.
Fred: Oh, I see. You think he should have gone into a field that would have insured him a higher standard of living.
Sarah: Exactly! Teaching is not the right job for Jim.

Effective paraphrasing is not a trick or a verbal gimmick. It comes from an attitude, a desire to know what the other means. And to satisfy this desire, you reveal the meaning his comment had for you so that the other can say whether it matched the meaning he intended to convey.

If the other's statement was general, it may convey something specific to you:

Larry: I think this is a very poor textbook.
You: Do you mean that it has too many inaccuracies?
Larry: No, the text is accurate, but the book comes apart too easily.

Possibly the other's comment suggests an example to you:

Laura: This text had too many omissions; we shouldn't adopt it.
You: Do you mean, for example, that it contains nothing about African Americans role in the development of America?
Laura: Yes, that is one example. It also lacks a discussion of the development of the arts in America.

If the speaker's comment was very specific, it may convey a more general idea to you:

Ralph: Do you have 25 pencils I can borrow for my class?
You: Do you just want something for them to write with? I have 15 ball-point pens and 10 or 11 pencils.
Ralph: Anything that will write will do.

Sometimes the other's ideas will suggest the inverse or opposite to you:

Stanley: I think the Teacher's Union acts too irresponsibly because the Administration has ignored them for so long.
You: Do you mean that the TU would be less militant now if the Administration had consulted with them in the past?
Stanley: Certainly, I think the TU is being forced to more and more desperate measures.

To develop your skill in understanding others, try different ways of:

1. Conveying your interest in understanding what they mean,
2. Revealing what the other's statement meant to you. Find out what kinds of responses are helpful ways of paraphrasing for you.

The next time someone is angry with you or is criticizing you, try to paraphrase until you can demonstrate that you understand what he or she is trying to convey as they intend it. Be a scientist of your own interactions – what effect does paraphrasing have on you and on the other?

PERCEPTION CHECK

Wallen's fourth tool, "perception check," consists of naming your hunch about what someone else is feeling. In other words, perception check is using feeling description to communicate your perception of someone else's emotion. For example, depending on your judgment about how they will take it and whether it will be useful, you might say, "you seem (sad, mad, glad, afraid)" or any variation thereof.

To generate a perception check you must pay attention to the other person's verbal and non-verbal sources of information (words, tone, body language and facial expressions), and take into account their circumstances (they just joined the company, they just lost a loved one, etc.). Then you match the external data with what you have felt in similar circumstances, or have felt when your verbal and non-verbal behavior was similar to that of the other person. Drawing on these sources of internal and external information, a perception check is then one's best guess about the other's emotions.

This may sound complicated. Like many processes of perception, when we break it down, it *is* complicated. It is also yet another constant and lightning quick process (like interpretation of meaning), usually occurring outside of conscious awareness. If you think about it, you will probably agree that you have hunches all the time about how others are feeling. Wallen helps us bring the process into awareness. This helps in two ways: we can get better and better at tuning in to others, and somewhat paradoxically, we can be less attached to our beliefs about what others are feeling.

In practical terms, perception check can help close gaps by providing a way to convey empathy and by increasing your understanding of the other by helping you find out whether your hunch matches their own beliefs about how they are feeling.

Keep in mind that emotions are, well, emotional, and people deny them in themselves and try to control them in others ("Don't feel sad"). Communication about emotion can be tricky. If a person believes you are pointing out their emotion as if it's a fault, they may respond defensively. None the less, perception check can have the desired impact, especially if you are acting with genuine empathy, and you are conveying that successfully to the recipient. Paying attention to and respecting the emotions of people you care about is important if you want to truly connect.

Paying attention to and respecting your own emotions is the surest way to hone your ability to empathize with others.

That brings us near the close of my chapter on Wallen's four skills. As I trust you can see, Wallen's Interpersonal Gap is potentially much more than just a theory. As corny as this may sound, *it is a way of (interpersonal) life.* Given that potential, further exploration is called for. My colleague and brother Chris wrote the following article to assist such exploration.

But first, let me say a little about "self-generation" (a concept Chris is about to introduce to you). Self-generation is what is coming from inside of you that you are accessing in interpersonal interactions. Sometimes this is current data, such as your feelings. Especially in reactive moments, it is past experience that you are projecting in the present onto others. As mentioned, authority figures are like blank screens for "projection." They remind us emotionally of the authority figures in our early lives, and it takes awareness to see them in the present as the people they really are. To the extent possible, it is important to be able to differentiate between and to be aware of what is truly current, and what is coming from the past. Try to remember that negative interpretations of others are more about past experiences (your hippocampus doing its job of carrying emotional memories) than they are about the person you are presently interacting with. That awareness will help you not get too attached to those interpretations, and that is vital for closing gaps and keeping your brain in open learner mode.

NOTE

1. Excerpted with permission from Chapter 4 of Crosby, G. (2008). *Fight, Flight, Freeze: Emotional Intelligence, Behavioral Science, Systems Theory & Leadership.* Seattle, WA. CrosbyOD Publishing.

Appendix C

DEI Behavior Description Quiz

Behavior description is one of the four skills identified by Dr. John Wallen in his communication model, *The Interpersonal Gap*. This skill is essential to self-awareness and to being open with others while minimizing misunderstanding as much as possible. It is also essential to effective leadership, supervision, and feedback. The skill is to describe the words and actions to which we are reacting. This is more difficult than it may sound. Most people place the cause of their own thoughts and feelings outside themselves ("You don't trust me") when a more accurate statement is something like, "based on what you did and/or said, I have come to the belief that you don't trust me."

If you can be precise about what was done or said ("You told me not to step on the ice"), you can get clearer about what you are reacting to, and over time become less reactive. If all you do is tell people your negative judgements of them as if those are all there is to "the facts," they will likely be offended and go into fight or flight mode. In contrast, if you can tell them what it was that they did or said that you are reacting to, you are each more likely to learn from the interaction and come to a mutual understanding.

Far too often interpersonal effectiveness suffers as a result of language that although intended as factual is subject to various interpretations. Engineers in their reports, supervisors in giving feedback, parents in their discipline, quality inspectors, employees attempting to be clear about concerns, all confuse phrases that make a judgment from those that report a fact (as close to an objective description of a behavior or condition as possible) and this confusion easily gives rise to conflict: "You're being careless" versus "Three jars were broken this past hour." "The second shift isn't working hard enough" versus "Production is down 40 cases today." A skillful person strives to communicate with specificity. They get it that a judgment/

interpretation not only inflames, but worse, it draws attention and energy away from the problem (i.e., three jars were broken) and towards fighting the accusation itself. The same holds true for sensitive DEI concepts such as micro-aggressions. "That was a micro-aggression" is likely to get a defensive response, whereas "when you said I'm a credit to my race, I felt offended," a description of behavior and feelings, is more likely to help the receiver engage in dialogue with you and consider the impact of their words.

Keep in mind that just because you perceive something as a micro-aggression, doesn't make that perception a fact. What is a fact is that you perceived it that way, and that your perceptions deserve respect. It's also possible that in the systemic ambiguity of inequality, racism, sexism, or whatever prejudice you are facing, that the person on the receiving end in any given moment (including you) has confirmation bias that takes in information (such as certain words or even just a frown) and assumes it to be a micro-aggression. I trust you agree that every frown from everyone that is different than you is *not* a micro-aggression. Instead, the wise individual has responsibility for sifting through their perceptions and *trusting themselves* while also *questioning themselves*. Otherwise, everything looks like a nail and the concept of micro-aggression, a potentially useful tool, becomes a clumsy hammer.

The ambiguity won't go away until we achieve real equality. Until then, when you believe there has been a micro-aggression, be specific about the behavior and the impact on you, and you may have the good fortune of influencing the other to assess their own behavior. You may also have the good fortune of discovering at times that you misunderstood. That may be an awkward moment, but if true it should also be a blessing and a relief.

ACTIVITY:

Take the following quiz to hone your understanding of behavior description:

The goal of the quiz is to distinguish between behaviorally specific statements and interpretations. Review the eighteen statements that follow and put an X beside the statements that you consider to be observable data (words or actions) versus interpretations (the observer's beliefs about the words and actions):

Behavior Description Quiz

1. ___ Nadine was discouraged.
2. ___ Jamar's voice got louder when he said, "Cut it out, Joe."
3. ___ Joe was trying to make Jamar mad.
4. ___ Nadine talked more than Jamar did.
5. ___ Nadine was aggressive.
6. ___ Joe was being racist.
7. ___ Li was not sincere.
8. ___ Jamar misinterpreted Joe.
9. ___ Joe said nothing when Jamar said, "Cut it out."
10. ___ Joe knew that Nadine was feeling discouraged.
11. ___ Joe invalidated Jamar. His behavior was a micro-aggression.
12. ___ April talked about the weather and the baseball game.
13. ___ April deliberately changed the subject.
14. ___ Roberto forgot the meeting.
15. ___ Camille didn't show respect to her boss.
16. ___ That's the third time you've started to talk while I was talking.
17. ___ The furnace repair was inadequate.
18. ___ Li did not look me in the eyes when she spoke to me.
19. ___ Camille said, "I expect to receive this report by 3:00 PM tomorrow."
20. ___ My boss is a micro-manager.

ANSWERS TO BEHAVIOR DESCRIPTION QUIZ

1. Nadine was discouraged – *interpretation*.

   This is a guess about Nadine's emotional state, undoubtedly inferred from statements and other behaviors (facial expression, tone of voice, posture. etc.), but a guess nonetheless.

2. Jamar's voice got louder when he said, "Cut it out, Joe" – *behavior description*.

   This is all based on observable data. You can hear a person's voice get louder, and you can hear their words. No interpretations (such as "Jamar was unprofessional," or "Jamar wasn't sure that Joe heard him") were added.

3. Joe was trying to make Jamar mad – *interpretation*.

   Here we are guessing at Joe's intentions. This type of judgment is more often than not an inaccurate assumption about intentions, and even if unspoken adds tension to the relationship between the judger (in this case whoever is forming this interpretation of Joe) and the person being judged.

4. Nadine talked more than Jamar did – *behavior description*.

   That's simply a fact. Somebody talked more than the other. There's no value judgment added in this sentence. An observer may judge either or both of them based on the behavior that has been described ("Jamar is timid," "Jamar is polite," "Nadine is domineering," "Nadine is assertive," etc.), but such interpretations are not included in the above sentence. Rather, the interpretations are in the eye of the beholder, and may be influenced by gender, racial, power, and other types of dynamics and bias.

5. Nadine was aggressive - *interpretation*.

   Especially when there is a power imbalance, what appears to be "aggressive" behavior to some is admired as "assertive" by others. For example, a form of sexism is judging woman as "aggressive" (or worse) while judging men exhibiting the same behaviors as "assertive" or "manly." Almost any behavior can be admired or not depending on how it fits our bias (pre-judgment) of how a certain person or type of person "should" behave.

6. Joe was being racist - *interpretation*.

"Racist" is a judgement, perception, or interpretation (words used interchangeably in this theory), not a behavior. Defining the word racist (or any other word) as an interpretation does not invalidate the judgment, hence in this example defining racist as an interpretation does not deny that racism exists. **The lesson here is simply that behavior description is the skill of being able to tell the difference between judgements and the behavior we are judging.**

Observable actions and/or statements are as close as we can get to "facts." While there may be general cultural agreement on what it means to be "racist," there are wide differences about how any judgment word translates into moment-to-moment daily behavior. As with all interpretations, no matter how touchy the topic, the process of interpretation is subjective.

As examples of the subjectivity of this judgment, ask the people you are with whether anyone can be "racist" or only "white" people can be racist. Ask them whether giving preference to a minority candidate is racist or progressive. If you start fighting, or are angry at this suggested test, please take a deep breath and get back to completing this assignment. There will be plenty of time for dialogue later, and clarity about behavior description may help decrease the tension in that dialogue.

Judgments, including "racist," are in the eye of the beholder. This is true whether only one person judges a behavior in a particular way, or whether everyone you know judges it the same way. The subjective nature of interpretation does not invalidate the interpretation. That conclusion would be a misunderstanding of this skill. **The skill is to be able to differentiate between what is the actual behavior and what is interpretation of the behavior.** Many people, especially in emotional situations, confuse the two and claim their judgments *are all there is to the facts.* That fusion of judgement (which is subjective) and behavior (which is objective IF we can see it, hear it, and describe it without bias) fuels conflict.

Let's return to our hypothetical "Joe." If someone wants to influence him, the odds of success go up if they can be behaviorally specific ("When you say, 'When will you people get over it,' I think you mean that you want minorities to keep their mouths shut," or "when you say 'I don't see color,' I'm afraid you are trying to sweep racism under the carpet"). Joe probably doesn't think of himself as racist, so without behavioral specificity, all that will likely come from accusing him of being racist is defensiveness and debate. "I am not!" "You are too!" "I'm not racist, you are!" "That's a micro-aggression!" "You're too sensitive!" You can see where that is headed, and it is probably nowhere good.

7. Li was not sincere - *interpretation.*

Judging a person's sincerity is a subjective process. We can observe that they aren't looking us in the eye (which has different implications in different settings and different cultures); we can see that they aren't smiling; we can hear that they repeated themselves, etc. Interactions are rich with observable data. Our perceptual biases will notice some of the data, while missing other information completely or noticing it beneath the level of our consciousness. We may conclude that someone is sincere or insincere based on the behavioral data, but even though interpretations are based on data, they are still interpretations.

8. Jamar misinterpreted Joe – *interpretation.*

Jamar's interpretation could be accurate. It could be inaccurate. Interpretation involves forming an opinion based on what we have observed. The common mistake that people make is to believe that their interpretations, and the interpretations of trusted others, are facts, and to lose sight that there are other possibilities. The only way to verify whether an interpretation is accurate or not is to verbalize your interpretation to the person you are interpreting. That is the essence of the skill known as paraphrasing.

9. Joe said nothing when Jamar said, "Cut it out" – *behavior description.*

Jamar's words and Joe's silence are observable behavior.

10. Joe invalidated Jamar. His behavior was a micro-aggression. – *interpretation*

These DEI terms may seem like facts, but they are none-the-less interpretations of behavior, such as the hypothetical moment above when Nadine talked more than Jamar did. Some observers might view that as an invalidation and a micro-aggression (or both), while others may not. Some readers might view *this explanation* as an invalidation and others may not. Whenever there is inequality there is increased ambiguity and tension, and it is even easier to mistake judgments as facts and to fight about the validity of the judgments.

It's less inflammatory to give behaviorally specific feedback and have dialogue about behaviors instead.

11. Joe knew that Nadine was feeling discouraged – *interpretation*.
12. April talked about the weather and the baseball game – *behavior description*.

    While this is behaviorally specific and good enough for the purpose of this test, it provides a low level of detail about April's behavior. Quotes, such as what April said about the weather and the baseball game, would add much more detail. At times less detail is good enough in behavior description, at other times more detail is important.

13. April deliberately changed the subject – *interpretation*.

    April may have changed the subject, but without further information (such as asking her) whether she did so deliberately is a matter of interpretation.

14. Roberto forgot the meeting – *interpretation*.

    Roberto didn't attend the meeting may be a fact. Whether he forgot, only Roberto knows for sure.

15. Camille didn't show respect to her boss – *interpretation*.

    Respect means different things to different people. For example, for some, it's a sign of respect if people will tell them when they are angry with them, while others believe anger is disrespectful.

16. That's the third time you've started to talk while I was talking – *behavior description*.

    The statement describes behavior. The behavior, if it is a persistent pattern by a man or men to talk when a female is talking, or for a member of a dominant ethnic group to talk when members of a minority group are talking, could reasonably be interpreted as a micro-aggression.

17. The furnace repair was inadequate - *interpretation*.

    Inadequate is an interpretation. Whether you claim it is "adequate" or "inadequate," both are interpretations and thus open to debate. To be specific you need to know more. For example, "after the furnace repair person came, the furnace still isn't maintaining heat within the specified range, and the noise that caused me to call the repair person in the first place is still happening."

18. Li did not look me in the eyes when she spoke to me – *behavior description*.

Eye contact varies from culture to culture, as do interpretations about it. This sentence only described the behavior, not a judgment about the behavior.

19. Camille said, "I expect to receive this report by 3:00 PM tomorrow" – *behavior description.*

This is a behavior description from two different angles. It is a quote. **Words are behavior**! They are public data. If you were being filmed, your words will be the same each time you watch the film, even though your judgements about yourself may change from viewing to viewing. That is evidence of the subjective nature of interpretation!

Use quotes to check meaning and to talk about moments. Repeating someone's words is a form of behavior description. Don't fight about whether you got the words right. If the other thinks or says they said something else, hold the possibility that you misheard (and especially hold that possibility if you were told the words second hand). Human perception is error likely especially if emotions are running high. If you differ about the words, let go and figure out together what you mean now and how to move forward.

The other angle here is that Camille's expectations are behaviorally specific. Whatever your reaction to her expectations, you know precisely when she wants the report. If you foresee problems in executing that task it would be wise to talk about it, but that is mostly a lesson for another day.

20. My boss is a micro-manager – *interpretation*

It's easy to believe this judgement is a fact, especially if your co-workers agree. It's also predictable that most, if they are the boss, will feel defensive if they are told this type of judgment. A far less combative approach is to be clear about what type of supervision would help you be even better at getting the job done. Perhaps you think you could make certain decisions, access certain types of information, do less reporting, spend less time being monitored, etc. Only you know what specific behavior leads you to the judgement that you are micro-managed. Offer feedback focused on behavior specifics, not on judgments.

Appendix D

T-Groups Adapted for the Workplace[1]

Be the change you wish to see in the world.

Mahatma Gandhi

FROM CONFLICT TO COLLABORATION

The T-Group workshop has just begun. The 24 participants and 3 faculty members have introduced themselves, and the CEO (who is himself participating) has briefly explained why he has sponsored this week-long workshop and follow-up session. The plant has been losing money for years, and he believes that people must learn a new way to work together if the plant is to survive. Relationships are tense, especially between management and labor. Because he trusts the facilitators, the CEO has invited twelve members of the Union leadership, including the Union President, who is barely on speaking terms with the CEO. There are layers of formal and informal reporting relationships and years of animosity in the mix. As the participants sit in a large circle to begin the week, there is no escaping the initial awkwardness. The Union President chooses to stand near the door, in his own words "uncertain" as to whether he will stay.

The workshop and a broader OD strategy were designed to help the organization decrease tension while increasing performance. The facilitator has already worked with the management team on their group dynamics and, with his colleagues, will be working with every team in the organization during the weeks and months to come. He has also met with Union leadership, to show respect, to inform, and to allow them to get their own feel for the strategy and his team of facilitators. It doesn't hurt that one of the facilitators used to be an electrician in a manufacturing plant.

Following the CEO's kickoff, the lead facilitator asks the participants to talk in pairs. Working in pairs is a critical part of the workshop structure. He explains that they will be doing this a lot throughout the week. He walks the room assigning pairs. The task is to talk about what they just heard…what they think and feel about it. Instantly 50% of the room goes from being quiet into conversation. The simple structure is repeated throughout the week, with different pairings, and is a big asset both to learning and to decreasing stress.

Now the room is buzzing with talk. The facilitator regains attention and invites anyone to speak. After an anxious silence, the conversation with the CEO begins. People admit their fears, "You guys are just here to brainwash us," and their hopes "We need to work together so maybe this will help." The CEO admits that he doesn't have all the answers and that he and the management team have made some mistakes. The HR Director explains why he thinks the workshop is needed. The Union VP says, "I don't know what he just said, but I'm against it!" The room goes silent. The HR Director begins to fight back. The facilitator says something like, "This is a good example of why we are here," and manages to lighten the mood without taking sides. Even though the facilitator is working for his customer (the CEO), neutrality when helping with interactions is vital to effective facilitation. Everyone relaxes. The President chooses to stay. The workshop proceeds.

INVITATION

What Is the Invitation?

Do you aspire to create a high performing work culture measured by the organization's metrics? Are your employees preoccupied with needless drama, characterized by blaming individuals and groups, avoiding direct conversations about difficult issues, silos, and other symptoms of ineffective culture? Do problems, such as quality issues, late delivery, safety incidents, low morale, unplanned outages, etc., plague the organization? Regardless of technological and other changes, the critical variable for organizational performance is how people interact, especially regarding difficult work issues and during moments of high emotional intensity.

Everyone at every level of the organization can become more emotionally mature and less prone to dramatizing interactions with peers and authority figures. When individuals learn through a group process the influence of their peers in the process plays a powerful role in taking the learning deeper and helping it stick. When a critical mass of a workgroup and/or organization go through a T-group learning process, the likelihood of sustained change is strong. If you relate to these issues, industry adapted T-groups are a reliable path to a work culture that can improve all of the above. Creating a High Performance Work Culture requires development of a critical mass of individuals and groups with high interaction skills.

PURPOSE

Why Use This Approach?

The industry-adapted T-group's unique purpose is examination and experimentation by the group members on their interpersonal and group dynamics. The outcome – as validated by participant ratings, the author's observations of participants over time, and business metrics dating back to the 1950s – is deep behavioral and work culture change resulting in high performance.

At their essence, T-groups provide a unique opportunity for each participant to examine,

- one's thoughts, feelings and wants from moment to moment (intrapersonal),
- what happens between oneself and others (interpersonal...for example, whether you have been understood as intended, and are understanding others as they intend),
- group dynamics (from the simple, such as who talks the most, to the complex, such as how the group handles conflict)
- and to get feedback from other participants and the facilitator.

This examination must to some extent be verbalized for feedback and maximum learning to occur. Topics in the traditional sense are less important than these verbal explorations, although deep conversations about work do occur during industry adapted T-groups.

SYSTEM

Who Needs to Be Involved?

We have used these methods with intact work teams, cross-functional project teams and a random mix from the same organization. Industry-adapted T-groups have been used as the basis for a two-year graduate program and in numerous Leadership Development courses. We have used them time and again as the foundation of a business culture change strategy in over 15 countries worldwide, with simultaneous translation, and with groups of functionally illiterate yet highly motivated learners. The approach is effective with groups of pastors and at church camps. In the right hands, the T-group methodology can be used anywhere, anytime to create real and lasting change.

Some only allow T-groups to be populated by strangers with no more than two participants attending from the same organization. However, Lewin's original T-group participants were not strangers to each other. They were community leaders who knew each other before and after the workshop. The benefit of T-groups populated by members from the same organization is that it is more like the original situation than a T-group populated by strangers. This is not to say that there is anything wrong with conducting T-groups populated by strangers. Either approach in the hands of skilled facilitators can result in deep learning and the author's father and mentor, Robert P. Crosby, mastered and continued to successfully use T-groups within organizations.

EXPERIENCE

How Does It Work?

Lewin knew that group change was more powerful than individual change... that pairing brings peer-to-peer influence to life, while also allowing some privacy for processing one's experience. In these workshops, people quickly get that they are all peers in being human, even while they have different roles in the organization. Kurt Lewin's original T-group emerged during a facilitated conversation between community leaders in Connecticut about racial tension. Not only did many of the participants know each other but also there was a clear topic. In contrast, a widely practiced T-group method is to start with ambiguity: no topic, no explanation of the structure. Learning comes from what emerges. This adds unique stress to the process, for better or worse.

Rather than starting with a T-group, and ambiguity, Crosby's process starts with an explanation of the process, including an agenda. Each participant has a manual which includes Learning Objectives, the Agenda, and other materials:

Day	Agenda
Monday	1. Workshop Overview 2. Neuroscience and EQ 3. Victim-Creator Accountability Model 4. T-group 5. The Interpersonal Gap 6. Behavior Description
Tuesday	1. Check-In (pairs reflect on most important learnings thus far, followed by group dialogue using T-group skills) 2. Emotional Intelligence 3. Feeling Description 4. T-group 5. Active Listening Skills 6. T-group
Wednesday	1. Check-In 2. Feedback Skills 3. T-group 4. Jay Hall Conflict Management Survey 5. T-group and other activities using the conflict survey results
Thursday	1. Check-In 2. Self-Differentiation, Self-Differentiated Leadership, Systems Thinking 3. T-group 4. Organizational Alignment 5. T-group
Friday (half day)	1. Check-In 2. T-group 3. Self Evaluation 4. Workshop Evaluation 5. Closing

After the opening, including dialogue with the sponsor about why the organization is holding the workshop, ground rules (full attendance, cell phones on silent) and introductions, the original workshop design for 24 participants begins its basic pattern of theory session (with all 24 participants together) followed by a T-group session (broken into two groups of 12 and in separate rooms), with that pattern repeating through the week. The workshop could also be as small as 6 and as large as 48, with 5 faculty – 1 for each T-group and 1 orchestrating the workshop and floating from T-group to T-group.

This mixing of theory and T-group practice is consistent with the early T-groups. Facilitators explain that the week flows from working on self-awareness and interpersonal skills, to systems thinking and application to work. Although there will be other deviations, such as which theory to start with, and what to teach in response to what emerges, the outcome remains essentially the same.

SAMPLE THEORY SESSION

The workshop can start with this simple theory session: The first assertion is that we were born with a completely open mind. We weren't burdened with fear-based thoughts such as, "I wonder if I will look stupid if I try to learn how to walk." The second assertion is that we are born with a full range of emotions. These assertions encourage us to recapture an open mind, and they frame the potential emotional intelligence (EQ) learning in a T-group. Along with dialogue that emerges while presenting, the participants are asked to talk in pairs about, "What does this theory have to do with me?" followed by a group discussion. This practice of engagement even during lectures is followed throughout the workshop.

Additional foundational theories explanations ease the participants into the week, and create a framework for "self-awareness." By the time they enter their first T-group, participants are already more attuned to their reactive responses of fight (verbal oppositional behavior) and flight (avoidance behavior) based on the neuroscience and EQ theories they have explored, and better understand their tendency to be reactive to tension.

They have already begun the process of shared learning and have some common focus.

This does not save them from ambiguity! Nothing can. No one knows what is going to happen next in life. One of the strengths of T-group learning is the focus on what is emerging. It's an opportunity to become more aware and skillful in the present and more organized in how one learns from experience.

THE FIRST T-GROUP OF THE WORKSHOP

Crosby's colleagues, Drs. John Scherer and Ron Short added an important structure to the T-group: an inside and outside group that helps participants manage their anxiety while accelerating their skill development (Figure D.1). Once split into two breakout rooms and two T-groups, each group of 12 splits (again assuming the original design for 24 participants), further into an "A" and "B" group. Six will be inside T-group (group A), the other six (group B) are seated in an outer circle, each assigned to silently observe a member of the inner circle in what we call a "learning partnership."

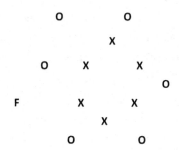

Key:

F = Facilitator,

O = Observer (outside group),

X = T-group members (inside group).

FIGURE D.1
Illustration of inside-outside T-group.

The observers complete notes in two columns: In the left column they note their partner's behavior while in the group (words, facial expressions, body language, tone of voice) and in the right column, their best hunch about their partner's emotions from moment to moment. This focus is derived from John Wallen's Interpersonal Gap model, as do many of our facilitator interventions.

The first group will be 'in' for approximately ten minutes. At the end of the ten minutes, the facilitator stops the action and directs the learning partners to get together and debrief for approximately 5 minutes. The observing partners share the behavior and emotion for the moment they thought was most important. No data dump of everything they have written down is necessary or meaningful. The intention is for the receiver of the feedback to do most of the talking and most of the work of reflecting on the feedback and their experience in the T- group. In most human interactions, feedback is received passively (and if there is tension, silently rejected). Instead T-group participants can learn how to actively receive feedback and to encourage active reception when they are giving feedback. Many participants learn as much or more from the observation task and the learning partner debriefs as they do from the actual T-group experience.

Deviations throughout the week include switching T-group facilitators (which tends to stir up authority issues), a 'total group' experience (everyone is 'in' without observers, including the facilitator), and a host of other possibilities, such as putting an empty chair in the T-group with an open invitation to the observers from group A to enter the group B (or vice versa) for brief interactions.

THE T-GROUP TASK

Another important difference between industry adapted T-groups and what has become the "traditional" T-group, is the T-group "task," which is explained before the first T-group of the week and repeated later if needed. It is also hung on the wall on a flipchart sheet as a visual for the participants, as are all the visuals drawn during the theory sessions. By the end of the week, the walls are covered with flip chart sheets. The T-group task is defined this way:

To verbalize,

- What I want,
- What I think (about myself, about others in the group, the facilitator, group dynamics),
- and What I feel (emotion)... here and now.

The facilitator also explains that unlike traditional teachers that keep themselves separate and in a sense above their students, the facilitator is part of the process, and holds themselves to the same standards (the T-group task) that they are teaching. Furthermore, because authority relationships are so emotional and dysfunctional in most organizations, the participants are encouraged to speak up if and when they are unhappy with the facilitator.

Facilitators in the a T-group for the workplace are active from the beginning in encouraging the task (more so than in other T-group models). If people are just offering thoughts (which is likely in their initial anxiety) ask, "What is your emotion now?" Encourage "I" language. Encourage the group to overcome their tendency towards indirectness by looking other participants in the eye and talking to them directly. Active encouragement of the task is essential to achieving the learning objectives.

Like most T-groups, there is no agenda (the agenda for the workshop is not the same as having an agenda for each T-group), and there are no designated leaders within the group (even if people in positions of formal authority are participating).

Whether relatively active or passive, eventually participants will get reactive towards the T-group facilitator. That is a critical moment in helping them learn how to be genuine while having differences. If the facilitator can engage at that moment in a manner where the participant feels respected, then the group members will likely become more honest about their differences within the group. The capacity to talk respectfully about differences is a critical performance variable in work culture. It's easy to talk about what you agree on and have in common. What people must get better at is clearing up misunderstandings and managing real differences.

Part of the task is to notice and articulate group dynamics/norms as they emerge. Who talks to whom? Who talks the most? Who talks the least? Is there a balance of participation? How does the group "decide" what to talk about? Do members look at and talk directly to each other? How does the group manage differences? These are the dynamics that determine the quality of work conversations, and these are the focus in a T-group. There is no harm in telling the participants exactly that. It is a tough enough learning task even when it is overtly and clearly stated.

THE INTERPERSONAL GAP

The foundation upon which the industry-adapted T-group sessions rests is Dr. John Wallen's Interpersonal Gap, a model reviewed on the first day, and assigned as follow up reading on the first night. The Interpersonal Gap identifies the degree of congruence and potential disconnect between a speaker's intention and the effect of the message "as received." Understanding this model helps people shift from just focusing on the sender during interactions, also taking responsibility as the receiver. The receiver interprets the message of the sender (words, facial expression, body language and tone of voice), and it is in the (mis)interpretations and listening assumptions of the receiver that many misunderstandings and reactive feelings are created.

Most, without awareness of the gap, simply blame the sender. Wallen's model encourages accountability when sending and receiving, and in doing so adds behavioral skills for reducing misunderstandings, and provides a vital framework for how to be open about issues and interactions without using inflammatory judgments/interpretations. By paraphrasing to check understanding, and by sticking with behavior and the impact on self, participants learn a new way to talk about and manage tense moments. These behavioral skills are not only critical for effective workplace feedback, but also to the feedback given throughout the workshop.

CHECK-INS

"Check-ins" in the mornings are another important part of the learning process. On the second morning, people are paired with a partner with whom they are to "check-in" first thing for the remainder of the week.

The task is to reflect on their learning, including from any interactions they had outside the workshop. A group discussion ensues, with some telling about their interactions and learnings. This dialogue, framed with the same task as the T-group, really becomes a whole group T-group and is often a source of some of the most important learnings of the week.

CLOSING

The closing is attended to the extent possible by the sponsor and the supervisors of each participant. The participants prepare by rating the session on two 1 to 10 scales, the first being Application to Work, and the second being Application to Life (outside of work). The average is around 8.5 on both scales (usually slightly higher on application to Life). The participants also prepare by identifying their most important learning, and by thinking in advance about their work relationship with their immediate supervisor ("How I want to be with my boss" & "What I want from my boss so I can do my job better").

The supervisors get to see the ratings and are made aware of the participants' preparation. The closing then consists of each participant talking about their learning. This is powerful because each participant's learning is unique to them and so they are the best source to articulate it. For many, it is also empowering to do so in the presence of the leader who is sponsoring the workshops. Furthermore, those in attendance at the closing get to learn from the participants and refresh their knowledge. Interaction is encouraged during this closing process, and skill-building continues. Finally, a graduation ceremony concludes the session.

SUSTAINING THE RESULTS

Follow-up and monitoring is vital to any successful implementation. This ranges from one to multiple sessions four to six weeks later. The Follow-Up starts with each participant speaking about their experiences since the initial workshop, reflecting on the theories they learned (both to jog their memories and as a starting point for coaching opportunities) and re-engaging their T-group learning. When integrated into a broader change strategy, participants can be coached and supported through this process in multiple settings (within their work teams for example) for years and even decades.

Critically, the top leader sponsoring the activity must be willing to participate themselves, so they can walk the talk and be seen walking the talk. The same is true for the facilitators, and for each participant. The ongoing challenge is to start with self rather than obsessing with what is "wrong" with others.

TECHNOLOGY

How Is Technology Leveraged?

T-groups require no electronic technology. All that is needed is a flipchart and markers, wall space for hanging flip chart generated visuals, chairs (no tables), and a room spacious enough that participants can talk privately in pairs and small groupings.

Beginning in 2020 my colleagues and I have begun experimenting with virtual T-groups. While in person work has many advantages, such as the ability to see the facial expressions and body language if working with more than one group, and the ability to have quick private conversation with participants during sessions and during breaks, we are pleased with the results. A plus of the virtual process is the access to video replay, which can be a powerful learning tool, and the obvious advantage that people can attend from anywhere on the globe who might otherwise never experience such learning. I believe there is room for both methodologies moving forward.

EVIDENCE

What Are the Theoretical & Empirical Foundations?

T-Groups were invented in 1946 by Kurt Lewin (1890-1947), Director of MIT's Research Center for Group Dynamics. In 1953, a young man, Robert P. Crosby, while becoming a Methodist Minister, found himself in a T-group at his seminary, led by Walter Holcomb. Holcomb had been influenced by Ken Benne, who had learned from Lewin. Crosby then attended a T-group workshop at National Training Laboratories (NTL), led by Drs. Ron Lippitt, Ken Benne, and Leland Bradford. Lippitt became Crosby's mentor for the next 29 years, while Crosby first applied the T-group concept to adult learning in the Methodist Church, then to a broader public, and finally to organizations. Along the way, he made some important adaptations to the T- group method presented here, which are at the core of its suitability for workplace learning.

When Kurt Lewin fled the Nazis and arrived in the United States, the study of authority relationships – including how a democracy could allow Hitler to rise to power, was near and dear to his heart. Crosby was drawn to this aspect of Lewin's work, and it became critical to his adaptation of the T-group method. Hierarchy, in Crosby's understanding, is not the problem. The problem is each human's struggle to be an authority figure and to relate to other authority figures. Crosby realized that T-groups can be an excellent way to work on relating effectively to both supervisors and reports, all the better when actual reporting relationships exhaust within the group. This was a somewhat radical departure from standard T-group convention.

While most T-group for the workplace workshops have a mix of participants from across an organization (usually from one location), they can also be run in smaller work teams. Contrary to the prevailing fear that the presence of authority figures will inhibit learning, participating and interacting in this type of learning with authority figures in the group leads to some of the most profound interactions and significant gains. T-groups are a "social technology." Esteemed Psychologist Carl Rogers wrote that T-groups and other group learning methods are "perhaps the most significant social invention of this century." The theoretical bases for this social invention include:

Theoretical Bases	Authors
The Interpersonal Gap. (Unpublished)	John Wallen
T-group Theory & Laboratory Method. New York, NY: John Wiley & Sons. 1964.	Leland Bradford, Jack Gibb, Ken Benne (Editors)
Transfer of Laboratory Training. NTL:Training News, 13(2). 1969.	Robert. P. Crosby & Richard Schmuck
The Civil Rights Origins of Organization Development. OD Practitioner. Spring. Vol 50. No.2. 2018.	Nadia Bello
A Failure of Nerve. New York, NY. Church Publishing. 2007.	Edwin Friedman
The Age of Heretics: A History of the Radical Thinkers Who reinvented	Art Kleiner

VALUES

What Are the Core Principles?

Facilitators encourage people with respect for boundaries, and by walking the talk, applying consistent behavioral standards to their own interactions with the group. The approach is grounded in respect for every individual. Groups and systems are stronger when there is effective engagement of the emotions and minds of every one who wants to be engaged.

Everyone at every level of the organization has the potential to become more emotionally mature and less prone to misunderstanding interactions with peers and authority figures. Participants interact openly about their immediate experience of each other, giving and receiving feedback throughout the process, practicing behavioral skills, and doing so within a group norm of caring and respect.

MASTERY

How Do I Become Confident and Competent?

Our industry adapted T-group and its application is described in detail in this chapter.

Facilitating T-groups helps one become more competent as a leader, as a group member, as an organization member, and in any relationship. You can experience a T-group through several organizations including the author's as well as the National Training Lab (NTL). The best way to learn this approach is through mentorship with an experienced T-group facilitator.

FREQUENTLY ASKED QUESTIONS

What Are Common Questions?

Question. What Happened to the T-group "Movement"?

Answer. In the 1960s and 1970s, T-groups became immensely popular. During that time most

"T-groups" lost the focus on group dynamics and gravitated towards focusing on individuals, not unlike a loose form of group therapy. Eventually, in the hands of a wider and wider circle of facilitators, some T-groups in organizational settings were marred by ugly and embarrassing confrontations, threatening the perceived value of T-group interactions significantly.

Question. Can't "Openness" Backfire?

Answer. Industry-adapted T-group workshops owe their success to clarity about the distinction between "Openness" about immediate interactions, which is encouraged, and "Personal Confession" (stories about one's past and one's personal life), which is not required. Clarity that feedback must be given as behaviorally specific and not laden with judgments (for example, stating that "When you spoke while I was speaking I felt frustrated" versus addressing the same behavior saying, "You were so rude") is also vital. Because of the clarity of the T-group task, facilitators rarely have to intervene or make the distinction between Openness and Personal Confession, but it is a line that facilitators carefully draw when necessary. In contrast, coaching and reminders about the use of behavior specifics instead of judgments is always necessary and repeated. It is a rare skill, even amongst experienced managers! When the line between behavior specific feedback and judgments gets blurred, T-groups can turn into a reactive mess instead of an effective learning experience.

CONCLUDING COMMENTS

Any Final Thoughts?

While it is possible to stubbornly stay outside the learning process during a T-group for the workplace workshops, it isn't easy. This is, in no small way, due to the brilliance of Lewin's understanding of group dynamics. It's hard to stay separate when your peers are participating, and even harder when the peer pressure is coming in the privacy of paired conversations. Most people are willing to give the process a chance, and, next thing you know, they are learning about themselves and trying on new behavior! It's tough to resist.

The same was true during the workshop that started this chapter. The process was rolling along, and shortly after the "Active Listening Skills" presentation, a critical incident occurred. Sitting in the same T-group, and talking to each other directly, the Union President looked the CEO in the eye and said, "I don't usually listen to you when we talk. I'm just wrapped up in what I am wanting to say." The CEO said, "I do the same thing. I don't listen to what you are saying either."

From that moment on, they committed to actually listen to each other and to being honest if they think it isn't happening. The two shifted from adversaries to collaborators for the remainder of that president's term, and the entire plant shifted into a more collaborative direction. It wasn't just a critical incident for the workshop – it was transformational for the organization. Among several emergent joint management and labor strategies that followed, they also became co-sponsors for a series of T-group based workshops, and the Union President became a reference for the author's work.

When a critical mass in an organization increases the capacity to foster a productive and safe work environment – high performance follows. This includes:

- giving clear direction,
- taking a stand for what you believe in,
- holding oneself and others accountable,
- fostering communication up and down the hierarchy,
- managing conflict,
- connecting with emotional intelligence (EQ) to all levels of the organization, and
- continually developing self, others, and the organization.

Participants consistently say that T-group learning enriches their personal and professional lives. Our hope is that T-group learning, with proper discipline, once again becomes a "movement."

METHOD PROFILE

Mastery Domain [Specialize/ Blend/ Innovate]	Modality	Sub-modality
Practicing	Personal Development	Organization Development
Typical Length of Engagement [1-3 hrs/ 1-3 days/ 1-3 mts/ 1-3 yrs]	**Size** [# of participants]	**Level of Application** [indivd/team/group/system/transsystem]
4-5 days	6 - 48 participants	individual/team/system
Technology [electronic/mechanical/hybrid]	**Format** [online/onsite/hybrid]	**Timing** [synchronous/asynchronous/hybrid]
mechanical/electronic	onsite and online	synchronous
Unique Requirement [logistic, parameter, principle]	**Required Training & Development** [DIY/Workshops/Adv. Training/Certif.]	**Proprietary Nature of Method** [proprietary/open-source]
no tables	mentorship strongly advised	open-source
Method Founder[s]	**Headquarters/ Homebase**	**Learning Community** [name, size]
Robert P. Crosby / Kurt Lewin	Seattle, WA, USA	www.crosbyod.com

NOTE

1. Reprinted with permission from Crosby, G. (2021c). *T-Groups Adapted for the Workplace.* The Change Handbook.

Appendix E

KRID[1]

KRID (Adapt/Adopt)
(Successfully Sharing Best Practices)

Most workplaces use best practices from other workgroups or organizations. Sometimes sharing a best practice has the unintended consequences of creating employees who instead of learning and adapting a new process, resist the new ideas entirely. This appendix will help you effectively share knowledge and best practices in various settings. Although specifically related to best practices, it is also a great way to recap large events where multiple workgroups have had similar experiences, such as the cascading of goal alignment (Chapter 3 of *Volume II*) or survey feedback (Chapter 4 of *Volume I*).

History: When, in the 1950s, Dr. Spencer Havilik experienced the City of Milwaukee shelve his water study (which, we now know, would have saved the city 100s of millions), it was for him the last straw. He found Dr. Ronald Lippitt at the Institute for Social Research, University of Michigan, and with others they founded the Center for Research in the Utilization of Scientific Knowledge (CRUSK).

Goal: To research the miss or unuse of knowledge, resistance to the same, and develop methodologies to effectively connect expertise (including research, theory, and successful practice knowledge) to practitioners/appliers who face problems/possibilities that could be enriched by the knowledge.

From this history and the nearly 30-year mentorship with Dr. Ronald Lippitt, Robert P. Crosby developed a step-by-step technique to successfully share best practices. KRID stands for Knowledge Retrieval Implication Derivation.

Here is a short lead-in to the process.

Most employees can remember a new program imposed by management, insisting that everyone follow the same practice. Many can also remember initiatives (quality initiatives, new business systems) that failed. These failed attempts are called "fads" or "flavor-of-the-month" programs. Why do they fail and what creates success in disseminating good practices so that results are achieved? First, let's review two extremes that guarantee failure.

Become a true believer in the practice and push it on everyone. This is the most popular implementation method. Companies spend mega-bucks on "cookie-cutter" approaches, and training companies flourish by marketing such packages. CEOs often forget the wisdom about managing for results, not for "activities." They count activities – how many people attend quality training or how many crews are now "self-directed" – rather than checking if such trainings or new practices are producing better results in productivity, safety, cost, and quality.

In this extreme, experts on the particular methodology or program being implemented are dispatched to convince, coerce, or otherwise manipulate the resisting parties to conform to the new approach. Consequently, even if the top executive mandated the change, intense resistance and sabotage of the essentials still occur in the new method.

Let the employees decide if they want to adopt the new program. In the other failure scenario, the new practice is suggested and left for individual or group discretion. A few adopt it, some adapt it to fit their needs, and many ignore it.

There is a better way. The key difference is between the words "adopt" and "adapt" –

Adopt = Swallow it whole
Adapt = Fit it to your needs
        – and in the paradoxical blending of these two in a unified construct.

Apply these fundamental principles and steps when sharing successful practices.

1. The successful practice must be presented, warts and all, as it is practiced. Presenters of this knowledge must not a) generalize to other situations, b) attempt to apply it for the audience, nor c) sell it.

Rather, they must share accurate data with genuine enthusiasm but no exhortations ("This is the greatest thing since sliced bread!") or admonitions ("You must do this or lose market share!").

2. As clearly as possible, measurable outcomes – for which all will be accountable – must be identified and communicated by the sponsoring executives. People will be held accountable for successful results rather than replicating the method.

3. Those receiving the knowledge about the successful practice must demonstrate their ability to accurately articulate the original practice. No arguing. Rather, repeat the words and paraphrase the meanings (i.e., "Here is what I heard you say, and I'm translating it into the following meanings. Do my meanings match your message?").

4. The receivers derive implications for their unique situation. Temporarily accepting the validity of the successful practice, they consider how to implement the process to fit their environment.

5. The initiating executive or key manager, perhaps in the midst of step four, clarifies those aspects, if any, of the practice that are so central that they are not negotiable. Thus, the receivers are clear about what must be *adopted* and what can be *adapted*. While striving for results and not activities as the goal, the executive may have compelling reasons (e.g., standardizing purchasing of costly equipment) to "edict" certain core elements. That which is to be adopted will be met by resistance, of course, which leads to the next step.

6. The initiating executive must listen, stay firm about the core, respect disagreement, and respect anger or frustration if it surfaces. After appropriate airing, they should restate the core (which may have shifted slightly – but genuinely, not as the result of placating but of careful listening) and then the firm expectation that people will follow the leader!

7. Work completion includes selecting and sequencing the practices to adapt, and planning additional training or resources to implement the adopted and adapted practices. Successful knowledge transfer is enhanced by understanding the adoption/adaptation distinction. One should minimize adoption and maximize adaptation while focusing on results instead of methods. Adaptation is a natural process because 1) situations to implement new practices are unique, 2) communicating a complex practice is likely to have misunderstandings, 3) humans are motivated most when using

their own creative juices, and 4) success increases with involvement and belief in the process by those who will complete the practice daily.

CONCLUSION

KRID remains one of the most practical and powerful ways to share knowledge in any organization that struggles with using learnings from internal or external sources. The process is simple to learn and can be adapted to serve your needs any time. Learn its foundations and add it to your tool kit.

NOTE

1. Reprinted with permission from Crosby, C. (2019). *Strategic Engagement: Practice Tools to Raise Morale and Increase Results Volume II: System-Wide Activities*, New York, NY. Business Expert press.

Bibliography

Allen, T. (2012). *The Invention of the White Race: The Origin of Racial Oppression in Anglo-America*. Volume Two. London, UK. Verso.

American Psychological Association. (2021). *Historical chronology: Examining psychology's contributions to the belief in racial hierarchy and perpetuation of inequality for people of color in U.S.* American Psychological Association. Retrieved from: https://www.apa.org/about/apa/addressing-racism/historical-chronology

Anderson, J. (2013). *British Corps of Colonial Marines (1808–1810, 1814–1816)*. Retrieved from: https://www.blackpast.org/global-african-history/british-corps-colonial-marines-1808-1810-1814-1816/

Blackmon, D. (2008). *Slavery by Another Name: The Re-Enslavement of Black Americans from the Civil War to World War II*. New York, NY. Anchor Books.

Bowen, M. and Kerr, M. (1988). *Family Evaluation: An Approach Based on Bowen Theory*. New York, NY. W.W. Norton & Company, Inc.

Brockell, G. (2020). The ugly reason 'The Star-Spangled Banner' didn't become our national anthem for a century. Washington, DC. The Washington Post. October 18, 2020. Retrieved from: https://www.washingtonpost.com/history/2020/10/18/star-spangled-banner-racist-national-anthem/

Campbell, J. (1988). *The Power of Myth*. New York, NY. Doubleday.

Cantu, E. and Jussim, L., (2021). *Microaggressions, Questionable Science, and Free Speech*. Texas Review of Law & Politics.

Carson, C. (1998). *The Autobiography of Martin Luther King Jr*. New York, NY. Grand Central Publishing.

Cartwright, S. (1851). *Diseases and Peculiarities of the Negro Race*. PBS. Retrieved from: https://www.pbs.org/wgbh/aia/part4/4h3106t.html

CDC. *Tuskegee Timeline*. Retrieved from: https://www.cdc.gov/tuskegee/timeline.htm

Chang, A., Meta, J., and Intagliata, C. (2021). *Beneath the Santa Monica Freeway Lies the Erasure of Sugar Hill*. NPR. May 4, 2021. Retrieved from: https://www.npr.org/2021/05/04/993605428/beneath-the-santa-monica-freeway-lies-the-erasure-of-sugar-hill

Chernow, R. (2017). *Grant*. New York, NY. Penguin Books.

Church, F. (2002). *The American Creed: A Biography of the Declaration of Independence*. New York, NY. St. Martin's Press.

Coates, T. (2014). *The Case for Reparations*. The Atlantic. June, 2014. Retrieved from: https://www.theatlantic.com/magazine/archive/2014/06/the-case-for-reparations/361631/

Coates, R., Ferber, A. and Brunsma, D. (2018). *The Matrix of Race: Social Construction, Intersectionality, and Inequality*. London, UK. SAGE Publications.

Coates, R., Ferber, A. and Brunsma, D. (2022). *The Matrix of Race: Social Construction, Intersectionality, and Inequality*. 2nd ed. London, UK. SAGE Publications.

Coontz, S. and Henderson, P. (1986). *Women's Work, Men's property: The Origins of Gender and Class*. London, UK. Verso.

Cowley, S. (2021). Racial Bias Skewed Small-Business Relief Lending, Study Says. *NY Times*. October 11, 2021.

Crosby, C. (2019). *Strategic Engagement: Practice Tools to Raise Morale and Increase Results Volume II: System-Wide Activities*. New York, NY. Business Expert Press.

Crosby, G. (2008). *Fight, Flight, Freeze: Emotional Intelligence, Behavioral Science, Systems Theory & Leadership*. Seattle, WA. CrosbyOD Publishing.

Crosby, G. (2021a). *Planned Change: Why Kurt Lewin's Social Science is Still Best Practice for Business Results, Change Management, and Human Progress*. Boca Raton, FL. Taylor & Francis Group.

Crosby, G. (2021b). *Spirituality and Emotional Intelligence: Wisdom from the World's Spiritual Sources Applied to EQ for Leadership and Professional Development*. Boca Raton, FL. Taylor & Francis Group.

Crosby, G. (2021c). *T-Groups Adapted for the Workplace*. The Change Handbook. The Collaborate Change Library. https://www.mylibrary.world

Danielle, B. (2017). *Sally Hemming's wasn't Thomas Jefferson's Mistress, She was his Property*. Washington, DC. Washington Post. July 7, 2017. https://www.washingtonpost.com/outlook/sally-hemings-wasnt-thomas-jeffersons-mistress-she-was-his-property/2017/07/06/db5844d4-625d-11e7-8adc-fea80e32bf47_story.html

Davis, K. (1990). *Don't Know Much About History*. New York, NY. HarperCollins.

DiAngelo, R. (2018). *White Fragility: Why It's So hard for White People To talk About Racism*. Boston, MA. Beacon Press.

Dillon, L. and Poston, B. (2021). The Racist History of Americas Interstate Highway Boom. *LA Times*. November 11, 2021. Retrieved from: https://www.latimes.com/homeless-housing/story/2021-11-11/the-racist-history-of-americas-interstate-highway-boom

Dyson, J. (1991). *Columbus: For Gold, God and Glory*. New York, NY. Simon and Schuster.

Evans, F. (2021). *How Interstate Highways Gutted Communities-and Reinforced Segregation*. History. October 20, 2021. Retrieved from: https://www.history.com/news/interstate-highway-system-infrastructure-construction-segregation

Ferre-Sadurni, L. (2019). What Happens When Black People Search for Suburban Homes. *NY Times*. November 18, 2019. Retrieved from: https://www.nytimes.com/2019/11/18/nyregion/fair-housing-discrimination-long-island.html?action=click&module=News&pgtype=Homepage

Francis, D. (2003). *Employers' Replies to Racial Names*. National Bureau of Economic Research (NBER). September, 2003. Retrieved from: https://www.nber.org/digest/sep03/employers-replies-racial-names

Frankl, V. (1949). *Man's Search for Meaning*. Boston, MA. Beacon Press.

Friedman, E. (1999). *A Failure of Nerve: Leadership in the Age of the Quick Fix*. New York, NY. Seabury Books.

Gaines, P. (2020). *USDA issued billons in subsidies this year. Black Farmers are still waiting for their share*. NBC News. October 28, 2020. Retrieved from: https://www.nbcnews.com/news/nbcblk/usda-issued-billions-subsidies-year-black-farmers-are-still-waiting-n1245090

General Assembly. (1691). *"An act for suppressing outlying slaves."* In *Encyclopedia Virginia*. December 07, 2020. Retrieved from: https://encyclopediavirginia.org/entries/an-act-for-suppressing-outlying-slaves-1691

Gray, R. (2015). *The Egyptian in all of us: First modern humans spread out of Africa into Europe and Asia from the Sinai Peninsula*. Retrieved from: https://www.dailymail.co.uk/sciencetech/article-3101197/The-Egyptian-modern-humans-spread-Africa-Europe-Asia-Sinai-peninsula.html

Gurman, A. and Kniskern, D. (1991). *The Handbook of Family Therapy*. Volume II. New York, NY. Routledge.

Hanh, T.H. (1991). *Peace is Every Step: The Path of Mindfulness in Everyday Life*. New York, NY. Bantam Books.

Hanson, V. (2001). *Carnage and Culture: Landmark Battles in the Rise of Western Power*. New York, NY. Anchor Books.

Kamin, D. (2020). Black Homeowners Face Discrimination in Appraisals. *NY Times*. August 25, 2020. Retrieved from: https://www.nytimes.com/2020/08/25/realestate/blacks-minorities-appraisals-discrimination.html

Kaplan, S. (2008). Blacks in Massachusetts and the Shays' rrebellion. Contributions in Black Studies: A Journal of African and Afro-American Studies. 2008, Sep; 8, Article 2.

Kendi, I. (2016). *Stamped from the Beginning: The Definitive History of Racist Ideas in America*. New York, NY. Bold Type Books.

Leibowitz, L. (1978). *Females, Males, Families: A Biosocial Approach*. Belmont, CA. Duxbury Press.

Lewin, K. (1997). *Resolving Social Conflicts & Field Theory in Social Science*. Washington, DC. American Psychological Association.

Lewin, K. (1999). *The Complete Social Scientist*. Washington, DC. American Psychological Association.

Lewis, T., Amini, A. and Lannon, R. (2000). *A General Theory of Love*. New York, NY. Random House.

Library of Congress. *Land Loss in Trying Times*. Retrieved from: https://www.loc.gov/classroom-materials/immigration/mexican/land-loss-in-trying-times/

Lilienfeld, S. (2017). *Microaggressions: Strong Claims, Inadequate Evidence*. January 11, 2017. Association for Psychological Science (APS). Sage Journals. Retrieved from: https://journals.sagepub.com/doi/10.1177/1745691616659391

Lilienfeld, S. (2019). *Microaggression Research and Application: Clarifications, Corrections, and Common Ground*. August 13, 2019. Perspectives on Psychological Science. Sage Journals. Retrieved from: https://pubmed.ncbi.nlm.nih.gov/31408611/

Manojlovik, B. (2014). *John Lewis*. South Orange, NJ. Seton Hall University. Retrieved from: http://blogs.shu.edu/diplomacyresearch/2014/01/20/john-lewis/

Marrow, A. (1969). *The Practical Theorist: The Life and Work of Kurt Lewin*. New York, NY. Teacher's College Press.

Martinez, E. and Kirchner, L. (2021). *The Secret Bias Hidden in Mortgage-Approval Algorithms*. The Markup.org. August 25, 2021. Retrieved from: https://themarkup.org/denied/2021/08/25/the-secret-bias-hidden-in-mortgage-approval-algorithms

McWhorter, J. (2020). *How 'White Fragility' Talks Down to Black People*. The Atlantic. July, 2020.

Merton, T. (2004). *A Year with Thomas Merton*. San Francisco, CA. Harper.

Milkman, K., Akinola, M. and Chugh, D. (2012). What happens before? A field experiment exploring how pay and representation differentially shape bias on the pathway into organizations. *Journal of Applied Psychology*, 100(6), 1678–1712.

Montagu, A. (1945). *Man's Most Dangerous Myth: The Fallacy of Race*. 2nd ed. New York, NY. Columbia University Press.

NAACP. *History of Lynching in America*. Retrieved from: https://naacp.org/find-resources/history-explained/history-lynching-america

National Institute of Health, National Library of Medicine. *AD 1493: The Pope asserts rights to colonize, convert, and enslave.* Retrieved from: https://www.nlm.nih.gov/nativevoices/timeline/171.html

New York Historical Society. *When Did Slavery End in New York State?* Retrieved: https://www.nyhistory.org/community/slavery-end-new-york-state

NY Times. (2021). *What the Tulsa race Massacre Destroyed.* May 24, 2021. Retrieved from: https://www.nytimes.com/interactive/2021/05/24/us/tulsa-race-massacre.html

Osbon, D. (1991). *A Joseph Campbell Companion: Reflections on the Art of Living.* New York, NY. HarperCollins Publishers.

Painter, N. (2010). *The History of White People.* New York, NY. W.W. Norton & Company.

Peele, T. and Willis, D. (2020). *Dropping affirmative action had a huge impact on California's public universities.* EdSource.org. October 29, 2020. Retrieved from: https://edsource.org/2020/dropping-affirmative-action-had-huge-impact-on-californias-public-universities/642437

Project Implicit. Retrieved from: https://implicit.harvard.edu/implicit/research/

Raj Bophal, B and Usher, J. (2007). *The beautiful skull and Blumenbach's errors: the birth of the scientific concept of race.* National Center for Biotechnology. BMJ. December 22, 2007. Information. Retrieved from: https://www.ncbi.nlm.nih.gov/pmc/articles/PMC2151154/

Ramirez, I., (2021). *10 examples of Environmental Racism and How it Works.* Yesmagazine.org. April 22, 2021. Retrieved from: https://www.yesmagazine.org/environment/2021/04/22/environmental-racism-examples

Robison, P. and Buhayar, N. (2021). *The National Association of Realtors Is Sorry About All the Discrimination.* Bloomberg Businessweek + Equity. December 21, 2021. Retrieved from: https://www.bloomberg.com/news/features/2021-12-21/real-estate-agents-want-to-fix-housing-discrimination-but-keep-their-commission

Ruiz, D.M. (1997). *The Four Agreements: A Practical Guide to Personal Freedom.* San Rafael, CA. Amber Allen Publishing.

Ruiz, D.M. and Ruiz, D.R. (2010). *The Fifth Agreement: A Toltec Wisdom Book.* San Rafael, CA. Amber Allen Publishing.

Schimmack, U. (2019). *The (lacking) predictive validity of the race IAT.* University of Toronto. Replicability-Index. Retrieved from: https://replicationindex.com/2019/02/06/raceiat-predictive-validity/

Silverman, D. (2019). *This Land is Their Land: The Wampanoag Indians, Plymouth Colony, and the Troubled History of Thanksgiving.* New York, NY. Bloomsbury Publishing.

Smithsonian Museum of American History. *What Does it Mean to be Human?* Retrieved from: https://amhistory.si.edu/starspangledbanner/the-lyrics.aspx

Smithsonian National Museum of Natural History. Retrieved from: https://humanorigins.si.edu/evidence/human-fossils/species/homo-sapiens

Sue, D. (2010). *Microaggression: More Than Just Race.* Retrieved from: https://www.uua.org/files/pdf/m/microaggressions_by_derald_wing_sue_ph.d._.pdf

Sue, D. and Spanierman, L. (2020). *Microaggressions in Everyday Life.* 2nd ed. Hoboken, NJ. Wiley.

Thurman, H. (1976). *Jesus and the Disinherited.* Boston, MA. Beacon Press.

Thurman, H. (2006). *Howard Thurman; Essential Writings.* Maryknoll, NY. Orbis Books.

Tolle, E. (1999). *The Power of Now.* Novato, CA. New World Library.

United Kingdom National Archives. *Emancipation.* Retrieved from: https://www.nation-alarchives.gov.uk/pathways/blackhistory/rights/emancipation.htm

United States National Archives. *National Archives Safeguards Original 'Juneteenth' General Order.* Retrieved from: https://www.archives.gov/news/articles/juneteenth-original-document

Wagenhiem, K. (1973). *Clemente!* New York, NY. Praeger Publishers.

Wallen, J. (1967). *The Interpersonal Gap.* Unpublished.

Watts, A. (1951). *The Wisdom of Insecurity: A Message for an Age of Anxiety.* New York, NY. Vintage Books.

Wausaw Daily Herald. (1963). *Welcome All Races And All Creeds, Minister Urges.* Wausaw, WI. Wausaw Daily Herald. February 19, 1963.

Welsh-Huggins, A. (2020). *Tests, background checks can thwart police diversity effort.* AP News. October 2, 2020. Retrieved from: https://apnews.com/article/race-and-ethnicity-civil-service-police-law-enforcement-agencies-lawsuits

Wiener, J. (2012). *Largest Mass Execution in US History: 150 years Ago Today. The Nation.* December 26, 2012. Retrieved from: https://www.thenation.com/article/archive/largest-mass-execution-us-history-150-years-ago-today/

Williams, M. (2019). Microaggressions: Clarification, Evidence, and Impact. Perspectives on Psychological Science. *Sage Journals.* 2020, Jan;15(1):3–26. Retrieved from: https://pubmed.ncbi.nlm.nih.gov/31418642/

Worden, R., McClean, S., Engel, R., Cochran, H., Corsaro, N., Reynolds, D., Najdowski, C., and Isaza, G. 2020). *The Impacts of Implicit Bias Awareness Training in the NYPD.* Albany, NY. The John Finn Institute.

Zinn, H. (1980). *A People's History of the United States.* New York, NY. Harper Perennial.

Index

Note: Page numbers followed by "n" refer to notes; and page numbers in *italics* refer to figures

Printed in the United States
by Baker & Taylor Publisher Services